A-Level

Biology

Exam Board: OCR A

Getting to grips with A-Level Biology can be strenuous, but with this CGP book your brain muscles* will be beautifully toned by the time the real exams arrive.

It's brimming with a massive range of exam-style questions covering both years of the OCR course — perfect for testing your skills and knowledge.

What's more, we've added a sprinkling of exam tips and a whole section of in-depth answers that'll tell you exactly how the marks are dished out for every question. There's no better way to shape up for the exams!

*Note from CGP: the rest of this book was written by Biology experts. This page was not.

A-Level revision? It has to be CGP!

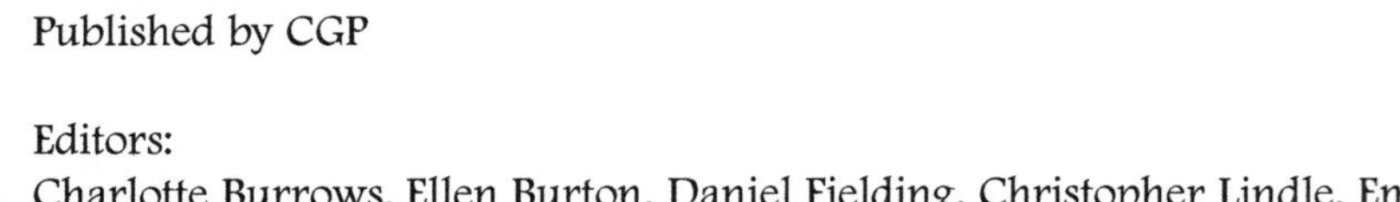

Published by CGP

Editors:
Charlotte Burrows, Ellen Burton, Daniel Fielding, Christopher Lindle, Emily Sheraton, Hayley Thompson.

Contributors:
Mark Ellingham, Emily Lucas, Ciara McGlade, Bethan Parry, Megan Pollard.

Phylogenetic tree on page 69: Jacobo Reyes-Velasco, Daren C. Card, Audra L. Andrew, Kyle J. Shaney, Richard H. Adams, Drew R. Schield, Nicholas R. Casewell, Stephen P. Mackessy, Todd A. Castoe; Expression of Venom Gene Homologs in Diverse Python Tissues Suggests a New Model for the Evolution of Snake Venom, Molecular Biology and Evolution, Volume 32, Issue 1, 1 January 2015, Pages 173–183. By permission of Oxford University Press.

Table 1 on page 78 based on the data from Conduction Velocity and Diameter of Nerve Fibers, J. B. Hursh, Vol. 127, Issue 1, July 1939, pages 131-139.

Maize graph on page 119 based on the data from "The linkage of certain aleurone and endosperm factors in maize, and their relation to other linkage groups" by C.B. Hutchison, published in Ithaca, N.Y. : Cornell University, 1922.

ISBN: 978 1 78294 919 0

With thanks to Janet Cruse-Sawyer, Glenn Rogers, Rachael Rogers, and Karen Wells for the proofreading.
With thanks to Ana Pungartnik for the copyright research.

Printed by Elanders Ltd, Newcastle upon Tyne

Illustrations by: Sandy Gardner Artist, email sandy@sandygardner.co.uk

Based on the classic CGP style created by Richard Parsons.

Contents

Use the tick boxes to check off the topics you've completed.

Module 1 (Development of Practical Skills) is tested in context throughout this book, alongside Modules 2 to 6.

Exam Advice

Good exam technique can make a big difference to your marks, so make sure you read this stuff carefully.

Get Familiar with the **Exam Structure**

If you're sitting the AS-level in Biology rather than the A-level, you'll be sitting a different set of exams to the ones described here.

For **A-level Biology**, you'll be sitting **three papers**:

Biological processes (Modules 1, 2, 3 and 5) **2 hours 15 minutes** **100** marks **37%** of your A-level	Multiple choice, short answer and extended response questions
Biological diversity (Modules 1, 2, 4 and 6) **2 hours 15 minutes** **100** marks **37%** of your A-level	Multiple choice, short answer and extended response questions
Unified biology (Modules 1 to 6) **1 hour 30 minutes** **70** marks **26%** of your A-level	Short answer and extended response questions

1) **All three papers** cover theory from **both years** of your course. This means you need to revise your **Year 1 Modules** (**1** to **4**) as well as your **Year 2 Modules** (**5** and **6**) for these exams.
2) **Module 1** relates to **practical skills**. The Module 1 theory is tested in context throughout this book, alongside Modules 2 to 6.

Your maths skills will also be tested in all three papers.

The **Quality** of Your **Extended Response** will be **Assessed**

In each of your three papers there will be **one or more extended response questions**. These questions are worth **6 or 9 marks** and require a **long answer**. They're shown with an **asterisk** (*) next to their number. You'll be awarded marks for the **quality** of your response as well as its **content**, so your answer needs to:

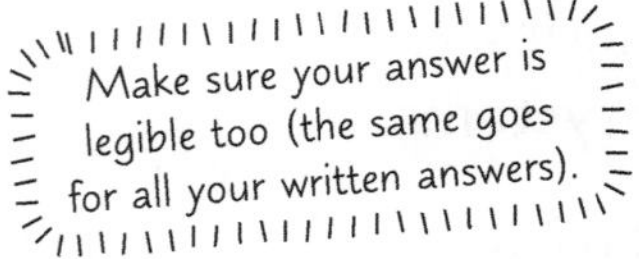

- Be written in **continuous prose** (so use paragraphs, not bullet points).
- Have a **clear** and **logical structure**.
- Use **appropriate scientific language**.
- Show **good reasoning** — i.e. show that you have thought about and understood the question, and can justify your answer.
- Include information that's **relevant** to the question.

Manage Your Time Sensibly

1) The **number of marks** tells you roughly **how long** to spend on a question — you've got **just over a minute per mark** in each paper. So if you get stuck on a short question, it's sometimes worth **moving on** to another one, and then **coming back** to it if you've got time **at the end**.
2) Bear in mind, you might want to spend a **bit longer** per mark on the **extended response** questions, in which case you'll have to spend a bit less time on the multiple choice and short answer questions.

Command Words Tell You **What You Need** to do in a Question

Here are some of the **most common ones**:

Command word	What to do
Give / Name / State	Give a brief **one or two word** answer, or a short sentence.
Describe	Write about what something's like in detail. E.g. describe the structure of a cell.
Explain	**Give reasons** or **causes** for something.
Outline	Write about the **main points** in a topic.
Suggest	Use your **scientific knowledge** to work out what the answer **might** be.
Discuss	Write about the **advantages** and **disadvantages** of something.
Calculate	Work out the **solution** to a mathematical problem.

Cell Structure — 1

No, no, not that type of cell — though revision can feel like a prison. This section's quite interesting, really...

For each of the questions 1-3, give your answer by writing the correct letter in the box.

1 The micrograph below shows part of a cell.

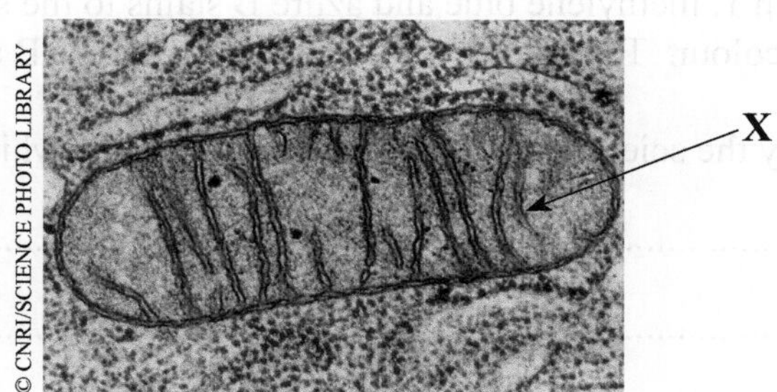

Which option, **A** to **D**, correctly identifies the structure labelled **X** in the micrograph?

A stroma **B** crista

C lamella **D** granum

Your answer B

(1 mark)

2 An organelle has the properties listed below.

- There are pairs of microtubules inside the structure.
- It is found on the surface of a cell.
- It is surrounded by a membrane.

Which organelle, **A** to **D**, is being described?

A cell wall **B** chloroplast

C flagellum **D** centriole

Your answer D

(1 mark)

3 The table below shows the role of three organelles in the production and secretion of proteins from a cell.

Which of the rows in the table, **A** to **D**, correctly identifies the functions of the organelles?

	Ribosome	Rough endoplasmic reticulum	Golgi apparatus
A	Packages proteins for transport.	Folds and processes proteins.	Makes proteins.
B	Makes proteins.	Packages proteins for transport.	Folds and processes proteins.
C	Folds and processes proteins.	Packages proteins for transport.	Makes proteins.
D	Makes proteins.	Folds and processes proteins.	Packages proteins for transport.

Your answer B

(1 mark)

4 A scientist observed the blood cells in a sample of blood. It is possible to distinguish between white and red blood cells because white blood cells contain a nucleus and red blood cells do not.

(a) Describe the function of a cell's nucleus.

....

....

(1 mark)

The scientist added eosin Y, methylene blue and azure B stains to the sample. Eosin Y stains the cytoplasm of cells an orange/pink colour. Together, methylene blue and azure B stain cell nuclei a blue/purple colour.

(b) Suggest and explain why the scientist used these stains to observe white blood cells in the sample.

....

....

....

(2 marks)

The scientist viewed the blood sample using a light microscope.

(c) Describe how the scientist could have used a light microscope to view cells on a prepared slide containing the blood sample.

....

....

....

....

....

....

(4 marks)

(d) (i) **Figure 1** shows an image of a white blood cell in the blood sample that the scientist observed. She measured the size of the cell to be 12 μm, using an eyepiece graticule. The scientist used the line (**X** to **Y**) to measure the size of the cell. Calculate the magnification of the image shown in **Figure 1**. Show your working.

If you need to measure something in an exam, do it in millimetres. This'll make it easier to convert to other units. For example, micrometres = mm × 1000 and nanometres = μm × 1000.

Figure 1

X Y

Magnification = ...

(2 marks)

(ii) The scientist calculated a percentage error of 0.4% when measuring cell size with the eyepiece graticule. Use this information to calculate the uncertainty of this measurement. Give your answer to one significant figure.

Uncertainty = ... μm

(2 marks)

5 Sperm cells are specialised for their function of delivering genetic material to the egg.

Figure 2 shows the structure of a sperm cell from an animal.

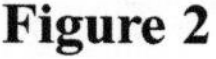

Figure 2

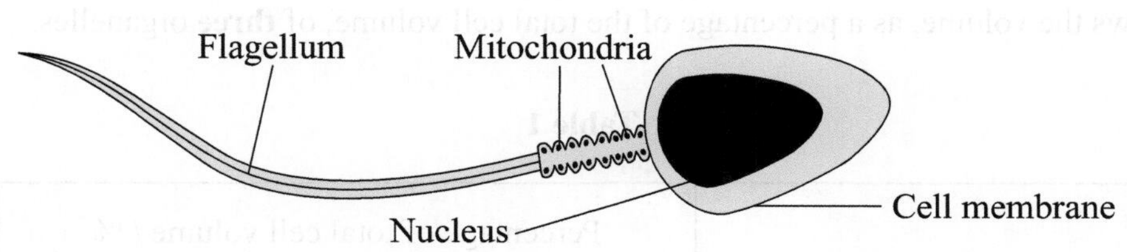

(a) Using **Figure 2**, give **one** similarity and **one** difference between a sperm cell and a bacterium.

....

....

....

....

(2 marks)

(b) (i) Suggest why the mitochondria are located close to the sperm cell's flagellum.

....

....

(1 mark)

(ii) A scientist wanted to observe the mitochondria in a sample of sperm.

Which type of microscope should the scientist use to study the internal structures of mitochondria? Explain your answer.

....

....

....

(2 marks)

(c) Dynein proteins are responsible for causing microtubules to bend.
A mutation in the *DNAH1* gene causes dynein proteins to no longer be expressed.
Suggest and explain how this may lead to male infertility.

....

....

....

(2 marks)

For questions on cell structure, you can be given a micrograph. It can be tricky to interpret these and to spot the different cell structures, but they are there. Trust me. To prepare yourself for the exam, make sure you learn what all the different cell structures look like.

Score

21

Cell Structure — 2

1 A team of scientists studied the organelles in **two** types of cell (**A** and **B**) taken from the body tissues of a eukaryotic organism.

Table 1 shows the volume, as a percentage of the total cell volume, of **three** organelles.

Table 1

Organelle	Percentage of total cell volume / %	
	Cell type **A**	Cell type **B**
Lysosomes	4	1
Rough endoplasmic reticulum	8	16
Nucleus	7	7

(a) The relative volume of the nucleus is the same in both types of cell. Suggest why.

....

....

(1 mark)

(b) The role of one of the two cell types is to ingest invading pathogens, and the other is to secrete enzymes.

Use **Table 1** to determine which of these two roles is carried out by cell type **A** and which is carried out by cell type **B**. Explain your answers.

....

....

....

....

....

....

(4 marks)

(c) Two other organelles that can be found in eukaryotes are mitochondria and chloroplasts. Compare the structure and function of these organelles to give **two** differences.

1. ....

....

2. ....

....

(2 marks)

2 A student observed the cells from the skin of an onion under a light microscope. To do so, he prepared a wet mount slide. He then added a stain.

(a) (i) Explain how the student could have added a stain to his wet mount slide.

....

....

....

(2 marks)

(ii) Give **one** safety precaution the student should have taken when preparing the slide.

....

(1 mark)

(b) The student used an eyepiece graticule to calculate the size of some of the onion cells. **Figure 1** shows the student's eyepiece graticule and stage micrometer. The stage micrometer measures in millimetres.

Figure 1

(i) Use **Figure 1** to calculate the size of **one** division on the student's eyepiece graticule, in micrometres. Show your working.

Answer = ... μm

(2 marks)

(ii) The student increased the magnification, so he needed to recalibrate the eyepiece graticule. Explain why the student needed to recalibrate the graticule.

....

(1 mark)

Another student calculated the size of an onion cell from an image. **Figure 2** shows the cell at × 100 magnification.

Figure 2

© Ed Reschke/Getty Images

(c) Using **Figure 2**, calculate the real length of the cell (**X** to **Y**) in micrometres. Show your working.

Answer = ... μm

(2 marks)

3 Microtubules are important components of cell structure. **Figure 3** shows the microtubules present in the cross-sections of **two** different organelles (**A** and **B**).

Figure 3

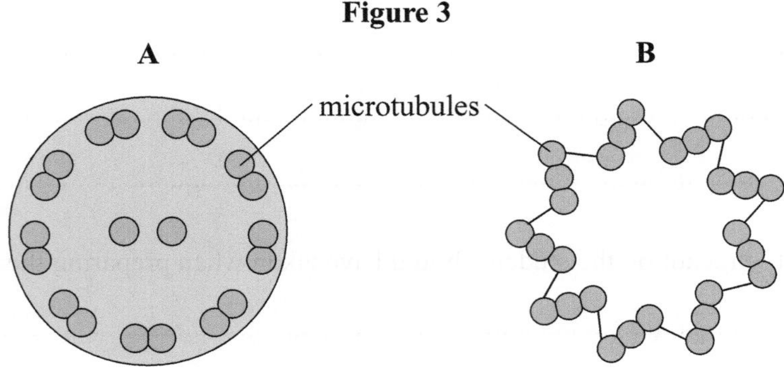

(a) (i) Suggest the identity of organelle **A**. Explain your answer.

....

....

(2 marks)

(ii) What is the function of organelle **B**?

....

....

(1 mark)

(b) The breakdown of the cytoskeleton in nerve cells has been linked to Parkinson's disease. People with Parkinson's disease can experience a lack of control of their muscles.

Nerve cells transmit nervous impulses to other cells, such as muscles, using neurotransmitter proteins. These proteins are released from vesicles transported to the surface of nerve cells.

(i) Suggest **two** reasons why cytoskeleton degradation in nerve cells could lead to a lack of muscle control.

1. ....

....

2. ....

....

(2 marks)

(ii) Abnormal function of certain organelles has been linked to some symptoms of Parkinson's disease. Suggest **one** organelle that may lead to some of these symptoms if it showed abnormal function in nerve cells. Explain your answer.

....

....

(1 mark)

EXAM TIP

Maths always manages to worm its way in. You really need to make sure you learn some formulas, like the one for magnification (magnification = size of image ÷ size of real object). And make sure you *really* know them — you need to be confident rearranging them.

Score

21

Biological Molecules — 1

Biological molecules are essential for living organisms — answering these questions is essential for your revision.

1 Which of the rows in the table, **A** to **D**, correctly identifies a phosphate ion?

	Chemical symbol	Cation	Anion
A	PO_4^{3+}		✓
B	PO_3^{4-}	✓	
C	PO_4^{3-}	✓	
D	PO_4^{3-}		✓

Your answer ☐

(1 mark)

2 The diagram below shows the structure of a molecule, called mucin.

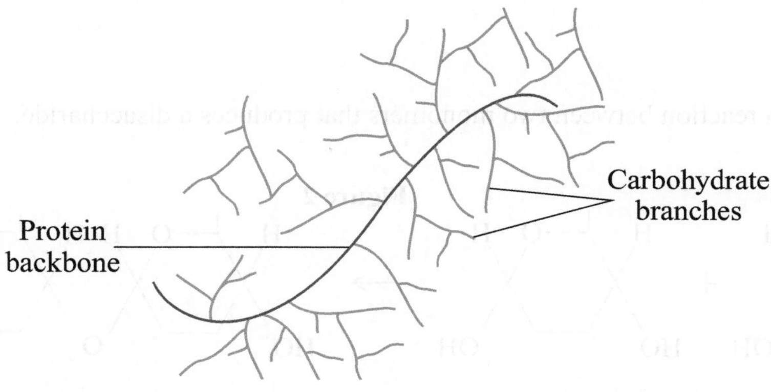

Which option, **A** to **D**, names the type of bonds present in a mucin molecule?

A glycosidic and ester bonds

B peptide and ester bonds

C glycosidic and peptide bonds

D peptide bonds only

Your answer ☐

(1 mark)

3 The table below shows information on four different molecules found in a cell.

Which of the rows in the table, **A** to **D**, describes the molecule that is the main component of cell membranes?

	Atoms in molecule	Variable group(s) present in molecule?
A	C, H, O, P	Yes
B	C, H, O	Yes
C	C, H, O	No
D	C, H, O, N	Yes

Your answer ☐

(1 mark)

4 **Figure 1** shows a polymer.

Figure 1

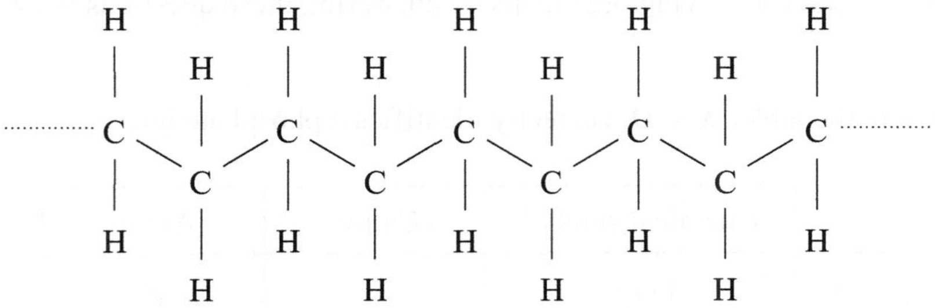

(a) What is a polymer?

....

(1 mark)

(b) (i) Draw a circle around a single monomer in **Figure 1**.

(1 mark)

(ii) Give **two** types of monomer found in biological molecules.

1. ....

2. ....

(1 mark)

5 **Figure 2** shows a reaction between two monomers that produces a disaccharide.

Figure 2

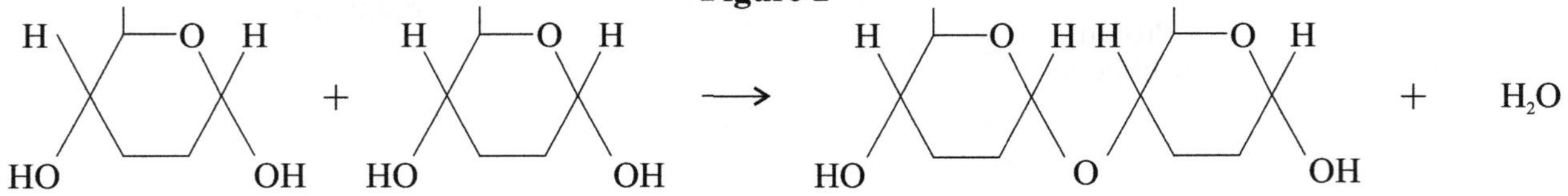

(a) (i) Name the monomers shown in **Figure 2**.

....

(1 mark)

(ii) Name the disaccharide produced in **Figure 2**.

....

(1 mark)

(iii) State the number of carbon atoms in the disaccharide produced in **Figure 2**.

Number of carbon atoms = ...

(1 mark)

(b) Disaccharides can be broken down.
Describe this reaction.

....

....

....

(3 marks)

6 Three molecules were tested and found to be proteins.

(a) Describe a test that can be carried out to determine whether or not a molecule is a protein. Include details of a positive result in your answer.

....

....

....

(2 marks)

Further analysis of two of the proteins showed that they had slightly different properties.

Protein **A** was soluble and contained four iron-containing prosthetic groups.
Protein **B** was roughly spherical in shape and soluble.

(b) (i) Suggest the name of protein **A**.

....

(1 mark)

(ii) It was concluded that protein **B** was insulin.
Explain why solubility is important for the function of insulin.

....

....

(1 mark)

(iii) Explain how the structure of insulin makes it soluble.

....

....

....

(2 marks)

(iv) The third protein was a fibrous protein, extracted from a sample of skin.
Suggest **two** properties of the fibrous protein.

1. ....

2. ....

(2 marks)

7 Animals living in hot, dry climates have developed behaviours that help them keep cool.

Kangaroos have been observed licking saliva onto their forearms in hot weather.

(a) Using your knowledge of the properties of water, explain why this behaviour helps the kangaroos to keep cool.

....

....

....

(2 marks)

Koalas have been observed to hug trees in hot weather.
This is thought to be because the trunks of trees are usually cooler than the surrounding air.

(b) (i) Tree trunks contain a lot of water.
Explain how this could contribute to the tree trunks being cooler than the surrounding air.

(2 marks)

(ii) With reference to the structure and bonding of water molecules, explain how water is able to flow up a tree trunk, from the roots to the leaves.

(3 marks)

8 Proteins are polymers of amino acids. **Figure 3** shows the amino acid alanine.

Figure 3

(a) (i) On **Figure 3**, circle and label the carboxyl group, the R group and the amino group.

(3 marks)

(ii) How is alanine different to the other 19 amino acids?

(1 mark)

(b) (i) Name the molecule released when a peptide bond is formed between **two** amino acids.

(1 mark)

(ii) Draw a diagram of the dipeptide formed from the reaction between **two** molecules of alanine.
Label the peptide bond.

(2 marks)

You need to be really familiar with the structure of proteins, lipids and carbohydrates. You might get asked to identify a molecule or one of its groups from a diagram. Practice drawing these molecules out at home to help you visualise them — and don't be afraid to take a minute to quickly sketch out a molecule in your exam if it helps you to answer the question.

Score

34

Biological Molecules — 2

1 Proteins have four levels of structure.

Figure 1 shows part of the secondary structure of a protein.

Figure 1

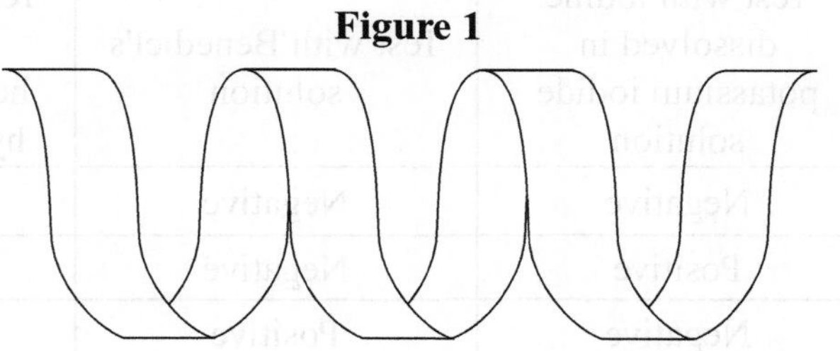

(a) (i) State which secondary structure is shown in **Figure 1**.

....

(1 mark)

(ii) Compare the bonding in the secondary and tertiary structures of a protein.

....

....

....

(2 marks)

Catalase is a globular, conjugated protein with a quaternary structure.

Catalase is an enzyme that catalyses the breakdown of hydrogen peroxide. In order to catalyse this reaction, the hydrogen peroxide molecules must bind to catalase's active site — this is an area of the protein with a specific 3D shape.

In humans, catalase is synthesised on ribosomes in the cytoplasm, but acts inside membrane-bound organelles known as peroxisomes.

(b)* Explain what the information above tells you about the structure of catalase and suggest how catalase's structure helps it to carry out its function.

....

....

....

....

....

....

....

....

....

(6 marks)

2 Three food samples (**A**, **B** and **C**), each containing carbohydrates, were tested using different techniques.

The results of these tests are shown in **Table 1**.

Table 1

Sample	Test Results		
	Test with iodine dissolved in potassium iodide solution	Test with Benedict's solution	Test with Benedict's solution (after heating with dilute hydrochloric acid)
A	Negative	Negative	Positive
B	Positive	Negative	Positive
C	Negative	Positive	Positive

(a) (i) Describe how to carry out a Benedict's test and what would indicate a positive result.

....

....

....

(2 marks)

The tests shown in **Table 1** allow the type of carbohydrate in each sample to be identified.

(ii) Using the information provided in **Table 1**, complete **Table 2** by placing a tick (✓) in the column that correctly identifies the type of carbohydrate present.

Table 2

Sample	Type of carbohydrate present		
	Reducing sugar	Non-reducing sugar	Starch
A			
B			
C			

(2 marks)

Two more samples were tested and found to contain the reducing sugar, glucose.

(b) (i) Describe how reagent test strips could be used to provide an indication of the glucose concentration in each sample.

....

....

....

(2 marks)

(ii) Give **one** other method of determining the glucose concentration in the two samples.

....

(1 mark)

3 **Figure 2** shows a type of biological molecule.

Figure 2

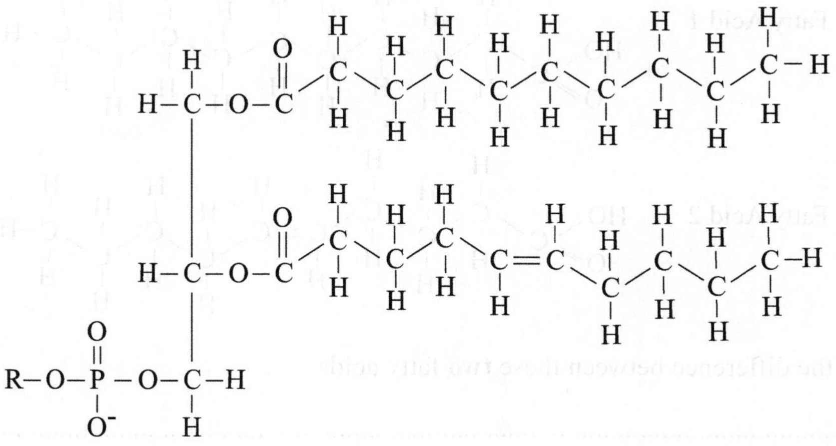

(a) Name the type of molecule shown in **Figure 2**.

Phospholipid

(1 mark)

A droplet of these molecules was placed in water.
The molecules took the arrangement shown in **Figure 3**.

Figure 3

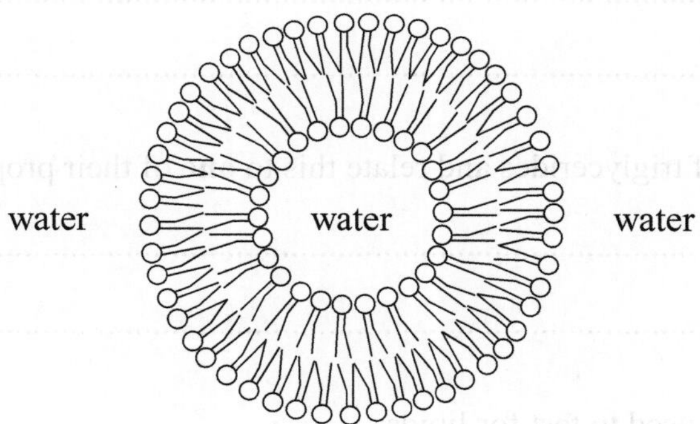

(b) (i) Explain why the molecules arranged themselves in this way.

(3 marks)

(ii) Describe **one** role that the molecules shown in **Figure 3** have in a cell.

(2 marks)

4 **Figure 4** shows two different fatty acids.

Figure 4

Fatty Acid 1

Fatty Acid 2

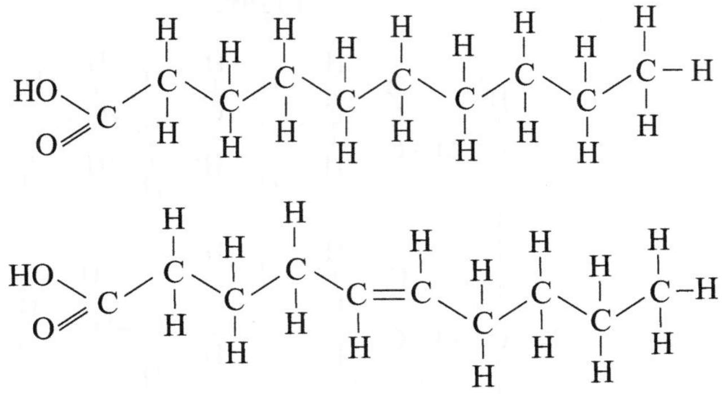

(a) (i) Explain the difference between these **two** fatty acids.

(2 marks)

Triglycerides contain fatty acids.

(ii) Describe how triglycerides are formed.

(3 marks)

(iii) Give **one** function of triglycerides and relate this to **one** of their properties.

(2 marks)

The emulsion test can be used to test for lipids.

(b) (i) Describe the emulsion test, including a positive result.

(2 marks)

(ii) An emulsion is droplets of one liquid suspended in another liquid.
Using this information, explain why lipids give a positive result in the emulsion test.

(1 mark)

Always make sure you read the instructions in an exam question carefully. If a question asks you to answer by placing ticks in a table and you put crosses in the table instead, you won't get the marks — even if your crosses are in the correct places. Harsh, but you have been warned.

Score

32

Biological Molecules — 3

1 Starch and cellulose are polymers of glucose. Starch is made of alpha-glucose molecules and cellulose is made of beta-glucose molecules.

(a) (i) Outline how starch is formed from alpha-glucose molecules.

....

....

....

(2 marks)

(ii) Draw the structure of beta-glucose below and explain how it is different from that of alpha-glucose.

....

....

(2 marks)

(iii) The beta-glucose molecules allow cellulose to form long, straight chains with multiple hydrogen bonds between the chains. Explain how this makes cellulose well-suited to its function.

....

....

(2 marks)

Starch is a mixture of two polysaccharides of alpha-glucose, amylose and amylopectin. The structures of amylose (**A**) and amylopectin (**B**) are shown in **Figure 1**.

Figure 1

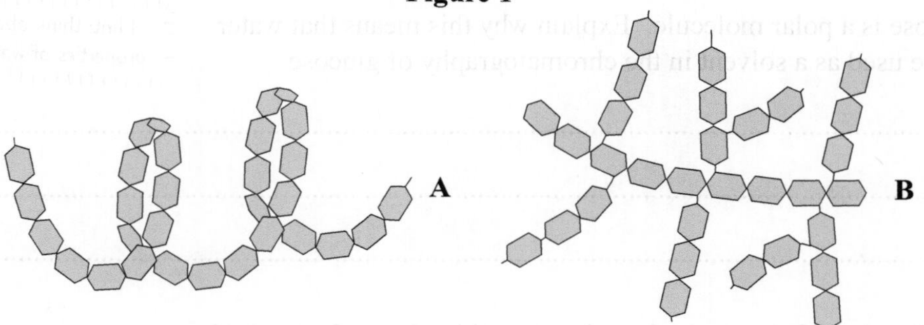

A

B

(b) Different starches are made up of different proportions of amylose and amylopectin. Using **Figure 1**, explain **one** advantage and **one** disadvantage of using amylose to store excess glucose, rather than amylopectin.

Advantage: ....

....

Disadvantage: ....

....

(2 marks)

2 A student was given three unknown samples of reducing sugar (**A**, **B**, **C**) to identify. She used paper chromatography to analyse the samples. The chromatogram produced is shown in **Figure 2**.

Figure 2

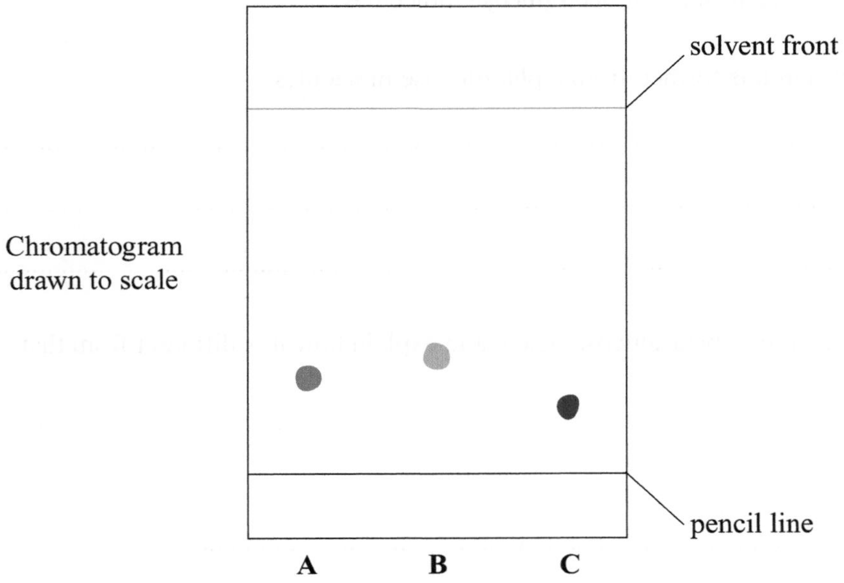

(a) (i) To produce her chromatogram, the student placed her prepared chromatography paper in a glass beaker containing a small amount of solvent. She then covered the beaker with a lid. Suggest why the student covered the beaker with a lid.

....

(1 mark)

(ii) Describe the role of a solvent in chromatography.

....

....

(1 mark)

(iii) Glucose is a polar molecule. Explain why this means that water can be used as a solvent in the chromatography of glucose.

Hint: think about the properties of water here.

....

....

....

(2 marks)

(b) (i) The R_f value of glucose in the solvent used by the student is 0.18.
Using **Figure 2**, determine which of the sugars (**A** to **C**) is glucose. Show your working.

Answer = ...

(2 marks)

(ii) Before the student could calculate the R_f values she dipped the chromatogram in Benedict's reagent. Suggest why the student needed to do this.

....

(1 mark)

3 A student wanted to investigate the concentration of glucose in different energy drinks. The student first produced four glucose solutions of different, known concentrations by diluting a 4.0 mM glucose solution. The volumes of distilled water and glucose solution he added to each test tube can be seen in **Table 1**. The total volume of each solution was 10 cm^3.

Table 1

Final concentration of glucose solution / mM	Volume of distilled water / cm^3	Volume of glucose solution / cm^3
4.0	0.0	10.0
	5.0	5.0
	7.5	2.5
	8.75	1.25

(a) Complete **Table 1** by filling in the three blank spaces with the correct final concentrations of glucose solution.

(1 mark)

(b) Describe how the student could use the glucose solutions he had prepared, along with a colorimeter, to determine the concentration of glucose in each energy drink.

....

....

....

....

....

(4 marks)

(c) (i) Give **one** negative control the student could use in his experiment.

....

(1 mark)

(ii) Explain why a control would be used in this experiment.

....

....

(1 mark)

(d) Some of the energy drinks investigated were coloured, while others were colourless. Explain why this may have reduced the accuracy of the student's results.

....

....

....

(2 marks)

EXAM TIP

Examiners love to test your maths skills, so there'll be several calculation questions in the exams. If a calculation question asks you to show your working, make sure you do. That way, even if you don't get the right answer, you might still pick up a mark for using the correct method.

Score

24

Nucleotides and Nucleic Acids — 1

Nucleotides are the building blocks of life — they join to form DNA and RNA, which ultimately control how every organism functions. This topic isn't too tricky, but here are some practice questions to keep you on your toes.

For each of questions 1-3, give your answer by writing the correct letter in the box.

1 Which of the rows in the table, **A** to **D**, correctly shows the molecules that make up ATP?

A	thymine	phosphate	adenine
B	phosphate	deoxyribose	adenine
C	ribose	phosphate	adenine
D	ribose	thymine	phosphate

Your answer ☐ **(1 mark)**

2 Which of the following options, **A-D**, is **not** needed to carry out a DNA precipitation reaction?

A detergent

B sodium chloride

C ethanol

D DNA helicase

Your answer ☐ **(1 mark)**

3 A DNA sequence before and after replication is shown below, on the left. The sequence is read from left to right. The table below shows which mRNA codons code for each type of amino acid.

DNA sequence before replication:
TACCTAGCT

DNA sequence after replication:
TACCTCGCT

Second mRNA base

First mRNA base	U	C	A	G	Third mRNA base
U	UUU - Phe UUC - Phe UUA - Leu UUG - Leu	UCU - Ser UCC - Ser UCA - Ser UCG - Ser	UAU - Tyr UAC - Tyr UAA - Stop UAG - Stop	UGU - Cys UGC - Cys UGA - Stop UGG - Trp	U C A G
C	CUU - Leu CUC - Leu CUA - Leu CUG - Leu	CCU - Pro CCC - Pro CCA - Pro CCG - Pro	CAU - His CAC - His CAA - Gln CAG - Gln	CGU - Arg CGC - Arg CGA - Arg CGG - Arg	U C A G
A	AUU - Ile AUC - Ile AUA - Ile AUG - Met	ACU - Thr ACC - Thr ACA - Thr ACG - Thr	AAU - Asn AAC - Asn AAA - Lys AAG - Lys	AGU - Ser AGC - Ser AGA - Arg AGG - Arg	U C A G
G	GUU - Val GUC - Val GUA - Val GUG - Val	GCU - Ala GCC - Ala GCA - Ala GCG - Ala	GAU - Asp GAC - Asp GAA - Glu GAG - Glu	GGU - Gly GGC - Gly GGA - Gly GGG - Gly	U C A G

A mutation occurred in the DNA sequence during replication. Which of the following, **A-D**, describes the result of the mutation when the corresponding mRNA sequence is translated?

A A serine (Ser) amino acid is replaced with an arginine (Arg) amino acid.

B There is no change to the amino acid sequence.

C An asparagine (Asn) amino acid is replaced with a glycine (Gly) amino acid.

D An aspartate (Asp) amino acid is replaced with a glutamate (Glu) amino acid.

Your answer ☐ **(1 mark)**

4 RNA molecules are single-stranded polynucleotides.

Figure 1 shows part of the structure of an RNA molecule.

Figure 1

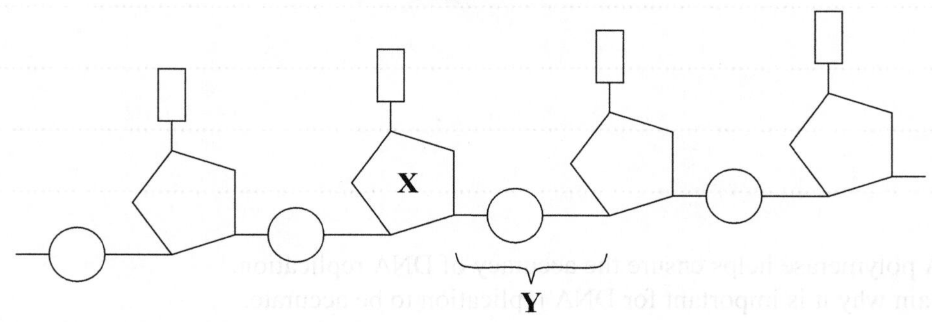

(a) (i) Name the structure labelled **X** in **Figure 1**.

....

(1 mark)

(ii) Name the bond labelled **Y** in **Figure 1**.

....

(1 mark)

Some RNA molecules are capable of folding into structures known as stem-loops. An example of a stem-loop structure is shown in **Figure 2**.

Figure 2

(b) (i) Looking at the sequence of the structure shown in **Figure 2**, explain how you can tell that this is part of an RNA molecule and not a DNA molecule.

....

....

(1 mark)

(ii) Using your knowledge of how DNA molecules can form a double helix, explain how the stem-loop structure shown in **Figure 2** is formed.

....

....

....

....

(3 marks)

(iii) Calculate the percentage of purine bases shown in **Figure 2**.

percentage of purine bases = ... %

(1 mark)

5 A scientist is investigating the role of enzymes in DNA replication.

(a) (i) Describe the roles that the enzymes DNA helicase and DNA polymerase play in DNA replication.

....

....

....

....

(3 marks)

(ii) DNA polymerase helps ensure the accuracy of DNA replication.
Explain why it is important for DNA replication to be accurate.

....

....

....

....

(3 marks)

The scientist mixes a bacterial DNA sample with the enzymes and substrates required for DNA replication. He does this in both the presence and the absence of ATP, and using active and inactive ATP hydrolase. ATP hydrolase is the enzyme that catalyses the breakdown of ATP. The scientist then measures the amount of DNA produced to determine whether DNA replication has taken place.

Some of the results of the investigation are shown in **Table 1**.

Table 1

DNA replication enzymes	ATP hydrolase	ATP	Has DNA replication occurred?
Present	Active	Present	Yes
Present	Active	Absent	No
Present	Inactive	Present	No
Present	Inactive	Absent	No

(b) (i) Describe the results shown in **Table 1**.

....

....

(1 mark)

(ii) Suggest an explanation for the results shown in **Table 1**.

....

....

....

(2 marks)

If you have to interpret the results of an unfamiliar experiment in the exam, don't panic — just make sure you read the method carefully. There will always be some important information there that will help you understand the results. If you can take a minute to piece it together with your existing biological knowledge, then you're sure to come out on top.

Score

19

Nucleotides and Nucleic Acids — 2

1 Leigh syndrome is a metabolic disorder that affects the central nervous system. It can be caused by a mutation in the MT-ATP6 gene.

Figure 1 shows **one** of the mutations in the MT-ATP6 gene that can cause Leigh syndrome. **Table 1** contains some of the DNA codons that code for particular amino acids.

Table 1

Amino acid	DNA codon
Isoleucine	ATT, ATC, ATA
Glutamate	GAA, GAG
Leucine	CTG, TTA, TTG
Methionine	ATG
Valine	GTT, GTC, GTA, GTG
Arginine	CGG, AGA
Alanine	GCT, GCC, GCA, GCG

Figure 1

Original gene: CAACCAATAGCCC**T**GGCCGTA

Mutated gene: CAACCAATAGCCC**G**GGCCGTA

(a) Give **one** piece of evidence from **Table 1** that shows the genetic code is degenerate.

....

....

(1 mark)

(b) (i) Describe the effect that the mutation shown in **Figure 1** will have on the mRNA sequence produced from the MT-ATP6 gene.

Hint: Figure 1 will be easier to read and interpret if you mark off every three bases with a slash, e.g. CAA/CCA/...

....

....

(1 mark)

(ii) Using **Table 1** for reference, describe the effect that the mutation shown in **Figure 1** will have on the primary structure of the protein produced from the MT-ATP6 gene.

....

....

(1 mark)

(c) Complete the following passage to show how mRNA from the MT-ATP6 gene is translated into a protein.

The mRNA attaches to the ribosome. tRNA molecules carry ....

to the ribosome. tRNA molecules attach to the mRNA via ....

rRNA in the ribosome catalyses the formation of a ....

between two .... The ribosome moves along the mRNA,

producing a polypeptide chain. The process continues until a ....

on the mRNA is reached.

(5 marks)

2 A team of scientists have developed a new drug. They want to investigate how the levels of three different mRNA molecules change when eukaryotic cells are treated with the drug.

To do so, they extract all of the mRNA from a sample of eukaryotic cells, and use an enzyme to convert the mRNA sequence into a complementary DNA (cDNA) sequence. They then determine the cDNA sequence and use it to identify the mRNA molecules that are present. The scientists analyse the data from treated and untreated cells to determine the level of mRNA expression.

(a) Outline how mRNA is produced from DNA by RNA polymerase.

....

....

....

....

....

....

(4 marks)

The results of the scientists' experiment are shown in **Figure 2**.

Figure 2

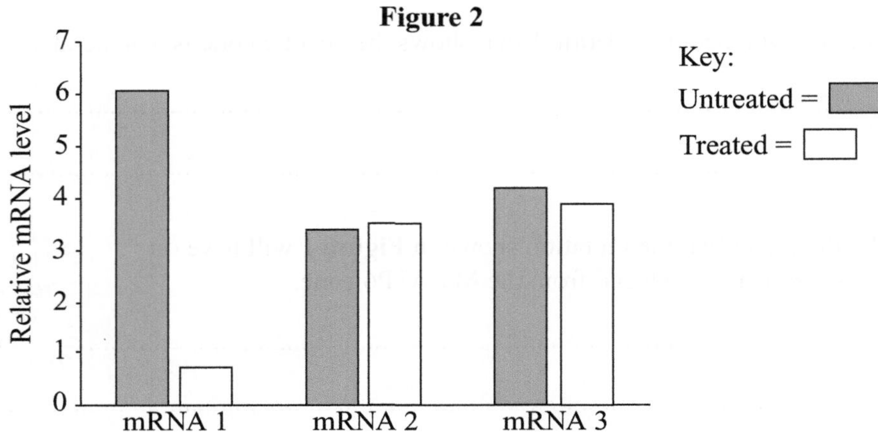

The scientists hypothesise that the new drug has two possible methods of action:
Method 1: By preventing RNA polymerase from working.
Method 2: By destroying particular mRNA sequences.

(b) (i) With reference to **Figure 2**, explain why the drug cannot be acting via Method 1.

....

....

....

(2 marks)

(ii) Explain how the results shown in **Figure 2** can be explained if the drug acts via Method 2.

....

....

....

(2 marks)

3* The scientists Meselson and Stahl carried out an experiment which showed that DNA replication is a semi-conservative process. The experiment used two types of nitrogen — heavy nitrogen and light nitrogen.

Meselson and Stahl grew *E. coli* bacteria in a nutrient broth which contained heavy nitrogen. Each time the bacteria divided, they replicated their DNA and took up heavy nitrogen from the broth to make new DNA nucleotides.

After several rounds of division, the heavy nitrogen was incorporated into all of the *E. coli* DNA. Meselson and Stahl then transferred the *E. coli* (bacterial generation 0) from the heavy nitrogen nutrient broth, to a nutrient broth containing only light nitrogen. They were left to divide several times.

Meselson and Stahl took a DNA sample from bacterial generation 0, and from the generations produced after each round of division in the light nitrogen broth. They then analysed the DNA to determine what percentage of the DNA contained only heavy nitrogen, both heavy and light nitrogen, or only light nitrogen. Some of the results of the experiment (bacterial generations 0-3) are shown in **Table 2**.

Table 2

Bacterial generation	Percentage of DNA with heavy nitrogen only	Percentage of DNA with both heavy and light nitrogen	Percentage of DNA with light nitrogen only
0	100	0	0
1	0	100	0
2	0	50	50
3	0	25	75

Using the information provided, explain how the experiment provides evidence that DNA replication is a semi-conservative process. You should include details of semi-conservative replication in your answer.

....

....

....

....

....

....

....

....

....

....

....

....

....

(6 marks)

Question 3* is a tricky one, there's no doubt about it. Not only does it ask you to interpret some unfamiliar experimental results, it also awards marks for the quality of your extended response. This means your answer should be well-structured, relevant and detailed. Take your time reading the information and think carefully about what your answer should include before you start.

Score

22

Enzymes — 1

Ahh, enzymes, now here's an interesting topic — these are important proteins that speed up lots of reactions. Most enzymes are really specific, and work best under optimal conditions. Now, let's see what you know...

For questions 1 and 2, give your answer by writing the correct letter in the box.

1 The rate of an enzyme-controlled reaction at **15 °C** is 0.8 cm³ min⁻¹. The optimum temperature for the reaction is 40 °C. The reaction has a Q_{10} of 2.

Which of the following options, **A** to **D**, gives the rate of reaction at **25 °C**?

A $0.4\ cm^3\ min^{-1}$

B $0.8\ cm^3\ min^{-1}$

C $1.6\ cm^3\ min^{-1}$

D $2.4\ cm^3\ min^{-1}$

Your answer ☐

(1 mark)

2 The rate of a chemical reaction involving an enzyme was recorded over 60 seconds, as substrate concentration was increased. The results are shown in **Figure 1**.

Which of the figures, **A** to **D**, shows what the reaction curve would look like for 60 seconds of the same reaction, in the presence of a competitive inhibitor?

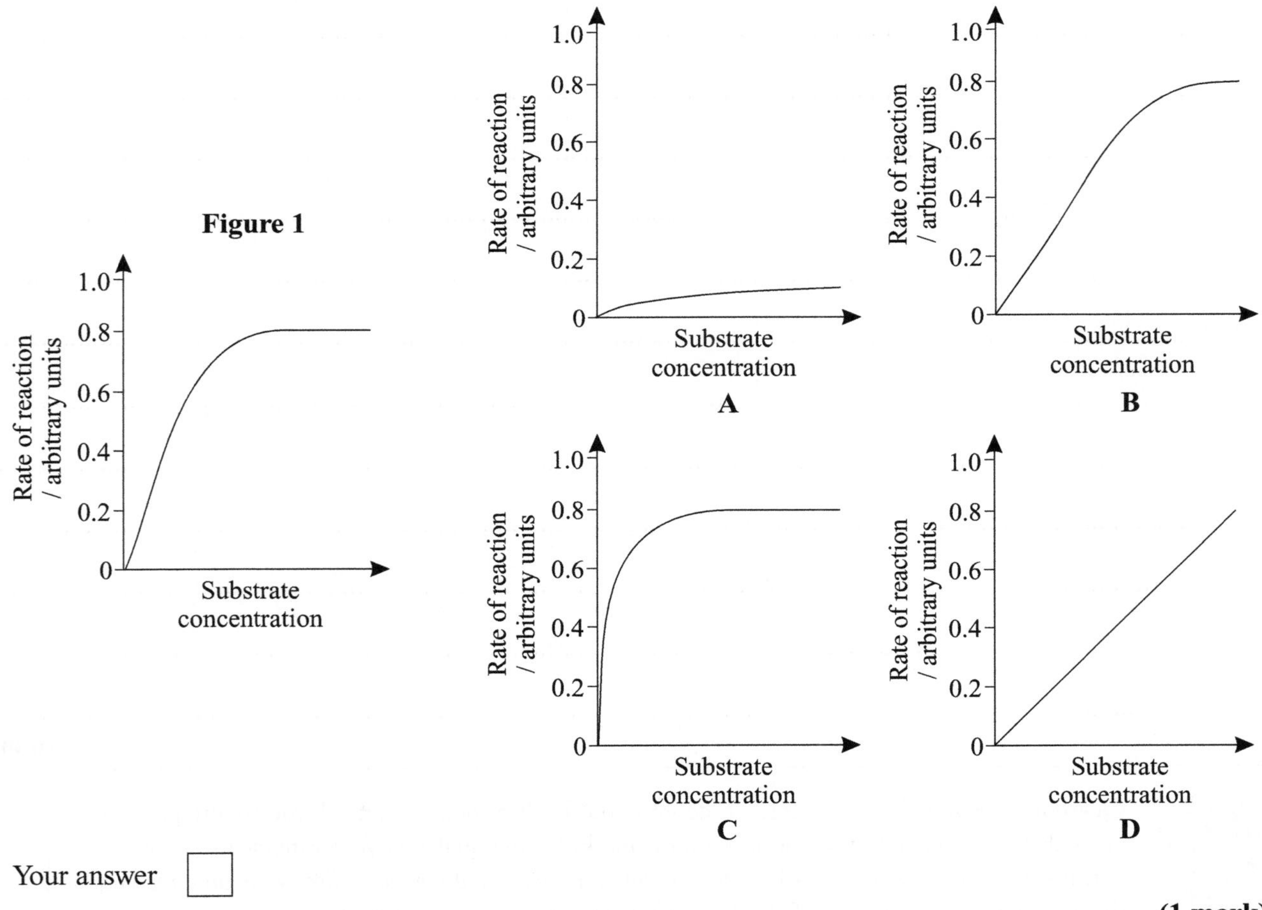

Your answer ☐

(1 mark)

3 **Figure 2** shows the activity of two different enzymes (**A** and **B**). The enzymes are involved in respiration. One enzyme is from an insect that lives in the UK and one is from an insect that lives in a tropical climate.

Figure 2

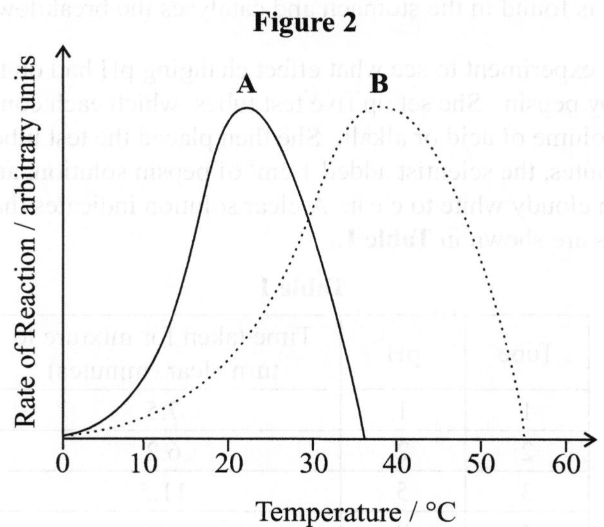

(a) Explain the shape of the curve for enzyme **A**.

....

....

....

....

(3 marks)

(b) Suggest which enzyme (**A** or **B**) is from the tropical insect. Explain your answer.

....

....

....

(2 marks)

Insecticides are chemicals that kill insects.
Scientists have developed an insecticide that works as a competitive inhibitor of enzyme **A**.

(c) Explain how the insecticide works.

You need to use information from the introduction to question 3, as well as your knowledge of how competitive inhibitors work, to answer this question part.

....

....

....

....

....

(4 marks)

The main factors that influence the rate of an enzyme-controlled reaction are temperature, pH, enzyme concentration and substrate concentration. It's important you understand how each factor affects the rate, so that you can interpret graphs like the ones in questions 2 and 3. You also need to learn how different types of inhibitor can affect enzyme-controlled reaction rates.

Score

11

Enzymes — 2

1 Pepsin is an enzyme that is found in the stomach and catalyses the breakdown of protein.

A scientist carried out an experiment to see what effect changing pH had on the breakdown of egg white, which contains protein, by pepsin. She set up five test tubes, which each contained 5 cm^3 of egg white suspension and a small volume of acid or alkali. She then placed the test tubes into a water bath set at 40 °C. After a few minutes, the scientist added 1 cm^3 of pepsin solution, and timed how long it took for the solutions to turn from cloudy white to clear. A clear solution indicates that all the protein has been broken down. The results are shown in **Table 1**.

Table 1

Tube	pH	Time taken for mixture to turn clear (minutes)
1	1	7.5
2	2	6.2
3	5	11.5
4	8	>15
5	11	>15

(a) Suggest why the temperature of the water bath was set to 40 °C.

....

....

(1 mark)

(b) The pH of the stomach ranges from pH 1.5 to pH 3.5.
The pH of the small intestine ranges from pH 6 to pH 7.
Use the results in **Table 1** to explain why pepsin is active in the stomach, but not in the small intestine.

....

....

....

....

....

(4 marks)

2 A student investigated how an enzyme-controlled reaction is affected by changes in enzyme concentration. The student used the enzyme catalase to break hydrogen peroxide down into water and oxygen.

(a) (i) The student used an extracellular source of catalase. In the human body, catalase is an intracellular enzyme. Explain the difference between extracellular enzymes and intracellular enzymes.

....

....

(1 mark)

(ii) Give **one** example of an enzyme that acts extracellularly in the human body.

....

(1 mark)

The results of the student's first experiment are shown in **Figure 1**.

Figure 1

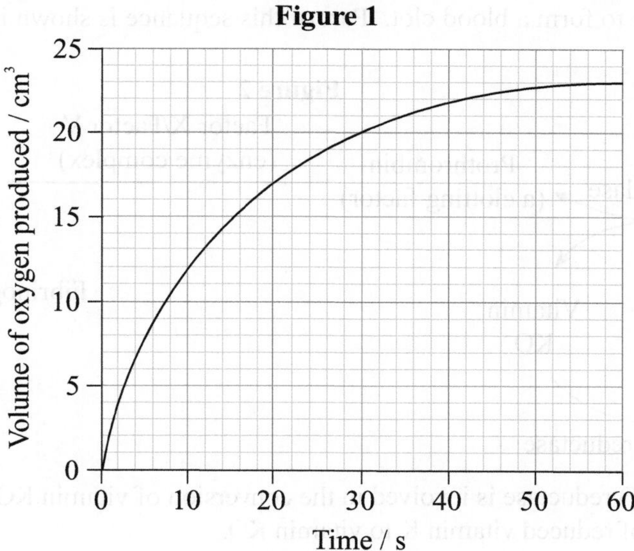

(b) Identify the dependent and independent variables in this investigation.

....

....

(1 mark)

The student collected the oxygen in a measuring cylinder submerged in water.
The measuring cylinder measured to the nearest 1 cm^3.

(c) Give the uncertainty of measurements associated with this measuring cylinder.

uncertainty = ... cm^3

(1 mark)

(d) Suggest **one** way that the student could have obtained more accurate results.

....

(1 mark)

(e) (i) Calculate the average rate of the reaction shown in **Figure 1** for the first 20 seconds. Show your working and include appropriate units in your answer.

rate = ...

(2 marks)

(ii) Calculate the initial rate of the reaction shown in **Figure 1**. Show your working.

To calculate the initial rate, you need to draw a tangent.

rate = ...

(2 marks)

(f) Sketch on the same axes the curve you would expect if the experiment were carried out with a higher enzyme concentration.

(1 mark)

3 There are many enzymes and coenzymes involved in the mechanism of blood clotting. These act in a sequence to form a blood clot. Part of this sequence is shown in **Figure 2**.

Figure 2

Precursor prothrombin → Carboxylase → Prothrombin (a clotting factor) → Factor X/Factor V (enzyme complex) → Thrombin (enzyme that activates clotting)

Reduced vitamin K (a coenzyme for carboxylase) → Vitamin KO

Vitamin KO → Vitamin KO reductase → Reduced vitamin K

Fibrinogen → Fibrin (a protein that traps platelets to form a blood clot)

(a) The enzyme Vitamin KO reductase is involved in the conversion of vitamin KO to reduced vitamin K, but not the conversion of reduced vitamin K to vitamin KO.
Use the induced fit model of enzyme action to suggest an explanation for this.

....

....

....

....

(3 marks)

(b) Reduced vitamin K acts as a coenzyme for carboxylase. What is meant by the term 'coenzyme'?

....

....

(2 marks)

Blood clots form to help repair wounds.
However if a clot forms in an artery or vein, it can cause problems by reducing blood flow.

(c) Warfarin is a medication that can be used to reduce the risk of blood clots forming in a blood vessel.
Warfarin interferes with the normal blood clotting mechanism by irreversibly inhibiting the action of the enzyme vitamin KO reductase.
With reference to **Figure 2**, explain why the action of warfarin could prevent blood clotting.

....

....

....

....

....

....

(4 marks)

Pen, pencil, ruler, calculator... Oh, that's just my shopping list for my exam. Sometimes examiners will ask you to draw, measure or calculate, so you need to make sure you've got all this stationery — a ruler that can measure in millimetres, a calculator, a pencil (for drawing graphs or diagrams) and a pen with black ink. In fact, make sure you've got a couple of spare pens too.

Score

24

Biological Membranes — 1

Cell membranes may look simple through a microscope, but nothing's as simple as it first seems. In fact, they're actually pretty complex and really important for cells. These questions will make sure your knowledge is tip top.

For each of questions 1-3, give your answer by writing the correct letter in the box.

1 The following options describe different types of movement across a cell membrane.

Which of the options, **A** to **D**, does **not** require the use of a transport protein or ATP?

A Enzymes being released from a cell via exocytosis.

B Glucose moving against its concentration gradient, from the intestinal lumen, into the cytoplasm of the cells of the intestines.

C Oxygen moving into the cell.

D Sodium ions diffusing into a cell from the extracellular fluid.

Your answer ☐

(1 mark)

2 A number of cells from a plant leaf are placed in a solution. The solution is hypotonic to the fluid inside the leaf cells.

Which of the following statements, **A** to **D**, describes what will happen to the leaf cells when they are placed in the solution?

A The cells will become flaccid.

B The cells will become turgid.

C The cells will burst.

D There will be no change in the cells.

Your answer ☐

(1 mark)

3 A student is investigating the effect of different factors on the rate of diffusion. He makes up some agar jelly containing red cabbage juice, and cuts it into cubes of 1 cm^3 and 3 cm^3. The student then places one of each cube size into separate beakers containing different concentrations of dilute ammonia solution. He then times how long it takes for the ammonia to diffuse into the agar cubes and turn them from red to green.

Which of the treatments, **A** to **D**, will result in the colour changing most rapidly?

A 1 cm^3 cube, ammonia concentration = 0.5 mol dm^{-3}

B 3 cm^3 cube, ammonia concentration = 0.5 mol dm^{-3}

C 3 cm^3 cube, ammonia concentration = 1.0 mol dm^{-3}

D 1 cm^3 cube, ammonia concentration = 1.0 mol dm^{-3}

Your answer ☐

(1 mark)

4 **Figure 1** models the arrangement of molecules in a typical cell membrane, observed from above.

Figure 1

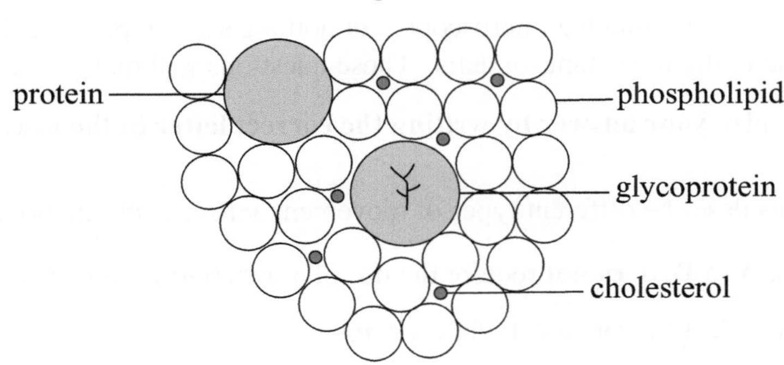

(a) (i) Describe the model illustrated in **Figure 1**.

....

....

(2 marks)

(ii) Explain the effect that a higher percentage of cholesterol would have on the model in **Figure 1**.

....

....

(2 marks)

(iii) State **two** roles of glycoproteins in the cell membrane.

1. ....

2. ....

(2 marks)

(iv) Describe what would happen to the structure of a cell membrane, if it was exposed to temperatures below 0 °C.

....

....

....

(2 marks)

(b) Cell membranes vary in structure due to the adaptation of specialised cells to their functions. For example, to conduct nerve impulses, a neurone cell relies upon the rapid movement of cations across its cell membrane.

(i) Suggest an adaptation that you might expect to observe in the cell membrane of a neurone cell. Give a reason for your choice.

....

....

(2 marks)

(ii) Low temperatures can reduce the speed at which nerve impulses are conducted. Suggest why.

....

....

....

(2 marks)

5 **Figure 2** shows part of the phospholipid bilayer in a cell-surface membrane.

Figure 2

Cell exterior — water potential = –0.5 kPa

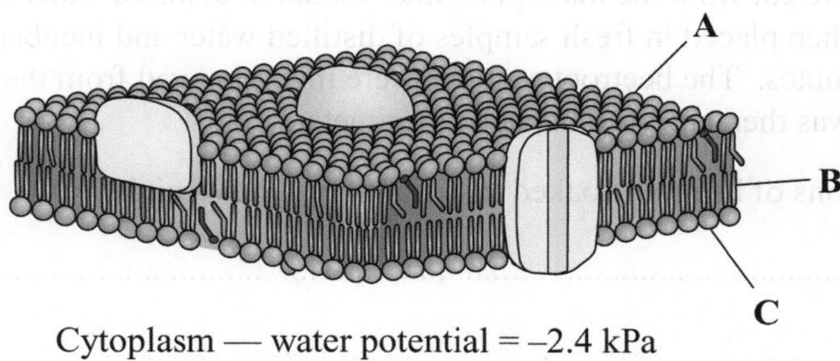

Cytoplasm — water potential = –2.4 kPa

(a) Which letter (**A-C**) represents the hydrophobic part of the phospholipid bilayer?

....

(1 mark)

(b) Explain how the phospholipid bilayer helps the membrane to carry out its function.

....

....

....

(2 marks)

(c) Using the information in **Figure 2**, describe the direction of movement of water across the cell membrane. Give a reason for your answer.

....

....

....

(2 marks)

6 Glucagon is a hormone that is released when there is not enough glucose in the blood. It binds to receptors on liver cells, causing the liver cells to break down stores of glycogen to glucose.

(a) Skeletal muscle cells also store glycogen.
Explain why glucagon affects liver cells, but not skeletal muscle cells.

....

....

....

(2 marks)

(b) REMD-477 is a drug that has a similar shape to glucagon. In the future, it might be used to treat diabetes because it is able to help keep the blood sugar level under control.
Suggest how REMD-477 helps keep the blood sugar level under control.

....

....

....

(2 marks)

7 Beetroot cells contain a vacuole. The vacuole contains red pigments called betalains, which are contained within the vacuole by a phospholipid membrane. A scientist wanted to investigate the effect of temperature on the permeability of this membrane.

Sections of beetroot were cut from the main plant and soaked in distilled water overnight. The cut sections were then placed in fresh samples of distilled water and incubated at different temperatures for 30 minutes. The beetroot sections were then removed from the water and discarded. Each sample of water was then analysed using a colorimeter.

(a) Why were the cut sections of beetroot soaked in distilled water overnight?

....

(1 mark)

(b) Suggest a negative control that could have been used in this investigation.

....

(1 mark)

Table 1 illustrates the results that were obtained from the colorimetry analysis. The percentage absorbance illustrates the proportion of transmitted light at blue/green wavelengths that was absorbed by the pigments in the water.

Table 1

Temperature / °C	Absorbance
20	0.05
30	0.16
40	0.35
50	0.60
60	0.73

(c) Explain, with reference to the structure of cell membranes, the results shown in **Table 1**.

....

....

....

....

....

(4 marks)

(d) A second investigation found that membrane permeability increased as the pH was decreased. Suggest an explanation for this.

....

....

....

(3 marks)

Examiners love a good practical question, so you'll need to brush up on terms like 'negative control'. When it comes to explaining results, be clear about what any table or graph is showing you — if the results for a colorimetry experiment show transmission of light rather than absorbance, the numbers will be the opposite way round to the ones above.

Score

33

Biological Membranes — 2

1 Mast cells are a type of immune system cell. They release a signalling molecule, called histamine, which triggers part of the immune response. Histamine is stored inside membrane-bound 'granules' in a mast cell's cytoplasm.

(a) Histamine is unable to diffuse across a mast cell's cell surface membrane. Suggest **one** reason why.

....

(1 mark)

(b) Suggest how mast cells release histamine into the blood.

....

....

....

(2 marks)

2 Plants contain a mixture of solutes. Depending on the relative concentrations of solutes inside a plant cell and its environment, water will move into or out of the cell by osmosis.

Some students wanted to investigate the water potential of white potato cells. To do so they incubated samples of white potato in different concentrations of sucrose solution. The mass of each sample was measured before and after the incubation. The change in mass was then calculated.

Figure 1 shows a calibration curve of the results.

Figure 1

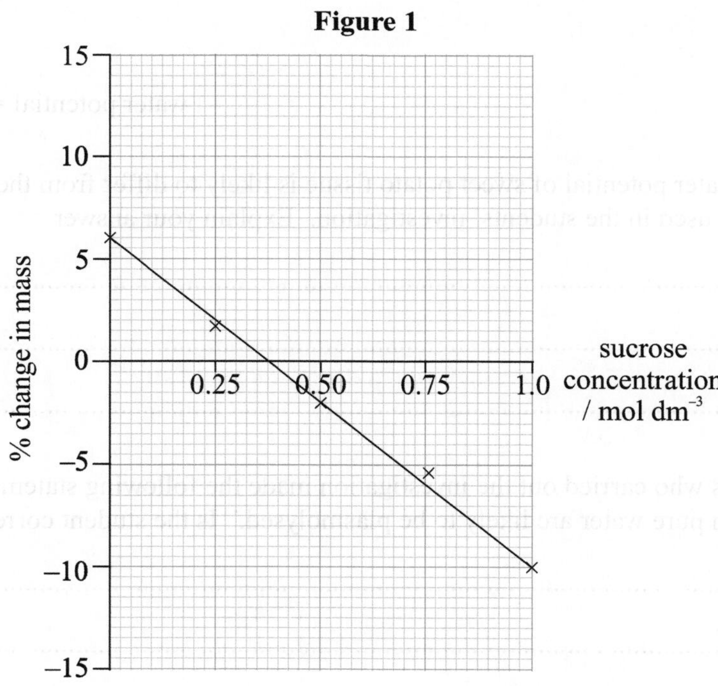

The students prepared the different concentrations of sucrose solution for their investigation using a stock solution of 1 mol dm^{-3} sucrose solution and distilled water.

(a) Complete **Table 1** to show the volumes of stock solution and water used to make up each concentration.

Table 1

Concentration of sucrose solution to be made up / mol dm^{-3}	Volume of 1 mol dm^{-3} sucrose solution used / cm^3	Volume of water used / cm^3	Final volume of solution to be made up / cm^3
1	20	0	20
0.75	15		20
0.5			20
0.25			20
0			20

(2 marks)

(b) Give **two** control variables for this investigation.

1. ....

2. ....

(2 marks)

Table 2 shows the relationship between sucrose concentration and water potential.

Table 2

Sucrose concentration / mol dm^{-3}	0.1	0.2	0.3	0.4	0.5	0.6	0.7	0.8	0.9	1.0
Water potential / kPa	–270	–540	–850	–1130	–1460	–1810	–2190	–2590	-3030	-3530

(c) Use **Table 2** and **Figure 1** to estimate the water potential of the potato tissue.
Show your working.

water potential = ... kPa

(2 marks)

(d) Suggest how the water potential of sweet potato tissue is likely to differ from the water potential of the white potato tissue used in the students' investigation. Explain your answer.

....

....

....

(2 marks)

(e) One of the students who carried out the investigation made the following statement:
'The potato cells in pure water are likely to be plasmolysed.' Is the student correct? Explain your answer.

....

....

(2 marks)

EXAM TIP

'Estimate' means you need to give an approximate value rather than calculate an exact answer. It needs to be a sensible estimate though, not just a stab in the dark guess, so you need to think about the best method to use to obtain your estimate.

Score

13

Cell Division and Cellular Organisation

Well, you're almost at the end of Module 2. Just one more section to get through. On you go then...

For each of questions 1-3, give your answer by writing the correct letter in the box.

1 Which of the following, **A** to **D**, correctly describes what is meant by the term 'homologous chromosomes'?

A Chromosomes in which the genetic information on each chromatid is identical.

B A pair of chromosomes in which each chromosome contains the same genes.

C Chromosomes that originate from the same parent cell prior to fertilisation.

D A pair of chromosomes in which each chromosome contains identical alleles.

Your answer ☐

(1 mark)

2 The human body has many different types of specialised cell, each of which is adapted to its function. Which of the rows, **A** to **D**, in the table below shows a correct adaptation for each cell type?

	Squamous epithelial cell	Neutrophil	Erythrocyte	Sperm cell
A	Joined to neighbouring cells via interlinking cell membranes	Has an acrosome containing digestive enzymes	Biconcave shape	Contains many lysosomes
B	Contains many lysosomes	Biconcave shape	Joined to neighbouring cells via interlinking cell membranes	Has an acrosome containing digestive enzymes
C	Joined to neighbouring cells via interlinking cell membranes	Contains many lysosomes	Biconcave shape	Has an acrosome containing digestive enzymes
D	Biconcave shape	Has an acrosome containing digestive enzymes	Joined to neighbouring cells via interlinking cell membranes	Contains many lysosomes

Your answer ☐

(1 mark)

3 The diagram below shows the main stages of the cell cycle. Which of the letters, **A** to **D** indicates the point in the cycle at which the attachment of chromosomes to the spindle is checked?

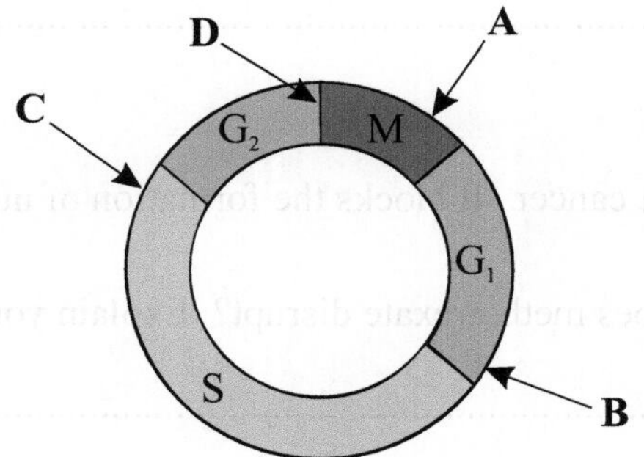

Your answer ☐

(1 mark)

4 A student investigated mitosis in an onion root tip.

(a) Explain why the student used the tip of the root for this investigation.

....

....

(1 mark)

(b) The student prepared a squash slide to view the cells.
Explain what is meant by a 'squash slide' and why the student prepared one for this investigation.

....

....

....

(2 marks)

The student's observations are shown in **Table 1**.

Table 1

Type of cell	Number of cells
Dividing	240
Non-dividing	80

(c) (i) Explain how the student was able to distinguish between dividing cells and non-dividing cells.

....

....

(1 mark)

(ii) Calculate the percentage of cells undergoing mitosis.

percentage of cells undergoing mitosis = ...%

(1 mark)

(d) The onion root tip contains stem cells.

(i) State **two** features of stem cells.

1. ....

2. ....

(2 marks)

(ii) Suggest **one** tissue type formed from the stem cells in a root tip.

....

(1 mark)

5 Methotrexate is a drug used to treat cancer. It blocks the formation of nucleotides within cells.

(a) (i) What stage of the cell cycle does methotrexate disrupt? Explain your answer.

....

....

(2 marks)

(ii) State why the cell cycle is unable to continue in cells that have been treated with methotrexate.

....

....

(1 mark)

(b) A low red blood cell count can be a side effect of taking methotrexate. Suggest why.

....

....

....

(2 marks)

6 A scientist is observing meiosis in the anthers of a diploid flowering plant.

(a) The scientist notes that some of the cells are undergoing anaphase II.

(i) Explain the difference between anaphase II and anaphase I.

....

....

....

(2 marks)

(ii) Outline the events that take place between the end of anaphase II and the completion of cell division.

....

....

....

(2 marks)

(b) Meiosis in the anthers produces pollen grains. A pollen grain is used to fertilise an ovum in the ovary of a female plant. Explain why meiosis is needed to produce a pollen grain.

....

....

....

(2 marks)

(c) Explain how meiosis creates genetic variation in plants.

....

....

....

....

....

....

(4 marks)

7 A scientist was studying the stages of the cell cycle.

The scientist used a microscope to observe some cells undergoing mitosis. **Figure 1** shows an image of one of these cells.

Figure 1

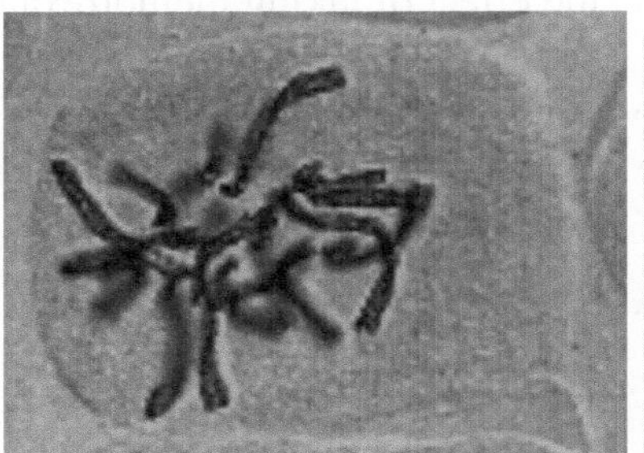

(a) Name the stage of mitosis shown in **Figure 1**. Explain your answer.

....

....

(2 marks)

Cyclins are proteins that play an important role in the cell cycle. A scientist recorded the concentration of two cyclins (**E** and **B**) during part of the cell cycle shown in **Figure 2**. He also recorded the mass of DNA present in the parent cell during this period (also shown in **Figure 2**).

Figure 2

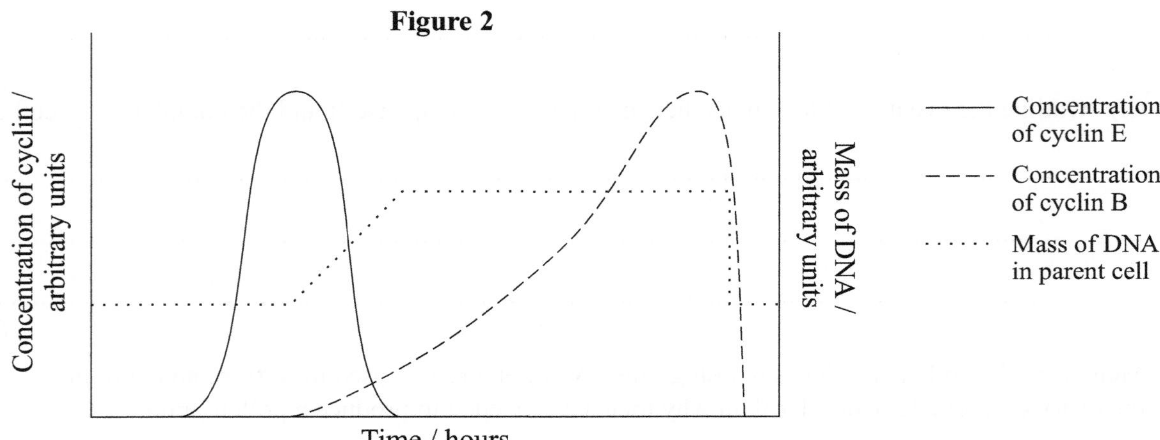

(b) Using the results shown in **Figure 2**, suggest the functions of cyclins **E** and **B** in the cell cycle.

....

....

....

....

....

....

(4 marks)

Exam questions on the cell cycle often describe a way that the normal cycle is altered and ask you to explain what effect this has. As long as you know what usually happens during the different stages of the cell cycle, you should be able to work out what happens if something changes. Make sure you're clued up on the different stages of interphase, mitosis and meiosis.

Score

32

Exchange and Transport — 1

If seeing 'Exchange and Transport Systems' got you excited about answering questions on the rail network, prepare to be disappointed. These are actually on how gases are exchanged in fish, insects, mammals and bacteria. Sorry.

For each of questions 1-3, give your answer by ticking the appropriate box.

1 The lungs contain various different cells and tissues, each of which has a different function. Which of the rows, **A** to **D**, in the table below shows the correct function for each component of the lungs?

	Goblet cell	Ciliated epithelium	Smooth muscle	Cartilage
A	Moves mucus away from the alveoli	Secretes mucus to trap microorganisms and dust	Provides support to the trachea and bronchi	Controls the diameter of the bronchioles
B	Secretes mucus to trap microorganisms and dust	Moves mucus away from the alveoli	Controls the diameter of the bronchioles	Provides support to the trachea and bronchi
C	Moves the mucus away from the alveoli	Provides support to the trachea and bronchi	Secretes mucus to trap microorganisms and dust	Controls the diameter of the bronchioles
D	Secretes mucus to trap microorganisms and dust	Controls the diameter of the bronchioles	Moves mucus away from the alveoli	Provides support to the trachea and bronchi

Your answer ☐ **(1 mark)**

2 The graph below shows the results of a spirometry test.

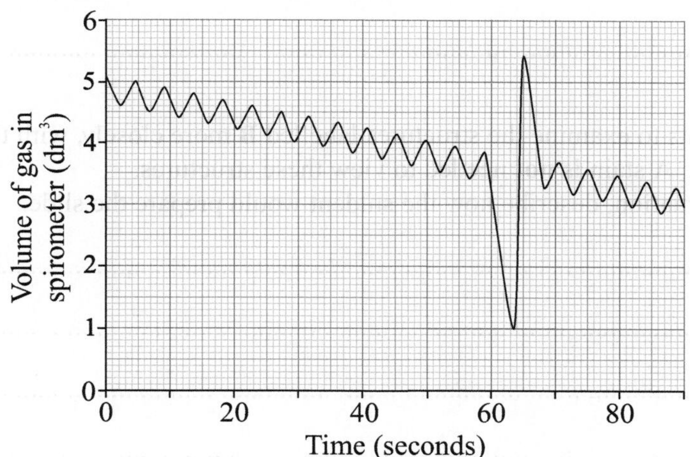

From the graph above, what is this individual's tidal volume?

A 2.1 dm^3 **B** 4.4 dm^3 **C** 0.5 dm^3 **D** 2.9 dm^3

Your answer ☐ **(1 mark)**

3 The following statements describe the process of ventilation in mammals. They are **not** in the correct order.

1 The external intercostal muscles and diaphragm muscles relax.
2 The pressure in the lungs decreases causing air to flow into the lungs.
3 The rib cage moves upwards and outwards, and the diaphragm flattens.
4 The pressure in the lungs increases and air is forced out of the lungs.
5 The external intercostal muscles and diaphragm muscles contract.
6 The rib cage moves downwards and inwards, and the diaphragm becomes curved.

Which option gives the correct order to describe the process of inspiration followed by expiration?

A 5, 3, 2, 1, 6, 4 **B** 1, 6, 4, 5, 3, 2 **C** 5, 6, 4, 1, 3, 2 **D** 1, 3, 2, 5, 6, 4

Your answer ☐ **(1 mark)**

4 A student dissected a grasshopper. As part of the dissection, she removed a piece of the grasshopper's exoskeleton.

(a) Suggest a tool that the student could have used to cut through the exoskeleton.

....

(1 mark)

(b) **Figure 1** shows a diagram of the grasshopper's gas exchange system.

Figure 1

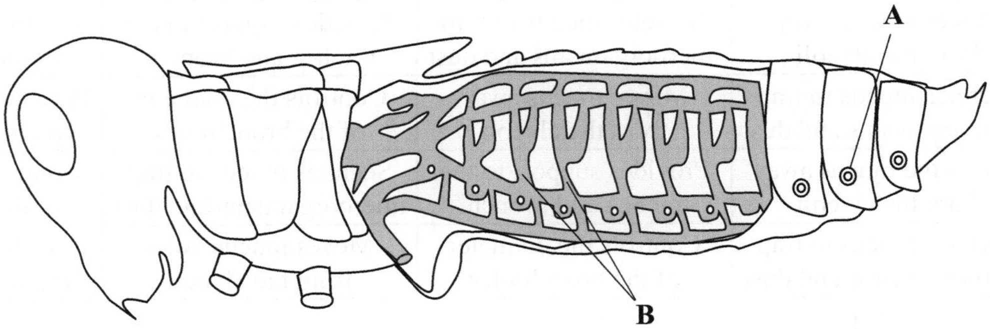

A

B

(i) Identify the structures labelled **A** and **B** in **Figure 1**.

A...

B ....

(2 marks)

(ii) The student wants to examine the structures labelled **B** more closely, with the use of a wet mount slide. A stain is **not** needed to view these structures.
Using this information, describe how the student would prepare the slide.

....

....

....

....

(3 marks)

(c) Explain how a grasshopper pumps air in and out of its body.

....

....

....

(2 marks)

(d) The grasshopper's gas exchange system contains fluid.
Describe how this fluid is involved in gas exchange.

....

....

....

(2 marks)

5 **Figure 2** shows a gill filament of a bony fish.

Figure 2

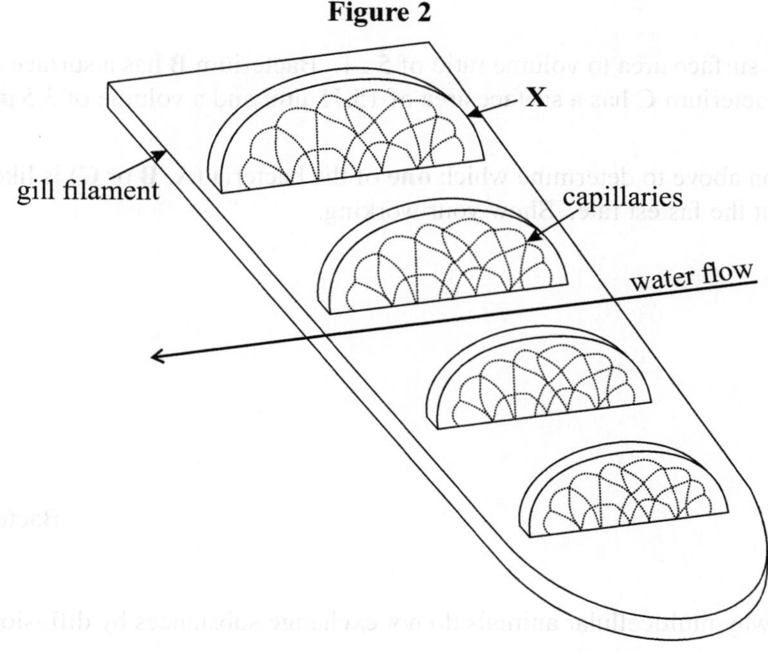

(a) (i) Name structure **X** on **Figure 2.**

....

(1 mark)

(ii) Draw an arrow on structure **X** to show the direction of blood flow.

(1 mark)

(iii) Label structure **X** to show where the highest and lowest concentrations of oxygen are found in the blood.

(1 mark)

(b) Explain **one** way in which the structure of the gill filament is adapted to its function.

....

....

(2 marks)

(c) Explain how changes in the buccal cavity of a bony fish allow the gills to be ventilated.

....

....

....

....

....

(4 marks)

Don't panic if you haven't carried out a practical task that you get asked about in the exams. You'll know the skills involved, even if you didn't use them for the same investigation. For example, you might have dissected the gas exchange system of a bony fish rather than an insect, but the principles of dissection and examining microscope slides are the same.

Score

22

Exchange and Transport — 2

1 Bacterium **A** has a surface area to volume ratio of 5 : 1. Bacterium **B** has a surface area to volume ratio of 84 : 22. Bacterium **C** has a surface area of 15.75 μm^2 and a volume of 3.5 μm^3.

(a) Use the information above to determine which **one** of the bacteria (**A**, **B** or **C**) is likely to be able to carry out gas exchange at the fastest rate. Show your working.

Bacterium: ....

(2 marks)

(b) Give **two** reasons why multicellular animals do not exchange substances by diffusion across their outer surface.

1. ....

....

2. ....

....

(2 marks)

2 Sharks exchange oxygen across their gill plates using a counter-current gas exchange system. **Figure 1** shows how the relative oxygen concentration of water changes with distance along a shark's gill plate.

Figure 1

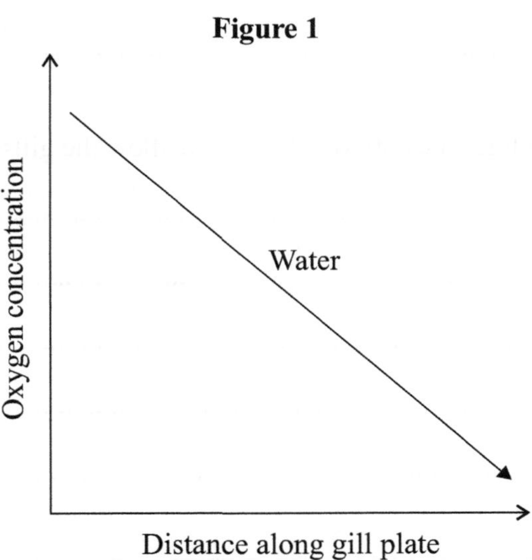

(a) On **Figure 1**, sketch the relative oxygen concentration of the blood flowing through the gill plate.

(1 mark)

Figure 2 shows how the relative oxygen concentrations of water and blood would change with distance along a shark's gill plate if gas exchange took place via a parallel flow system.

Figure 2

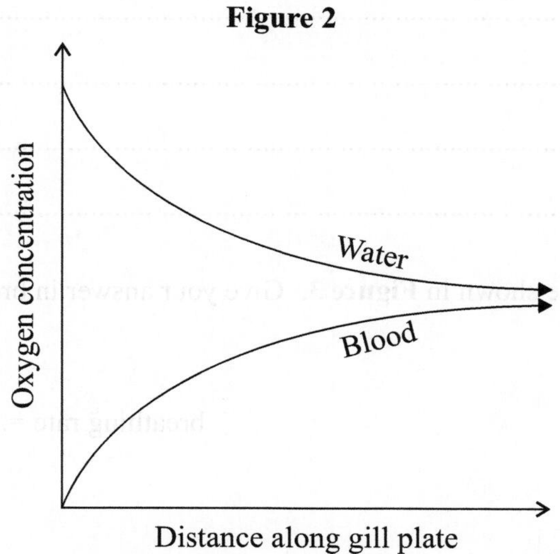

(b) Use **Figure 2** to explain why a parallel flow gas exchange system would be less efficient than a counter-current gas exchange system.

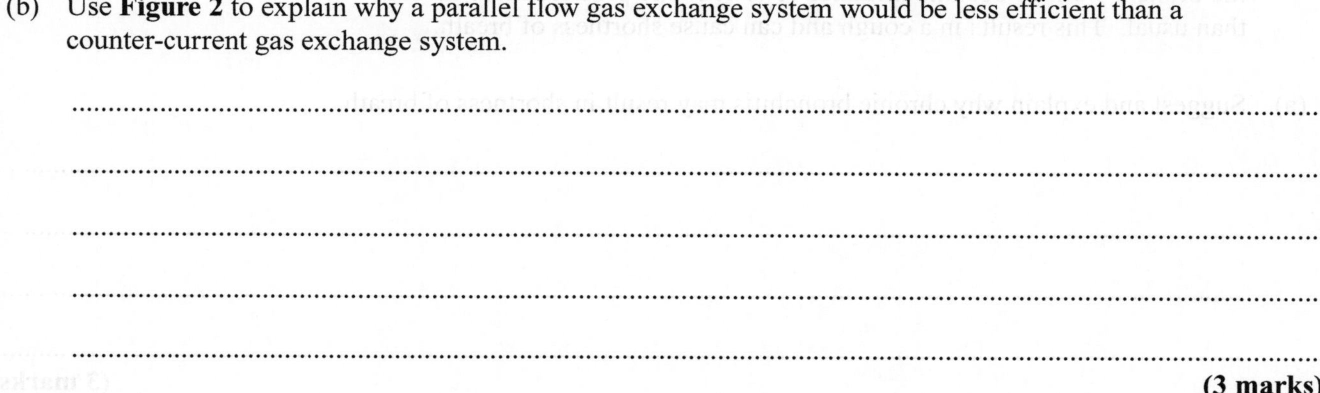

(3 marks)

3 Intrapulmonary pressure is the pressure inside the lungs.
Figure 3 shows how intrapulmonary pressure changes during breathing.

Figure 3

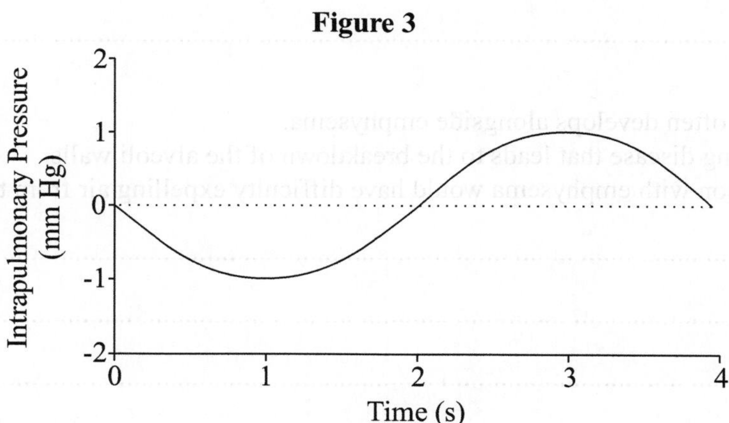

(a) State the time in **Figure 3** at which the lung volume is at its smallest.

....

(1 mark)

(b) State the time period in **Figure 3** during which air is being taken into the lungs.
Explain your answer.

....

....

....

....

(3 marks)

(c) Calculate the breathing rate shown in **Figure 3**. Give your answer in breaths min^{-1}.

breathing rate =.................................. breaths min^{-1}

(1 mark)

4 Chronic bronchitis is a long-term infection of the bronchi. This causes the bronchi walls to become inflamed (swollen) and produce more mucus than usual. This results in a cough and can cause shortness of breath.

(a) Suggest and explain why chronic bronchitis may result in shortness of breath.

....

....

....

....

(3 marks)

(b) Explain how the concentration gradients of oxygen and carbon dioxide are maintained between the alveoli and the blood in a healthy person.

....

....

....

(2 marks)

(c) Chronic bronchitis often develops alongside emphysema.
Emphysema is a lung disease that leads to the breakdown of the alveoli walls.
Suggest why a person with emphysema would have difficulty expelling air from their lungs.

....

....

....

(2 marks)

EXAM TIP

Ah, 'context'... the examiners just love it. That's why, instead of asking you bog standard questions about diffusion or ventilation in the lungs, they're more likely to get you to apply your knowledge to a context — for example, by telling you all about a disease that interrupts lung function and then getting you to work out why that's the case. If you've learnt your stuff, you'll be fine.

Score

20

Transport in Animals — 1

More questions about transport now — this time they're all about circulatory systems in animals. If your heart rate is quickening in panic at the thought of this stuff coming up in the exams, you better get practising now.

For each of questions 1-3, give your answer by writing the correct letter in the box.

1 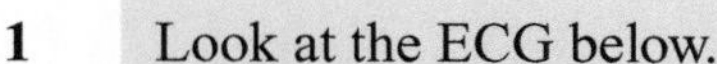
Look at the ECG below.

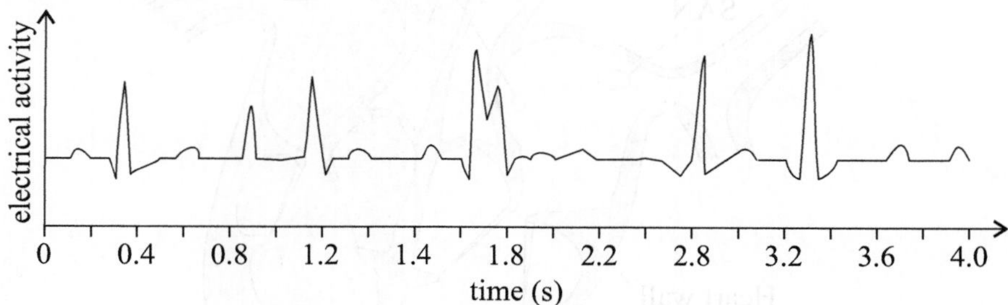

What abnormal heart activity is displayed in this ECG?

A fibrillation

B an ectopic heartbeat

C tachycardia

D bradycardia

Your answer ☐

(1 mark)

2 Which of the following statements related to the function of haemoglobin is/are correct?

Statement 1: At low partial pressures of oxygen, oxygen is loaded onto haemoglobin, forming oxyhaemoglobin.

Statement 2: Oxyhaemoglobin more readily dissociates into haemoglobin and oxygen when the concentration of carbon dioxide in the blood is high.

Statement 3: Fetal haemoglobin has a higher affinity for oxygen than adult haemoglobin.

A 1, 2 and 3

B 1 and 2 only

C 2 and 3 only

D 1 only

Your answer ☐

(1 mark)

3 During the cardiac cycle, blood enters the heart through the vena cava and pulmonary vein. The following statements describe the rest of the cardiac cycle. They are **not** in the correct order.

1: The atria contract, forcing blood through the atrioventricular valves.

2: The wave of electrical activity is detected by the atrioventricular node and passed along the bundle of His and the Purkyne tissue.

3: The ventricles contract, forcing blood through the semi-lunar valves.

4: The sino-atrial node sends out a wave of electrical activity.

5: Blood leaves the heart through the aorta and pulmonary artery.

Which option gives the correct order of events in rest of the cardiac cycle?

A 1, 4, 2, 3, 5

B 4, 3, 2, 1, 5

C 3, 5, 4, 2, 1

D 4, 1, 2, 3, 5

Your answer ☐

(1 mark)

4 Electrical impulses in the heart are generated by the sino-atrial node (SAN) and conducted across the muscle tissue in a highly coordinated sequence.

Figure 1 shows a diagram of the heart. The SAN and atrio-ventricular node (AVN) are labelled.

Figure 1

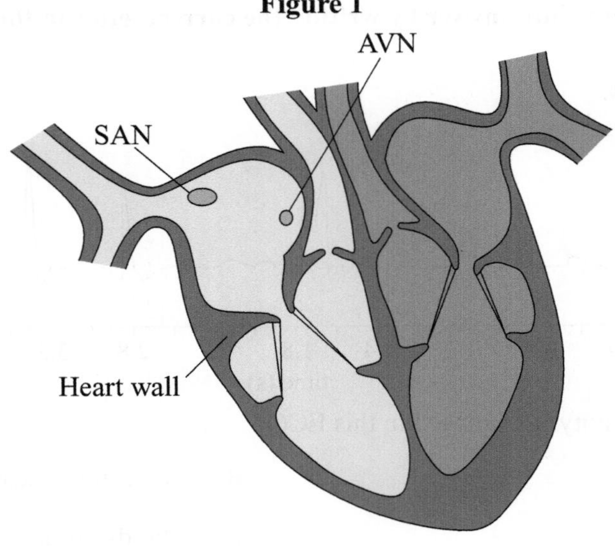

(a) Describe the function of the AVN.

....

(1 mark)

The heart wall contains muscle tissue and collagen, which acts as a structural support.
Collagen does not conduct electricity.

(b) Explain why the collagen in the heart wall also has a role in helping to ensure that the ventricles contract at the right time.

....

....

....

(2 marks)

5 **Figure 2** shows a cross-section of the human heart.

Figure 2

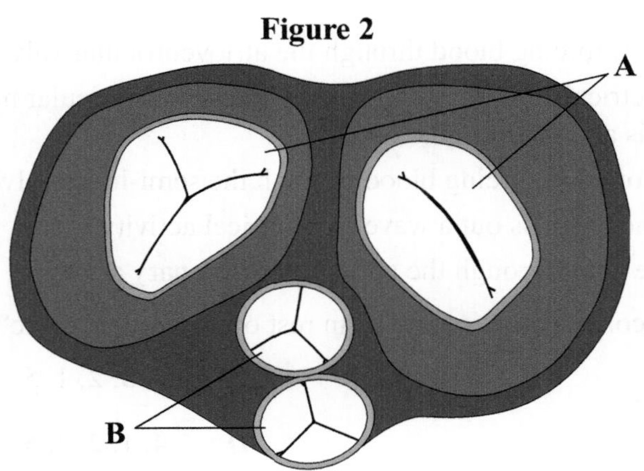

(a) What is the role of the valves labelled **A** in **Figure 2**?

....

....

....

(2 marks)

(b) In terms of pressure changes in the heart, explain what causes the valves labelled **B** in **Figure 2** to open.

....

....

(1 mark)

(c) Cardiac output is the volume of blood pumped out of the left ventricle in one minute. Scientists investigated the effect of body position on heart rate and cardiac output. **Table 1** shows their results.

Table 1

	Standing up	Lying down
Mean heart rate (bpm)	74	57
Mean cardiac output (cm^3 min^{-1})	4700	4700
Mean stroke volume (cm^3)		

(i) The stroke volume is the volume of blood that is pumped out by the left ventricle in one cardiac cycle. Use the information in **Table 1** to complete the table to show the mean stroke volumes. Give your answers to three significant figures. Show your working.

(2 marks)

(ii) The scientists ensured that the participants of the investigation had been in the required position for five minutes before they recorded these measurements. Suggest why.

....

....

(1 mark)

(iii) Suggest why there is a difference in heart rate between standing up and lying down in **Table 1**.

....

....

(1 mark)

(iv) Explain why the scientists used 'mean' measurements.

....

....

(1 mark)

EXAM TIP

Try not to leave anything blank in the exam, especially multiple choice questions. You won't lose marks for wrong answers, so you might as well try narrowing down your options, then give your best guess. It can be easier than it looks to rule things out — e.g. if you have to choose the right sequence of events, think about whether certain things must happen before others.

Score

14

Transport in Animals — 2

1 A student carried out a dissection of a mammalian heart.
Figure 1 shows the external structure of the heart.

Figure 1

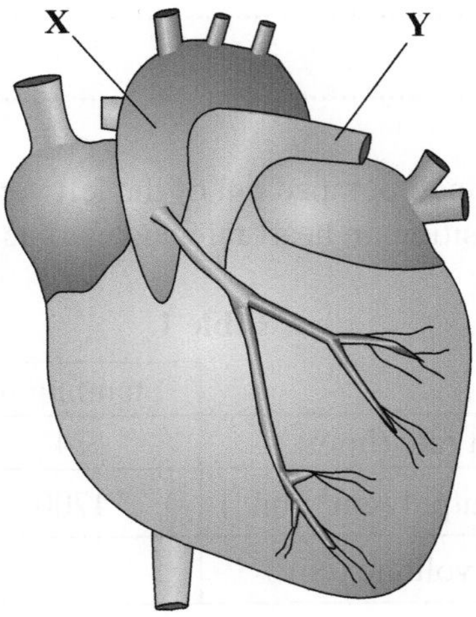

X Y

(a) (i) Name the blood vessels labelled **X** and **Y** on **Figure 1**.

X: ....

Y: ....

(2 marks)

The student struggled to identify the blood vessels attached to the heart.
He was also unable to tell which were arteries and which were veins.

(ii) Describe how feeling the inside of the blood vessels would have allowed the students to tell the difference between an artery and a vein.

....

....

(1 mark)

(b) Sketch a line on **Figure 1** to show where the student would need to make a cut to see inside the left ventricle.

(1 mark)

(c) Name the blood vessel that can be seen on the surface of the heart in **Figure 1**.

....

(1 mark)

The student produced a biological drawing of the heart.

(d) Give **one** instruction that the student would need to follow in order to produce a clear and useful drawing.

....

(1 mark)

2 Lymph is formed from tissue fluid, which is formed in capillary beds.

(a) Lymphoedema is a condition that develops when a person's lymphatic system does not function correctly. The main symptom is the swelling of parts of the body.

(i) Suggest why lymphoedema causes swelling.

....

....

(1 mark)

(ii) State **two** ways in which the composition of lymph is different from the composition of blood.

1. ....

2. ....

(2 marks)

(b) **Table 1** shows the hydrostatic and oncotic pressures along a capillary bed.

Table 1

	Arteriole end of capillary bed	Venule end of capillary bed
Hydrostatic pressure (mmHg)	33	16
Oncotic pressure (mmHg)	26	26

(i) Explain the difference in hydrostatic pressure at the arteriole and venule ends of the capillary bed.

....

....

(2 marks)

(ii) Suggest why the oncotic pressure remains the same at each end of the capillary bed.

....

....

....

(2 marks)

(c) Capillary beds are important exchange surfaces.
Explain **one** way in which the structure of capillaries helps them carry out their function.

....

....

(1 mark)

3 **Figure 2** shows the oxygen dissociation curve for a person who is exercising, alongside a person who is not exercising.

Figure 2

(a) Explain why the percentage saturation of haemoglobin with oxygen is lower at point **A** in **Figure 2** than at point **B**.

....

....

....

(2 marks)

(b) (i) Explain why the Bohr effect means that the oxygen dissociation curve for the person exercising is to the right of the oxygen dissociation curve for the person who is not exercising.

....

....

....

(2 marks)

(ii) Describe the roles of carbonic anhydrase and carbonic acid in the Bohr effect.

....

....

....

....

(3 marks)

4 **Figure 3** shows the pressure changes in an individual's heart during the cardiac cycle.

Figure 3

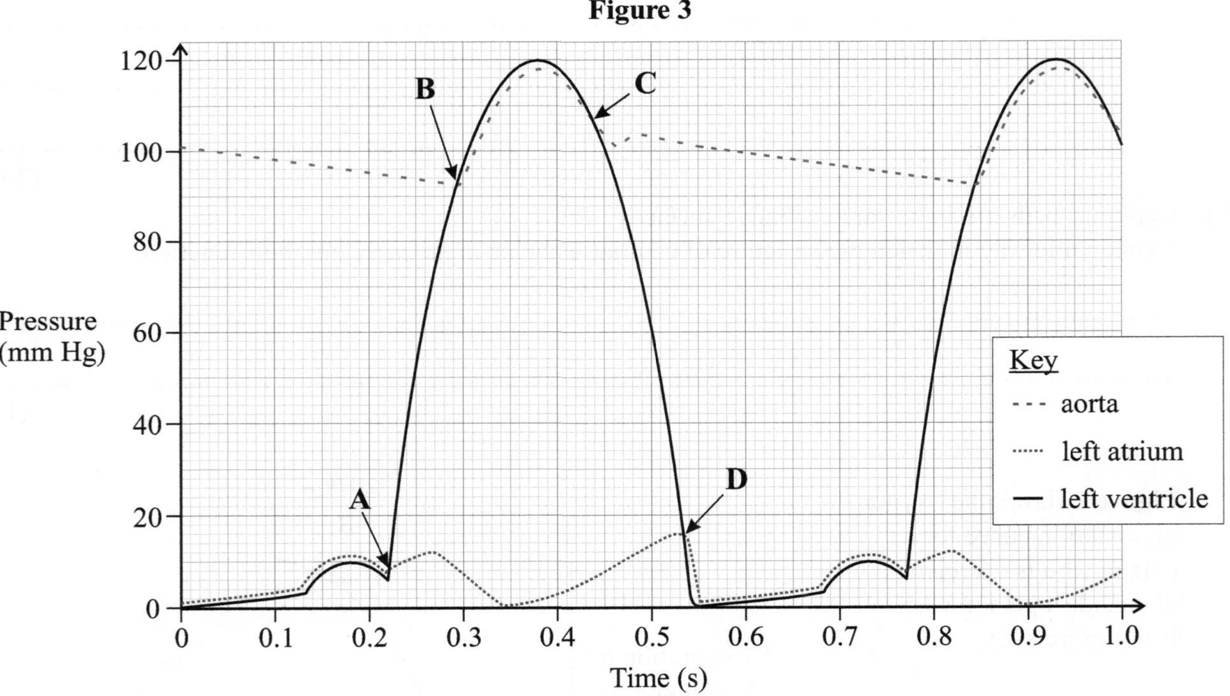

(a) Calculate the heart rate for the individual shown in **Figure 3**.

.... beats per minute

(1 mark)

(b) When on **Figure 3** does the left atrium first start to contract?

Hint: when a chamber contracts, there's a sudden rise in pressure inside the chamber.

.... seconds

(1 mark)

(c)* Explain the events that are occurring at points **A** to **D** on **Figure 3**.

....

....

....

....

....

....

....

....

....

....

....

....

....

(6 marks)

(d) Explain the difference between the maximum pressures of the left atrium and the left ventricle of the heart.

....

....

....

(1 mark)

(e) Using your own knowledge and information from **Figure 3**, explain **one** way in which the aorta is adapted for its function.

....

....

....

(2 marks)

Don't worry if you're presented with an unfamiliar graph in the exam. Just make sure you read the key carefully (if there is one) and the labels on the axes too. Don't try to answer any questions until you're sure you understand exactly what the graph is showing.

Score

32

Transport in Plants

Now's the time to find out whether you can remember everything you should know about transport in plants, or whether you've got a memory like a sieve tube element.

For each of questions 1-3, give your answer by writing the correct letter in the box.

1 The rate of transpiration in plants is affected by a variety of factors, including light intensity, temperature, humidity and wind speed. In the table below, which of the rows **A** to **D** corresponds to the set of conditions that would give the fastest rate of transpiration?

	Light intensity	Temperature	Humidity	Wind speed
A	low	high	low	low
B	high	high	low	high
C	high	high	high	high
D	low	low	low	low

Your answer ☐

(1 mark)

2 Which of the statements, **A** to **D**, related to the transport of water in plants, is **incorrect**?

A Water travels down a water potential gradient to enter a plant through the root hair cells.

B Water must travel from the root hair cells through the root cortex to reach the xylem.

C When water is transported through areas of the plant via the apoplast pathway, it is transported through the non-living parts of plant cells, such as the cell walls.

D Water molecules moving through the apoplast pathway pass through plasmodesmata.

Your answer ☐

(1 mark)

3 Which of the following statements about adaptations of hydrophytes is/are **true**?

Statement 1: Hydrophytes have stomata in sunken pits and a thick waxy layer on their epidermis.

Statement 2: Stomata are usually only found on the upper surface of hydrophytes' leaves.

Statement 3: Air spaces in the tissues of hydrophytes can act as a store of oxygen for use in respiration.

A 1, 2 and 3

B 1 and 2 only

C 2 and 3 only

D 3 only

Your answer ☐

(1 mark)

4 A student used a potometer to investigate transpiration in a plant. **Figure 1** shows how the potometer was set up. The student closed the tap, then took the capillary tube out of the beaker of water long enough for an air bubble to form. She then recorded the amount of time it took for the air bubble to move between the two markers, and used it to calculate the transpiration rate.

Figure 1

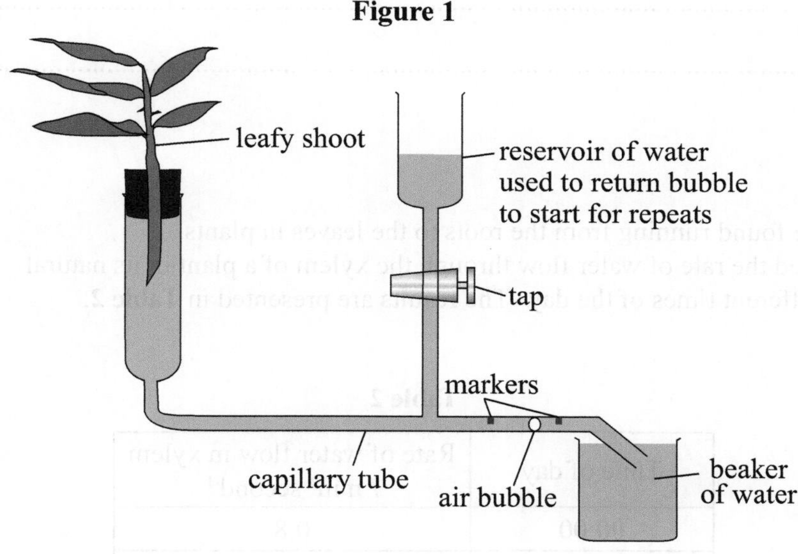

(a) When setting up this experiment, it is important that water does not touch the leaves. Using your knowledge of water transport in plants, explain why.

....

....

....

(2 marks)

(b) Suggest **one** other precaution that must be taken when setting up this experiment.

....

(1 mark)

(c) Suggest and explain why measuring the time it takes for the air bubble to move between the two markers may not result in an accurate estimation of the plant's transpiration rate.

....

....

....

(2 marks)

The student used the potometer to investigate the effect of temperature on the transpiration rate. The results are shown in **Table 1**.

Table 1

Temperature / °C	Mean transpiration rate / cm^3 per minute
20	0.20
30	0.34
40	0.85
50	1.24
60	1.36

(d) Explain the relationship between the temperature and the transpiration rate in **Table 1**.

....

....

....

....

(3 marks)

5 Xylem vessels are found running from the roots to the leaves in plants. Scientists measured the rate of water flow through the xylem of a plant in its natural environment at different times of the day. The results are presented in **Table 2**.

Table 2

Time of day	Rate of water flow in xylem / mm^3 $second^{-1}$
00:00	0.8
06:00	2.8
12:00	4.5
18:00	3.0

(a) Using your knowledge of water transport in the xylem, explain the difference in the results between 00:00 and 12:00 in **Table 2**.

....

....

....

....

(3 marks)

(b) In order to investigate the structure of the xylem, the scientists also carried out a dissection of the plant's stem.

(i) Suggest why the scientists kept the dissected plant tissue in water until they were ready to view the cells.

....

....

(1 mark)

(ii) Suggest a further step that the scientists would have carried out in order to observe the xylem vessels under a microscope.

....

....

(1 mark)

(iii) Describe **one** way in which the position of xylem vessels differs between the stem and the root of a dicotyledonous plant.

....

....

(1 mark)

6 **Translocation in a plant describes the movement of solutes to where they are needed within the plant.**

(a) When treated with metabolic inhibitors, translocation in a plant stops. Explain why.

....

....

....

(2 marks)

Figure 2 represents the flow of solutes in the phloem of a tree, according to the mass flow hypothesis.

Figure 2

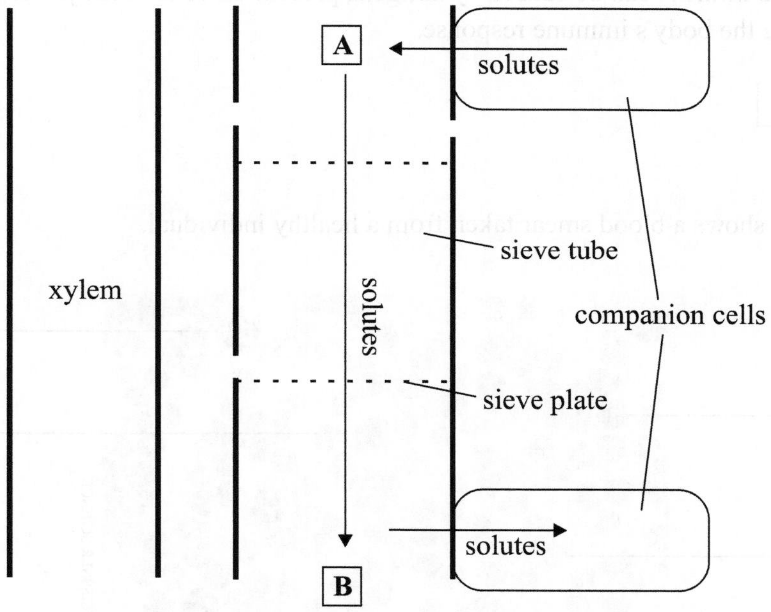

(b) Explain why the pressure at point **A** in **Figure 2** will be higher than that at point **B**.

....

....

....

....

....

(4 marks)

EXAM TIP

Make sure you pay attention to whether a question is asking you to 'describe' or 'explain' — they don't mean the same thing. 'Describing' means giving an account of something, e.g. saying how a variable changes in a table or graph, whereas 'explaining' means setting out reasons behind it, e.g. saying why the variable changes.

Score

23

Disease and the Immune System — 1

These questions are about disease and the immune system. Your primary response is going to want you to turn away from this page, but make sure you stick at it. You want to get those memory cells activated for your exam.

For questions 1 and 2, give your answer by writing the correct letter in the box.

1 Rheumatoid arthritis is an autoimmune disease that causes inflammation of the joints. Which of the following statements, **A** to **D**, related to rheumatoid arthritis is **true**?

A Rheumatoid arthritis can be caused by the body failing to produce antibodies against foreign antigens in the joints.

B Rheumatoid arthritis can be caused by the body mistakenly producing antibodies against antigens present on cells in the joints.

C Rheumatoid arthritis can be caused by the body producing excess antibodies in response to the presence of foreign antigens in the joints.

D Rheumatoid arthritis can be caused by antigens present on cells in the joints suppressing the body's immune response.

Your answer ☐ **(1 mark)**

2 The image below shows a blood smear taken from a healthy individual.

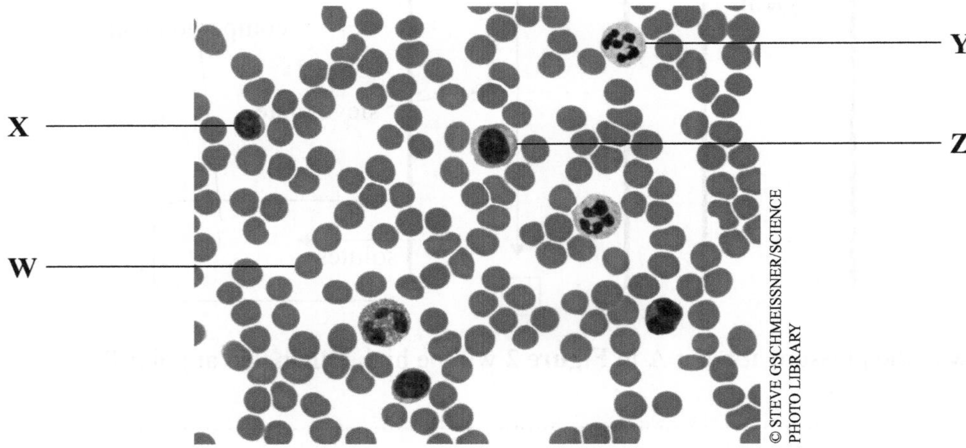

Which of the rows, **A** to **D**, in the table below correctly identifies the cells labelled **W** to **Z**?

	W	X	Y	Z
A	Lymphocyte	Monocyte	Neutrophil	Red blood cell
B	Red blood cell	Monocyte	Lymphocyte	Neutrophil
C	Lymphocyte	Neutrophil	Monocyte	Red blood cell
D	Red blood cell	Lymphocyte	Neutrophil	Monocyte

Your answer ☐ **(1 mark)**

3 **Figure 1** shows an antibody. The antibody acts as an agglutinin.

Figure 1

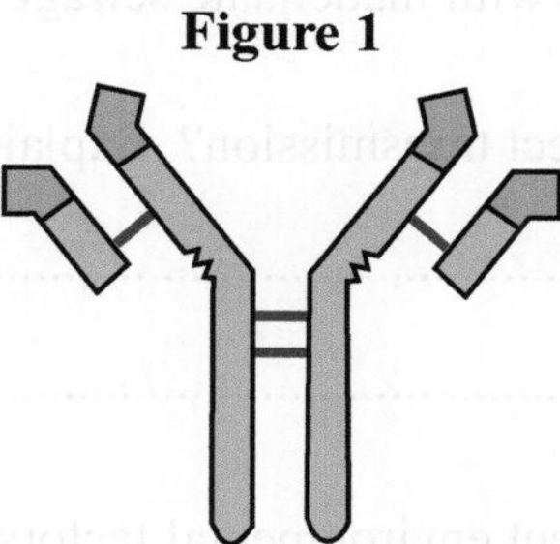

(a) (i) Describe the role of this antibody in the immune response.

....

(1 mark)

(ii) Name a type of cell that produces antibodies.

....

(1 mark)

(iii) Describe **two** ways in which the structure of the antibody shown in **Figure 1** is adapted to its function.

1. ....

2. ....

(2 marks)

Some antibodies have a more complex structure, made up of several monomers joined together. This is shown in **Figure 2**.

Figure 2

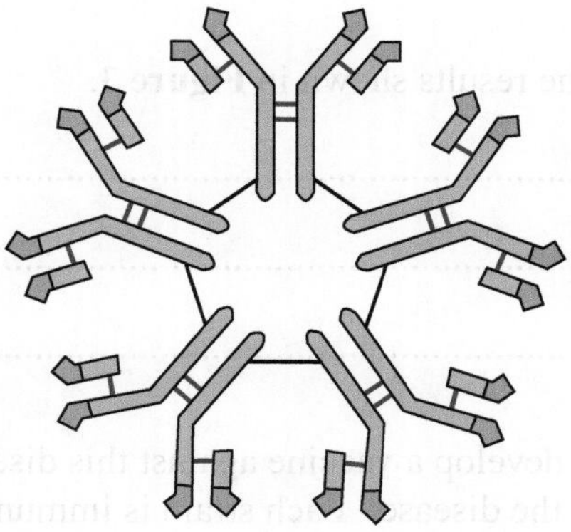

(b) Suggest and explain **one** advantage of the structure in **Figure 2**, compared to that in **Figure 1**.

....

....

(2 marks)

(c) Some cells can produce antibodies at a rate of 2000 molecules per second. Calculate how many antibodies would be produced by one of these cells in one hour. Show your working. Give your answer in standard form.

Number of antibodies = ...

(2 marks)

4 Scientists are investigating the transmission of a diarrhoeal disease that can be fatal in young children. The disease can be contracted by drinking water contaminated with infected faeces. For this reason, it is common in low-income countries with inadequate sewage and drinking water systems.

(a) Does this disease show direct or indirect transmission? Explain your answer.

....

....

(1 mark)

The scientists investigated how different environmental factors influenced the spread of this disease in a particular low-income country. **Figure 3** shows some of their results.

Figure 3

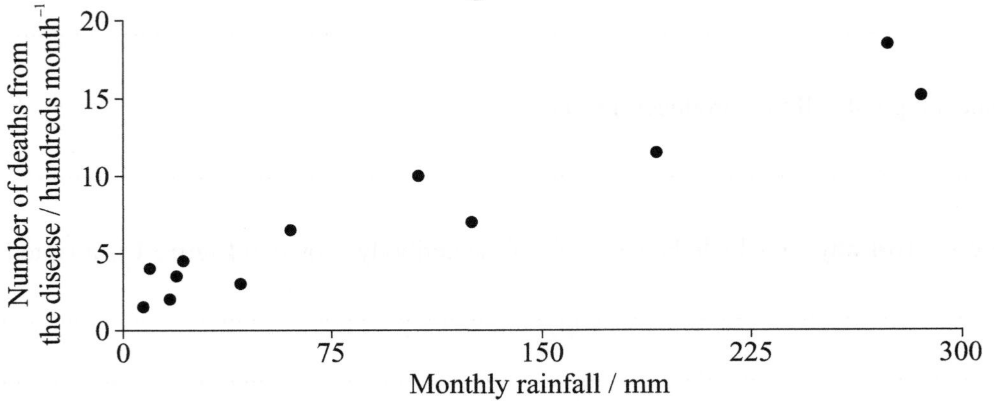

Number of deaths from the disease / hundreds month^{-1}

20, 15, 10, 5, 0

0, 75, 150, 225, 300

Monthly rainfall / mm

(b) (i) What conclusion can be drawn from the results shown in **Figure 3**?

....

....

(1 mark)

(ii) Suggest an explanation for the results shown in **Figure 3**.

....

....

....

(2 marks)

(c) Other scientists are attempting to develop a vaccine against this disease. There are several different strains of the pathogen that cause the disease. Each strain is immunologically distinct.
Suggest and explain why this may make it difficult to develop an effective vaccine against the disease.

....

....

....

....

(3 marks)

EXAM TIP

Make sure you understand what a graph is showing before you launch into your answer. You should ~~double~~ triple check the axis labels — you don't want to talk about the number of cases of the disease, for example, if the graph's talking about the number of deaths from the disease.

Score

17

Disease and the Immune System — 2

1 Corn plants that are being eaten by caterpillars release a chemical. The chemical's odour attracts a species of wasp that lays its eggs in the caterpillars. When the eggs hatch, the caterpillars are killed.

(a) Suggest **one** way in which a corn plant's response to being eaten may help to defend it against infection by pathogens.

....

....

(1 mark)

(b) Describe **one** way in which a corn plant may be able to limit the spread of an invading pathogen between its cells.

....

....

(1 mark)

2 Phagocytosis is an important step in the immune response of humans.

(a) When a person is wounded, phagocytes migrate from different areas of the body to the site of the wound.

(i) Explain what causes phagocytes to migrate in this way.

....

....

(2 marks)

(ii) Suggest a benefit of the phagocytes' migration response.

....

....

(1 mark)

(b) Describe what happens when a phagocyte comes into contact with a pathogen.

....

....

....

....

(3 marks)

IgG is an opsonin. Some people do not produce enough IgG.

(c) Explain how phagocytosis may be affected by a reduced level of IgG in the blood.

....

....

....

(2 marks)

3 **Figure 1** shows a person's immune responses following two separate infections with the same strain of bacteria.

Figure 1

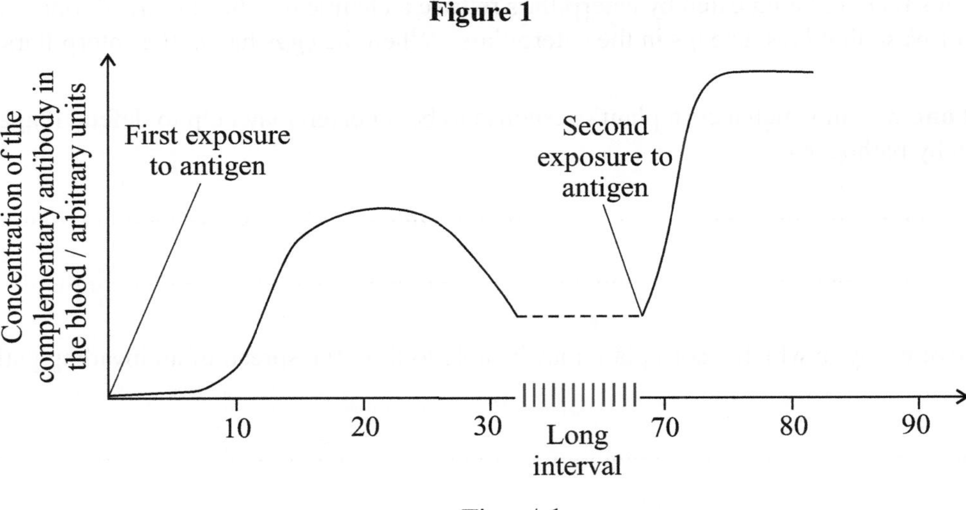

(a) (i) Explain the shape of the curve for the primary immune response.

Remember, 'explain' means 'give reasons for'. Don't just describe the shape of the curve here.

....

....

....

....

....

....

(4 marks)

(ii) Using the information shown in **Figure 1**, explain why the person shows no symptoms following the second exposure to a bacterial antigen.

....

....

....

(2 marks)

Tetanus is a disease caused by *Clostridium tetani* bacteria. The bacteria secrete a toxin that can cause serious muscle spasms. Tetanus can be treated with a mixture of anti-toxins and antibiotics.

(b) Explain why anti-toxins are an effective treatment for tetanus but cannot be used to cure the disease.

....

....

....

....

(3 marks)

4 **Group B streptococcus (GBS) is a bacterium that can be carried, without harm, in a healthy human body. However, if a newborn baby becomes infected with GBS, it can lead to meningitis or other serious diseases.**

GBS is typically passed on from a carrier mother to her baby during birth. Scientists are currently working to develop a vaccine against GBS, which will be given to pregnant women.

(a) (i) Suggest why a pregnant woman may be vaccinated against GBS even if she carries it without harm.

....

....

(1 mark)

(ii) Explain how the vaccine would lead to the production of memory cells against GBS.

....

....

....

....

....

(4 marks)

When a baby breastfeeds, it receives some of its mother's antibodies. This gives the baby immunity against the diseases its mother is immune to.

(b) Describe two differences between the immunity obtained from breastfeeding with the immunity obtained from a vaccine.

1. ....

....

2. ....

....

(2 marks)

Meningitis is the inflammation of the protective layers around the brain and spinal cord.

(c) (i) Using the information provided, explain how the non-specific immune response to a GBS infection could lead to meningitis.

Hint: this question is really asking you how the non-specific immune response against bacteria could lead to inflammation.

....

....

....

....

(3 marks)

(ii) Meningitis can be treated with antibiotics. Explain why it might become a problem to treat meningitis with antibiotics in future.

....

....

(1 mark)

5 **Figure 2** shows a simplified model of the different antigens present on red blood cells from different blood types.

Figure 2

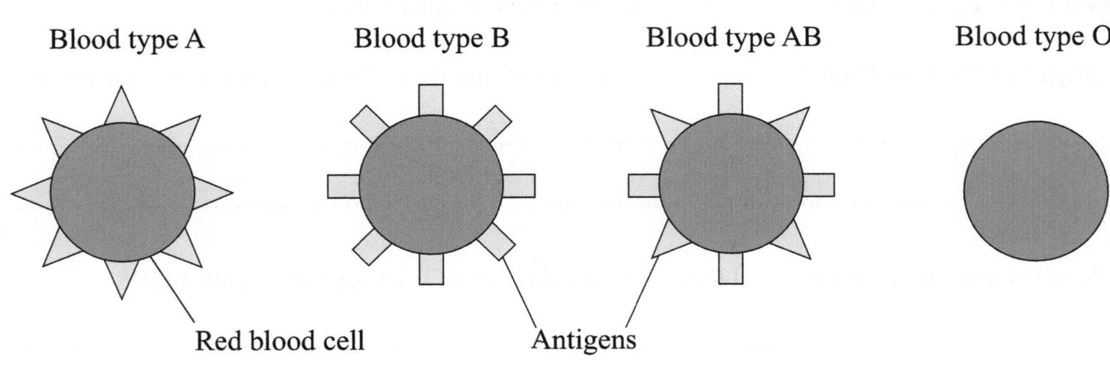

(a)* Using the information in **Figure 2**, explain what would happen if a person with blood type A received a transfusion of blood type B.

....

....

....

....

....

....

....

....

....

....

....

(6 marks)

(b) Explain why anyone can receive type O blood.

....

....

(1 mark)

(c) Agglutinins can be used to determine whether a person has type O blood. Suggest how.

....

....

(2 marks)

EXAM TIP

When answering exam questions — especially ones like 5 (a)*, where you'll be marked on the quality of your extended response — it's important to use the correct, scientific terms. There are a lot of scientific terms in this topic (e.g. phagocytosis, opsonin and antigen to name just a few) so make sure you learn what they all mean <u>and</u> how to spell them.

Score

39

Biodiversity

There's a lot you need to know about biodiversity — what it is, how to measure it, which factors affect it, and how to conserve it. You know what that means... here's a bunch of questions about all those things. Enjoy.

For each of questions 1-3, give your answer by writing the correct letter in the box.

1 Some students are investigating the species present in a coastal habitat. They draw a straight line from the coast, heading inland, and then use quadrats to sample 1 m^2 areas at regular intervals along the line. What type of sampling, **A** to **D**, are the students using?

A random sampling

B systematic sampling

C stratified sampling

D opportunistic sampling

Your answer ☐

(1 mark)

2 Which of the following statements about *in situ* and *ex situ* conservation methods is/are **true**?

Statement 1: *In situ* conservation might involve preventing the introduction of non-native species that threaten local species.

Statement 2: An advantage of *ex situ* conservation is that it is easier to control the environment than with *in situ* conservation.

Statement 3: Marine conservation zones are an example of *ex situ* conservation.

A 1, 2 and 3

B 1 and 2 only

C 2 and 3 only

D 1 only

Your answer ☐

(1 mark)

3 A scientist is using Simpson's Index of Diversity to compare the level of biodiversity in four different habitats. The results are shown in the table below.

Habitat	Simpson's Index of Diversity
A	0.64
B	0.24
C	0.72
D	0.45

Based on the information above, which of the following statements is/are definitely **true**?

Statement 1: Habitat A has a higher species richness than Habitat D.

Statement 2: Habitat B has the highest biodiversity.

Statement 3: Habitat C is more diverse than Habitat D.

A 1, 2 and 3

B 1 and 3 only

C 3 only

D 2 only

Your answer ☐

(1 mark)

4 Scientists investigated the diversity of plants in an ungrazed field. The data obtained is shown in **Table 1**.

Table 1

Species	Number of individual plants counted in different quadrats					Mean number counted
Rapeseed	24	46	32	28	32	
Common sunflower	1	0	2	1	1	
Common poppy	8	12	6	10	8	
Creeping thistle	13	14	7	15	13	

(a) (i) Complete **Table 1** to show the mean number of each species counted.

(1 mark)

(ii) Using the mean values you added to **Table 1** and the formula provided below, calculate Simpson's Index of Diversity for plants in this field. Show your working.

$$D = 1 - \left(\sum \left(\frac{n}{N}\right)^2\right)$$

where n = total number of individuals of one species and N = total number of organisms of all species

$D =$ ....

(2 marks)

(b) Suggest a method that the scientists could have used to randomly place the quadrats in the field.

....

....

(1 mark)

The scientists then gathered data in a second field on which farm animals were allowed to graze. The mean number of creeping thistle was much lower in the second field than in the first.

(c) The scientists wanted to determine if the difference in means between the two fields was significant. State which statistical test they could have used to determine this. Explain your choice.

....

....

(2 marks)

(d) Further investigations in both fields showed the species diversity of the grazed field to be lower than that of the ungrazed field. Suggest an explanation for this.

....

....

....

(2 marks)

5 Scientists wanted to investigate the impact of different farming practices on ladybird biodiversity. To do so, they counted the number of different ladybird species on organic and conventional farms. This allowed them to compare the species richness of the ladybirds in the different types of farm.

(a) Explain why it may have been more useful for the scientists to compare indexes of diversity for their investigation.

....

....

....

(2 marks)

The scientists' data can be seen in **Figure 1**. The error bars indicate standard deviation.

Figure 1

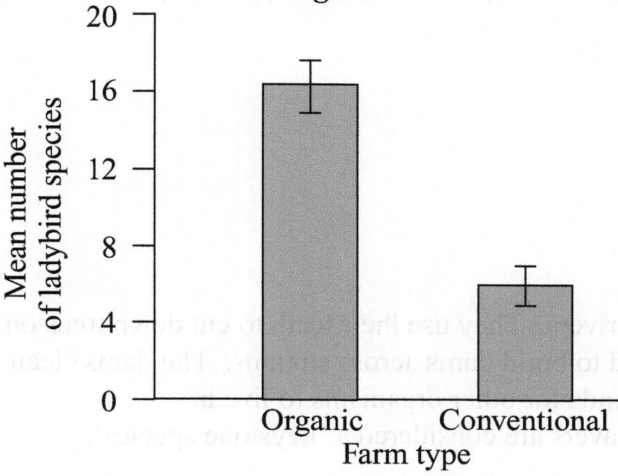

(b) The scientists concluded that conventional farming had a much greater impact on the number of ladybird species than organic farming. Use the data in **Figure 1** to evaluate this claim.

....

....

....

....

....

(3 marks)

Many of the conventional farms studied by the scientists practised continuous monoculture.

(c) (i) Explain **one** reason why continuous monoculture has a negative impact on biodiversity.

....

....

(1 mark)

(ii) Explain **one** economic reason **against** growing crops using continuous monoculture.

....

....

....

(2 marks)

6 A captive breeding programme is being carried out with beavers. Genetic samples are taken from the beavers, so that the proportion of polymorphic gene loci can be monitored.

(a) (i) Suggest why it is important to monitor the proportion of polymorphic gene loci in this population of beavers.

....

....

....

(2 marks)

(ii) 165 loci in the genome of the beaver population are sampled.
132 of the gene loci have only one allele present, while the rest have more than one allele.
Calculate the proportion of the gene loci that are polymorphic. Show your working.

....

(2 marks)

(b) Beavers live in and around rivers. They use their teeth to cut down trees on the river bank, which they use for food and to build dams across streams. The dams clean the water and create new ponds and wetlands for other organisms to live in.
Suggest **one** reason why beavers are considered a 'keystone species'.

....

....

(1 mark)

(c) It is hoped that members of the captive beaver population could eventually be released into wild. This is part of an attempt to increase the biodiversity of their natural river habitat.
Suggest **one** way in which human population growth may have reduced the biodiversity of this habitat.

....

....

(1 mark)

(d) Conservation agreements can help to improve biodiversity.
Describe how **one** international or local conservation agreement protects species or habitats.

....

....

....

(2 marks)

EXAM TIP

A maths question might seem simple if you're given the formula, but it's still easy to make mistakes. You need to make sure that you're substituting the correct numbers into the formula. For example, with the formula for Simpson's Index of Diversity, make sure you don't get 'N' (number of all organisms) and 'n' (number of individuals of one species) mixed up.

Score

27

Classification and Evolution — 1

You might not classify this section among the most fun things you could be doing right now, but you really ought to have a go at these questions about classification and evolution. It'll be worth it in the end.

For questions 1 and 2, give your answer by writing the correct letter in the box.

1 The statements below describe the features of four different types of single-celled organism.

Blepharisma japonicum: A protozoan with a nucleus that occurs in water or soil.
Nitrospira moscoviensis: An organism with no nucleus and a helical shape that can oxidise nitrites.
Stipitococcus capensis: A type of algae found in freshwater that contains chlorophyll and is capable of photosynthesis.
Brettanomyces bruxellensis: A saprotrophic organism with a cell wall made of chitin commonly used in the production of beer.

Which row, **A** to **D**, of the table below gives the correct classification for each of these organisms according to the five kingdom classification system?

	Blepharisma japonicum	*Nitrospira moscoviensis*	*Stipitococcus capensis*	*Brettanomyces bruxellensis*
A	Fungi	Protoctista	Protoctista	Fungi
B	Protoctista	Prokaryotae	Protoctista	Fungi
C	Prokaryotae	Fungi	Plantae	Animalia
D	Fungi	Prokaryotae	Plantae	Protoctista

Your answer ☐

(1 mark)

2 The diagram below shows a simple phylogenetic tree for a number of types of reptile.

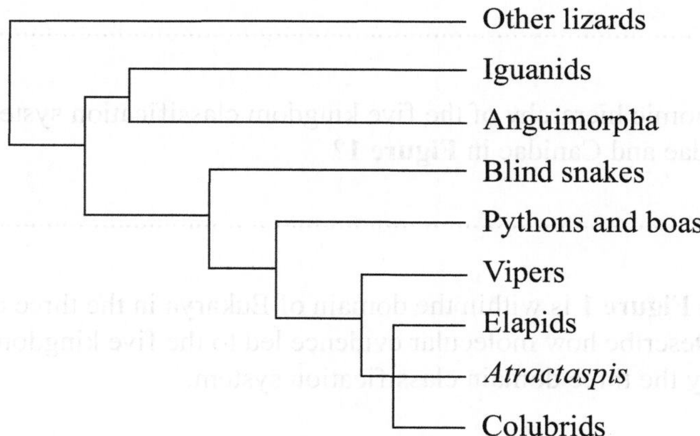

On the basis of this diagram, which of the following statements is/are true?

Statement 1: Iguanids are more closely related to Anguimorpha than other lizards.

Statement 2: Blind snakes are more closely related to pythons and boas than vipers.

Statement 3: Elapids are more closely related to *Atractaspis* species than colubrids.

A 1, 2 and 3

B 1 and 2 only

C 2 and 3 only

D 1 only

Your answer ☐

(1 mark)

3 **Figure 1** is a phylogenetic tree. It shows how different species from the order Carnivora are related.

Figure 1

(a) The plural of genus is genera.
How many different genera are represented in **Figure 1**?

....

(1 mark)

(b) Which **two** species in **Figure 1** are most closely related? Give a reason for your answer.

....

....

(1 mark)

(c) Which level of the taxonomic hierarchy of the five kingdom classification system is represented by the groups Felidae, Mustelidae and Canidae in **Figure 1**?

....

(1 mark)

(d) The phylogenetic tree in **Figure 1** is within the domain of Eukarya in the three domain classification system. Describe how molecular evidence led to the five kingdom classification system being replaced by the three domain classification system.

....

....

....

....

(2 marks)

There are quite a few terms you need to know for this topic, so make sure you learn them all. Most of the five kingdoms are easy to remember, but try not to get Prokaryotae and Protoctista confused — even though they're similar words and are both made up of fairly simple organisms, there's a crucial difference in that Protoctista are eukaryotic.

Score

7

Classification and Evolution — 2

1 The golden spiny mouse is a species of small mammal found in the Middle East, often living in hot desert habitats. It has a high water intake through its diet, which includes snails, insects and green vegetation. It is also able to make highly concentrated urine. It has spiny fur, which it can spread out when threatened, so that it appears larger than it is.

(a) Describe how **one** physiological adaptation increases the chance of survival in golden spiny mice.

....

....

(1 mark)

(b) The fur of golden spiny mice is a golden-brown colour, which is a similar colour to the ground in the desert habitats that they usually live in.
Explain how this fur colour may have evolved through natural selection.

....

....

....

....

....

....

(4 marks)

(c) Golden spiny mice are also known as *Acomys russatus*.
Explain why there is this other name for the species.

....

....

....

(2 marks)

(d) Five adult golden spiny mice were captured from two populations in different areas and weighed.
The results are shown in **Table 1**.

Table 1

	Mass of mouse / g				
Population 1	43.9	39.9	42.6	43.1	37.4
Population 2	44.8	39.8	51.5	50.2	46.0

(i) Two of the individuals from the Population 2 sample are over 50 g.
Explain the potential causes for this variation in mass.

....

....

....

(2 marks)

(ii) Calculate the standard deviation for the results from Population 1, using the formula:

$$s = \sqrt{\frac{\sum (x - \overline{x})^2}{n - 1}}$$

Give your answer to three significant figures.

....

(2 marks)

(iii) Suggest how it could be determined whether there is a significant difference between the two populations shown in **Table 1**.

....

(1 mark)

2 The theory of evolution by natural selection is attributed to Charles Darwin. However, Alfred Russel Wallace also contributed to its formulation.

(a) Describe Wallace's contribution to the formulation of the theory of evolution by natural selection.

....

....

....

(2 marks)

Since Darwin and Wallace's work was first published, more evidence for the theory of evolution by natural selection has been discovered. For example, some fossils of an extinct dinosaur species called *Archaeopteryx* have been found. These fossils had some features of land dinosaurs, such as long, bony tails and teeth, and some features of modern birds, such as wings and flight feathers.

(b) Suggest how *Archaeopteryx* fossils could support the theory of evolution.

....

....

....

(2 marks)

(c) Molecular evidence for evolution has also been found.
Describe how molecular evidence can be used to support the theory of evolution by natural selection.

....

....

....

(2 marks)

3* The European corn borer is a species of moth. It is a pest that has caused large losses to corn crops in Europe and North America.

To reduce the impact of the European corn borer on corn yield, Bt corn was developed. Bt corn is a type of corn that has been genetically modified so that it produces a pesticide. The pesticide selectively kills the larvae of European corn borers when they eat it. However, natural selection may mean that some European corn borer populations have developed resistance to the pesticide produced by Bt corn.

As a result of this, farmers are advised to plant areas called 'refuge areas' next to the Bt corn crop. These refuge areas contain non-Bt corn to attract the European corn borers that have not been exposed to the Bt corn. These European corn borers can eat and lay their eggs in the refuge areas. The Bt-resistant European corn borers will also enter these refuge areas and breed with the European corn borers present there.

Using the information above, discuss how the planting of refuge areas may reduce the spread of Bt corn resistance and have implications for human populations.

(6 marks)

If you get a question like 1(b) in the exams, you must make sure your answer relates to the specific context in the question. In other words, don't just write about how natural selection works in general — you need to relate it to the evolution of fur colour in golden spiny mice in particular. Think about how having golden-brown fur might make the mice better adapted.

Score

24

Communication and Homeostasis — 1

Cell communication is vital for survival — it's how the body is able to respond to stimuli and regulate its internal conditions. This topic might seem tricky, but after these questions you'll know it backwards... and forwards...

For questions 1 and 2, give your answer by writing the correct letter in the box.

1 The nervous system is made up of a complex network of neurones and other cells.

Which row, **A** to **D**, in the table below gives the correct function of each type of neurone?

	Motor neurone	Sensory neurone	Relay neurone
A	Transmits nerve impulses from the CNS to effectors	Transmits nerve impulses from receptors to the CNS	Transmits nerve impulses directly between receptors and effectors, bypassing the CNS
B	Transmits nerve impulses between the other two types of neurone	Transmits nerve impulses from the CNS to effectors	Transmits nerve impulses from receptors to the CNS
C	Transmits nerve impulses from the CNS to effectors	Transmits nerve impulses from receptors to the CNS	Transmits nerve impulses between the other two types of neurone
D	Transmits nerve impulses directly between receptors and effectors, bypassing the CNS	Transmits nerve impulses from the CNS to effectors	Transmits nerve impulses from receptors to the CNS

Your answer [C]

(1 mark)

2 In humans, the concentration of glucose in the blood is tightly regulated.

Which of the following options, **A** to **D**, correctly describes the physiological changes that occur following a large meal?

A After a large meal, the blood glucose concentration rises. This stimulates β-cells in the pancreas to release insulin. Insulin then acts on various effectors to increase the permeability of cell membranes to glucose, and activate glycogenesis.

B After a large meal, the blood glucose concentration rises. This stimulates α-cells in the pancreas to release insulin. Insulin then acts on various effectors to decrease the permeability of cell membranes to glucose, and activate gluconeogenesis.

C After a large meal, the blood glucose concentration rises. This stimulates β-cells in the pancreas to release glucagon. Glucagon then acts on various effectors to decrease the permeability of cell membranes to glucose, and activate gluconeogenesis.

D After a large meal, the blood glucose concentration rises. This stimulates α-cells in the pancreas to release glucagon. Glucagon then acts on various effectors to increase the permeability of cell membranes to glucose, and activate glycogenesis.

Your answer [A]

(1 mark)

3 **Figure 1** shows a cross-section through a neurone cell membrane while it is at rest.

Figure 1

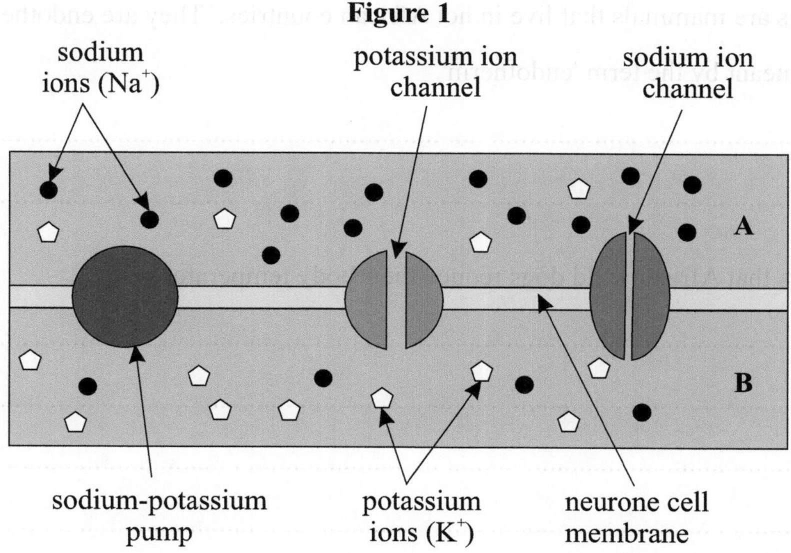

(a) When a neurone is at rest, the outside of the cell membrane is positively charged compared to the inside. State why.

The presence of Na^+ and K^+ ions since its channels aren't open

(1 mark)

(b) Explain why there is a greater concentration of sodium ions on side **A** of the cell membrane shown in **Figure 1**.

(2 marks)

(c) State why sodium ions on the outside of the cell do not move across the cell membrane shown in **Figure 1**.

(1 mark)

(d) Outline how the movement of potassium ions across a neurone cell membrane establishes a resting potential.

(3 marks)

(e) Explain why sodium ion channels are not evenly distributed across the surface of a myelinated neurone.

(3 marks)

4 Mammals and reptiles control their body temperature in different ways.

African wild dogs are mammals that live in hot African countries. They are endotherms.

(a) Explain what is meant by the term 'endotherm'.

....

....

(1 mark)

(b) Explain **two** ways that African wild dogs reduce their body temperature.

1. ....

....

2. ....

....

(4 marks)

(c)* African wild dogs are active during the day and at night, despite the temperature becoming considerably cooler at night. Unlike African wild dogs, the majority of lizard species, which are reptiles, are not active at night.

Explain the responses which allow African wild dogs to maintain their body temperature at night, and why most lizard species are not active at night.

....

....

....

....

....

....

....

....

....

(6 marks)

(d) In desert environments, the temperature can become exceedingly hot during the day. Give **one** way that lizards living in this environment can reduce their body temperature.

....

(1 mark)

(e) Komodo dragons are very large lizards. Unlike smaller lizards, Komodo dragons can maintain a fairly constant body temperature more easily throughout the day. Suggest why.

....

....

....

(2 marks)

5 A Pacinian corpuscle is a mechanoreceptor found in the skin, which detects pressure stimuli. **Figure 2** shows a simplified diagram of a Pacinian corpuscle at rest.

Figure 2

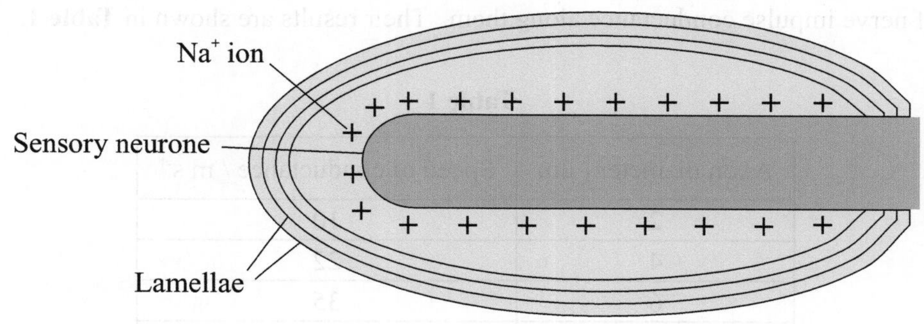

(a) Outline how the Pacinian corpuscle shown in **Figure 2** will change when exposed to a pressure stimulus.

....

....

....

....

(3 marks)

(b) Give **one** reason why the change you explained in part **(a)** may not lead to the generation of an action potential.

....

....

(1 mark)

(c) Give **one** reason why the change you explained in part **(a)** may lead to a high frequency of action potentials.

....

....

(1 mark)

(d) A Pacinian corpuscle converts one form of energy into another. What does this mean the Pacinian corpuscle is acting as?

....

(1 mark)

(e) Suggest an explanation for why there are several different types of mechanoreceptor in the skin.

....

....

....

(2 marks)

There's a lot to remember when it comes to cell communication, so it's a good idea to really get to grips with the basics when revising, so you can easily apply them to any exam context. Try constructing a table that shows the structure and function of different types of neurone. Or draw a rough graph of an action potential and talk yourself through how one is generated.

Score

34

Communication and Homeostasis — 2

1 A group of scientists investigated how the diameter of different myelinated neurones affected the speed of nerve impulse conductance along them. Their results are shown in **Table 1**.

Table 1

Axon diameter / μm	Speed of conductance / m s^{-1}
2	10
4	22
6	35
8	46
10	58
12	70

(a) Describe how nervous impulses are conducted along myelinated neurones.

....

(1 mark)

(b) Draw a suitable graph to show the results in **Table 1**. Include a line of best fit.

(2 marks)

(c) Use the graph you have drawn to predict the speed of conductance in a myelinated neurone with a diameter of 7 μm.

.... m s^{-1}

(1 mark)

(d) The scientists repeated the investigation in non-myelinated neurones.
Suggest how their results may have been different to the results shown in **Table 1**.

....

....

(1 mark)

2 Synapses can be excitatory or inhibitory, or both.

Figure 1 shows the interaction between a group of neurones. The synapses that connect Neurones A and B to Neurone D are excitatory. The synapses that connect Neurone C to Neurone D are inhibitory. Neurones A and B release the neurotransmitter acetylcholine and Neurone C releases the neurotransmitter GABA.

Figure 1

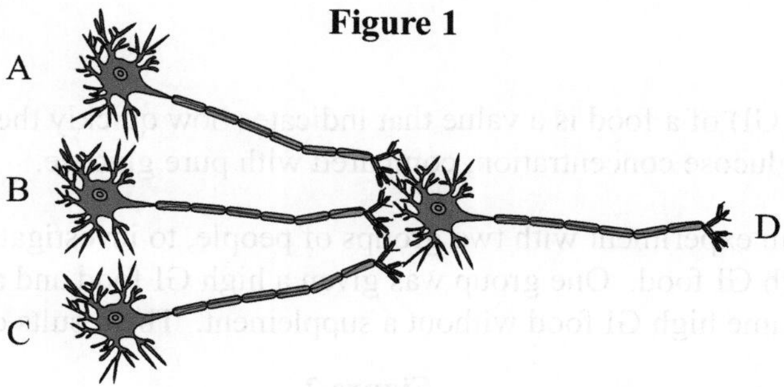

Table 2 shows what happens when a nervous impulse arrives at the end of each neurone in **Figure 1**.

Table 2

Neurones activated by an impulse	Action potential initiated in Neurone D
A + B	Yes
B + C	No
A + C	No
A + B + C	Yes

(a) Describe the effect that GABA has on the potential difference across the postsynaptic membrane of Neurone **D**.

....

(1 mark)

(b) Explain how **Table 2** shows that acetylcholine is released at an excitatory synapse and GABA is released at an inhibitory synapse.

....

....

....

....

(2 marks)

(c) Explain why an action potential is initiated in Neurone **D** when Neurones **A**, **B** and **C** are activated by an impulse, but not when Neurones **A** and **C** are activated by an impulse.

....

....

....

....

(2 marks)

Acetylcholinesterase (AChE) is an enzyme found at cholinergic synapses, which breaks down acetylcholine. Metrifonate is a drug which inhibits AChE.

(d) At another synapse, Neurone **X** is activated and triggers an action potential in Neurone **Y** by releasing acetylcholine. Explain what might happen at the synapse if metrifonate was present in the synaptic cleft between Neurones **X** and **Y**.

....

....

....

....

(2 marks)

3 The glycaemic index (GI) of a food is a value that indicates how quickly the food increases blood glucose concentration, compared with pure glucose.

Scientists conducted an experiment with two groups of people, to investigate the effect of taking a supplement with a high GI food. One group was given a high GI food and a supplement, and the other group was given the same high GI food without a supplement. The results can be seen in **Figure 2**.

Figure 2

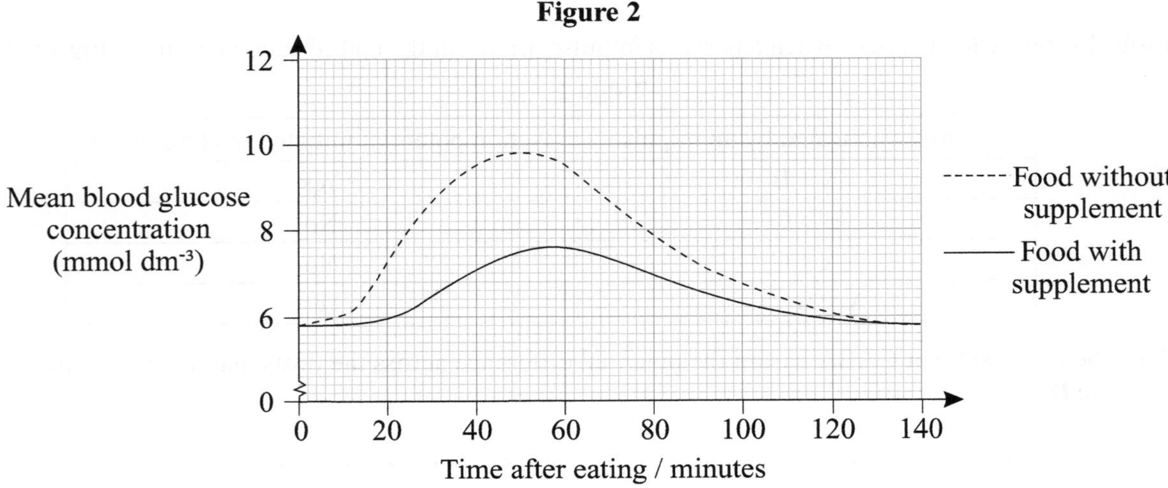

(a) Calculate the percentage difference in mean blood glucose concentration for the food with supplement, compared to the food without supplement, when the blood glucose concentration has reached its peak.

....

(1 mark)

(b) Describe the impact of the high GI food with the supplement on blood glucose concentration, as shown in **Figure 2**.

....

....

....

....

(2 marks)

The food supplement is being considered for use in patients with Type 2 diabetes.

(c) Suggest and explain why this food supplement might be considered useful for people with Type 2 diabetes.

....

....

....

....

....

(3 marks)

(d) State **two** ways that Type 2 diabetes is usually managed.

1. ....

2. ....

(2 marks)

4 Disopyramide is a drug that can be used to treat people who have an irregular heartbeat. The drug works by blocking some sodium and potassium ion channels on cardiac cell membranes. Overall the action of disopyramide can increase the duration of an action potential. Cardiac cells receive action potentials in the same way as neurones.

(a) Explain how an action potential is triggered in a cardiac cell.

....

....

....

....

....

....

(4 marks)

(b) Explain how blocking potassium ion channels increases the duration of an action potential.

....

....

....

(3 marks)

(c) Suggest and explain why people with a heartbeat that is too fast might be prescribed disopyramide.

....

....

(2 marks)

If you're asked to draw a graph in the exams or plot data of any kind, like Q1, remember that the independent variable goes on the *x*-axis and the dependent variable (the thing you're measuring) goes on the *y*-axis. Be careful to plot your points accurately too — there's usually only 1 plotting mark up for grabs and if you put just one of the points in the wrong place, you won't get it.

Score

29

Communication and Homeostasis — 3

1 Cortisol is one hormone involved in the 'fight or flight' response to stress.

(a) Where in the adrenal gland is cortisol released from?

....

(1 mark)

The mechanism of cortisol activation is shown in **Figure 1**.

Figure 1

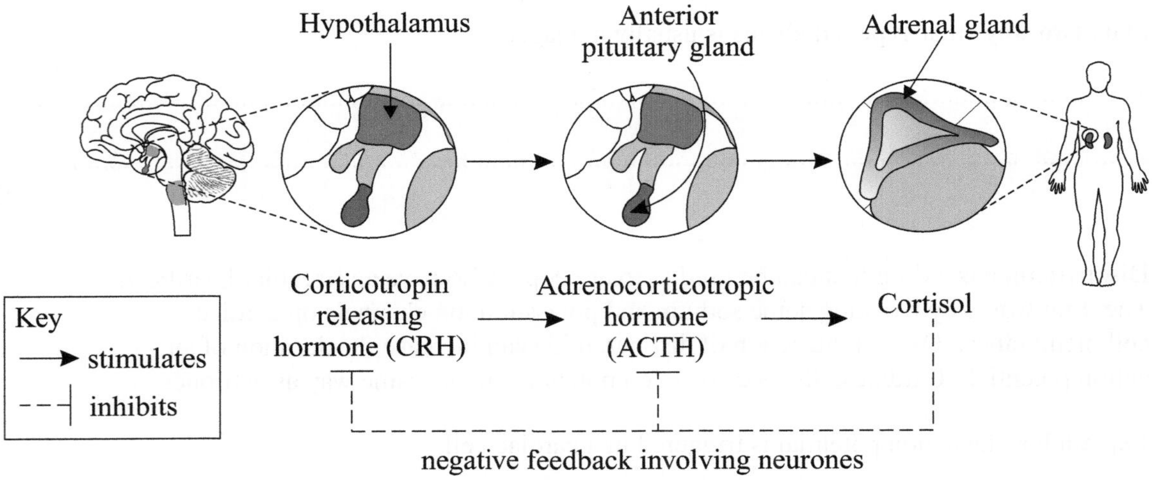

(b) When a stress stimulus is detected, neurones in the hypothalamus are stimulated to secrete CRH. Explain what type of cell signalling is occurring during this stage.

....

....

(2 marks)

(c) ACTH stimulates the adrenal gland to produce cortisol. Explain what type of cell signalling is occurring during this stage.

....

....

(2 marks)

(d) Alcohol depresses the action of neurones. Using **Figure 1**, suggest and explain **one** consequence that frequently drinking large of amounts of alcohol could have on the body.

....

....

....

(3 marks)

2 Insulin, glucagon and adrenaline all have an effect on blood glucose concentration.

(a) Describe how insulin increases the transport of glucose into cells.

....

....

(2 marks)

(b) Describe **one** other mechanism of insulin action that helps to regulate blood glucose concentration.

....

....

(1 mark)

(c) Insulin is secreted from the β-cells in the pancreas when a high blood glucose concentration is detected. Explain the process that leads to insulin secretion from the β-cells.

....

....

....

....

....

....

....

(5 marks)

The action of glucagon is said to be antagonistic to that of insulin.

(d) Describe the role of glucagon in the regulation of blood glucose concentration.

....

(1 mark)

(e) Describe **two** mechanisms of glucagon action.

1. ....

....

2. ....

....

(2 marks)

Adrenaline is released from the adrenal glands.
Athletes often experience a large increase in their adrenaline levels before they compete.

(f) Explain how the action of adrenaline might increase the performance of an athlete.

....

....

....

(2 marks)

3 During exercise, the body experiences changes in core body temperature.

(a) Explain why it is necessary for homeostatic mechanisms to resist these changes.

....

....

....

(2 marks)

(b) Negative feedback mechanisms enable the body to maintain its core temperature during exercise. What is meant by negative feedback?

....

....

(1 mark)

Intense exercise under hot conditions can cause body temperature to increase above 37.5 °C. The resulting condition is referred to as hyperthermia. When body temperature rises above 40 °C, a person is classed as having severe hyperthermia.

(c) Suggest how severe hyperthermia can cause life-threatening disruption to metabolic processes.

....

....

....

....

(2 marks)

People with severe hyperthermia often stop sweating, which causes their body temperature to continue to rise.

(d) What type of feedback mechanism is happening at this point? Explain your answer.

....

....

(2 marks)

4 Scientists measured the concentration of glucose in the blood of a group of people with Type 1 diabetes. They compared the results to a control group without diabetes. Prior to the blood test, each person had fasted for eight hours. The results can be seen in **Table 1**.

Table 1

	Mean value (± standard deviation)	
	People with Type 1 diabetes	People without diabetes
Glucose / mg per 100 cm^3	148.68 (± 13.89)	73.29 (± 8.13)

(a) Suggest why each person had to fast for eight hours prior to the blood test.

....

....

(1 mark)

(b) Explain the results shown in **Table 1**.

....

....

....

(3 marks)

(c) (i) The scientists conducted a statistical test to determine whether the difference in the results for patients with Type 1 diabetes and individuals without diabetes was significant. Suggest a statistical test that could have been carried out and give a reason for your choice.

Statistical test: ....

Reason: ....

(2 marks)

(ii) The probability value of the statistical test was found to be less than 0.05. Explain what this shows.

....

....

....

(2 marks)

(d) Describe the cause of Type 1 diabetes.

....

....

(2 marks)

(e) Type 1 diabetes can be treated with insulin injections. Insulin used to be extracted from animal pancreases, but now scientists are able to make human insulin.

(i) What organisms are mostly used to make human insulin today?

....

(1 mark)

(ii) Suggest **one** advantage to a person with Type 1 diabetes of being able to inject human insulin rather than animal insulin.

....

(1 mark)

(f) Explain **one** type of treatment that could be used to potentially cure Type 1 diabetes in the future.

....

....

....

....

(3 marks)

People with Type 1 diabetes sometimes develop hypoglycaemia, which is where their blood glucose concentration becomes too low. This can happen when too much insulin is injected.

(g) Explain why it is important to prevent blood glucose concentration from becoming too low.

....

....

(1 mark)

EXAM TIP

For questions like Q1, it's important to know the difference between positive and negative feedback — negative feedback aims to prevent a change in state from happening, so acts against the change. It's how homeostasis works. But positive feedback acts with the change in state, and keeps it moving in a particular direction. This means positive feedback isn't always a good thing...

Score

44

Excretion — 1

Excretion — it doesn't sound like the most pleasant of topics, but it's important stuff that you'll need to know for your exams. Have a go at these questions. They're just about livers and kidneys — it doesn't get *too* gross.

For each of questions 1-3, give your answer by writing the correct letter in the box.

1 Which of the following, **A** to **D**, takes place in the proximal convoluted tubule of a kidney nephron?

A Sodium and chloride ions are filtered out of the blood into the tubule.

B Water moves into the tubule from the surrounding tissue by osmosis.

C Glucose, amino acids and vitamins are reabsorbed from the tubule into the blood.

D Glucose is absorbed from the blood into the tubule.

Your answer ☐

(1 mark)

2 The image below shows a section of a kidney under a light microscope.

Which label, **A** to **D**, on the diagram below shows where ultrafiltration takes place within the kidney?

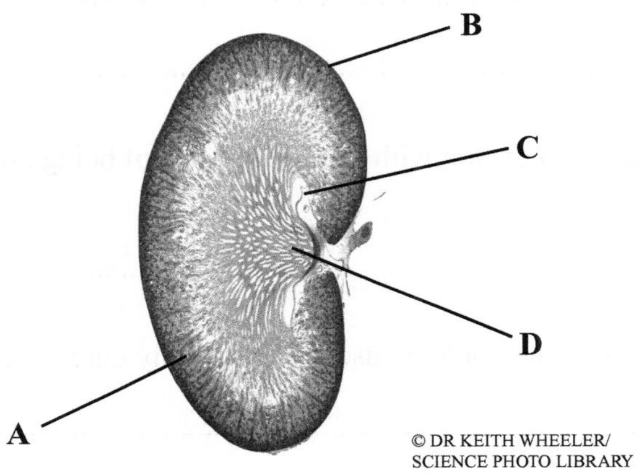

© DR KEITH WHEELER/ SCIENCE PHOTO LIBRARY

Your answer ☐

(1 mark)

3 Paracetamol is a commonly used painkiller. Scientists have determined that doses of 150 mg per kg body weight in one 24 hour period are likely to cause liver damage.

Which of the following individuals, **A** to **D**, might experience liver damage as a result of their paracetamol intake?

A An individual weighing 63 kg who has ingested 6 g of paracetamol in 24 hours.

B An individual weighing 75 kg who has ingested 9 g of paracetamol in 24 hours.

C An individual weighing 62 kg who has ingested 2 g of paracetamol in 24 hours.

D An individual weighing 80 kg who has ingested 12 g of paracetamol in 24 hours.

Your answer ☐

(1 mark)

4 There are several different tests that can help doctors to diagnose and then treat kidney disease.

(a) One test involves estimating an individual's glomerular filtration rate (GFR).
The GFR can be estimated for children using the following formula:

$$\text{GFR (ml/min/1.73m}^2) = (0.41 \times \text{height in cm}) \div \text{creatinine in mg/dl}$$

Table 1 shows the details used to estimate the GFR of four children.

Table 1

Child	Age	Height (m)	Creatinine (mg/l)	GFR (ml/min/1.73m^2)
1	11	1.65		10.7
2	12	1.42	120	4.85
3	8	1.14	165	2.83
4	6	1.12	79	5.81

(i) Explain what is meant by the glomerular filtration rate **and** how it can be used to indicate whether a patient has kidney disease.

....

....

....

(2 marks)

(ii) Estimate the creatinine level in mg/l for **Child 1**, using the information in **Table 1** and the formula for GFR given above. Give your answer to 3 significant figures. Show your working.
1 dl = 0.1 l

.... mg/l
(2 marks)

(b) A urine microalbumin test can also be used to diagnose kidney disease.
It tests for the presence of albumin (a protein) in a person's urine.
Explain why a urine microalbumin test could help a doctor to diagnose kidney disease in a patient.

....

....

....

(2 marks)

Kidney disease can lead to kidney failure. This can be treated using haemodialysis.

(c) During haemodialysis, blood flows through a dialysis machine in the opposite direction to dialysis fluid.
The blood is separated from the dialysis fluid by a partially permeable membrane.

(i) Explain the function of the partially permeable membrane in a haemodialysis machine.

....

....

....

(2 marks)

(ii) Suggest why the blood flows in the opposite direction to the dialysis fluid.

....

....

(1 mark)

(d) Explain **two** ways in which kidney failure may lead to health problems.

1. ....

....

2. ....

....

(4 marks)

5 A scientist wants to compare the size of kidney medullas relative to the size of whole kidneys in sheep and pigs. She obtains three kidneys from both animals from an abattoir. The sizes of the kidneys differ.

(a) Suggest and explain **two** factors that the scientist should have kept the same for all of the kidneys she sourced to make her comparison valid.

1. ....

....

2. ....

....

(4 marks)

(b)* Plan a method that the scientist could use to compare the average medulla size relative to the overall size of the kidney for the two species. You should include details of the measurements the scientist should take and any calculations she should carry out.

....

....

....

....

....

....

....

....

....

(6 marks)

EXAM TIP

Make sure you pay attention to the units in calculation questions — sometimes values will need converting into the correct units before they can be plugged into an equation or given as an answer. You should learn how to convert between standard S.I. units, e.g. g and mg, or nm, μm and mm. Non-standard conversions (like dl to l) will usually be given to you in the question.

Score

26

Excretion — 2

1 **Figure 1** shows a light micrograph of part of the cortex of the kidney magnified by × 300.

Figure 1

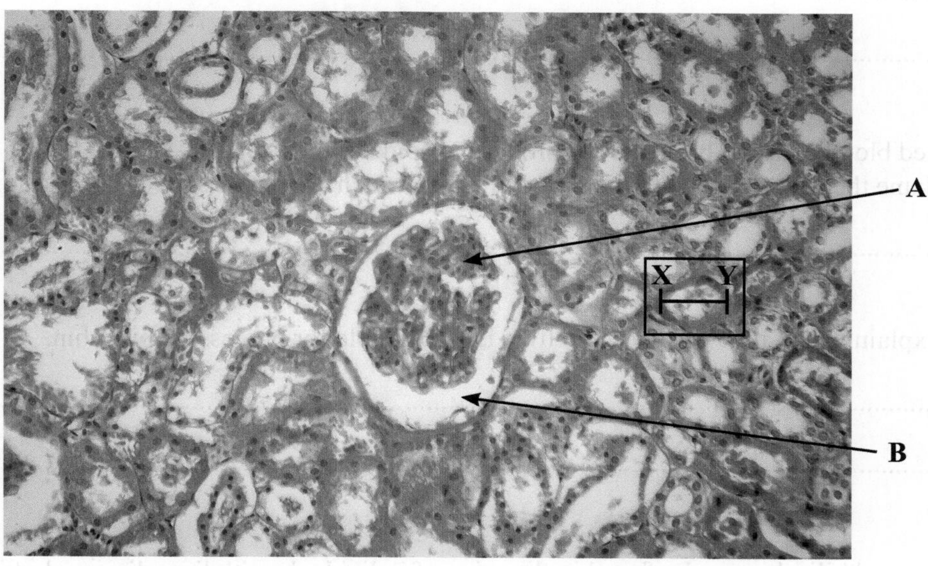

(a) Name the structures labelled **A** and **B** on **Figure 1**.

A ....

B ....

(2 marks)

(b) The structure in the box in **Figure 1** is part of a distal convoluted tubule.

(i) The width of the distal convoluted tubule is indicated by the line **X** to **Y**. Calculate the real width of the tubule in μm.

> You'll need to rearrange the magnification formula (magnification = image size ÷ object size) for this question.

.... μm

(2 marks)

(ii) Explain why the distal convoluted tubules and collecting ducts of a kidney nephron change in permeability when the water content of the blood falls.

....

....

....

....

....

....

(4 marks)

2 When red blood cells die, the haemoglobin they contain is broken down. One of the products of this breakdown is the protein bilirubin. High levels of bilirubin in the blood can be toxic, so the bilirubin released after the cells die is processed in the liver.

(a) (i) Through which **two** main blood vessels do red blood cells enter the liver?

1. ....

2. ....

(2 marks)

(ii) Red blood cells are broken down in the sinusoids of the liver.
Name the cells attached to the sinusoid walls, which are responsible for breaking down red blood cells.

....

(1 mark)

(iii) Explain which type of cell in the liver is responsible for processing bilirubin.

....

....

(1 mark)

Unprocessed bilirubin can be found in the urine of individuals with liver disease, but is not found in the urine of healthy individuals. Diagnostic tests for bilirubin often involve diazo, a reactant that causes a colour change on contact with bilirubin molecules.

(b) A hospital patient is suspected of having liver disease.
Suggest how the doctors might use a diagnostic test involving diazo to test for signs of liver damage.

....

....

....

....

....

....

(3 marks)

3 Some kinds of liver disease are associated with a decrease in the activity of enzymes involved in the ornithine cycle.

Suggest and explain why a decrease in the activity of these enzymes could cause problems for a person's health.

....

....

....

(2 marks)

4 Loops of Henle in the kidneys help to reabsorb water from the urine.

Figure 2 shows a simple diagram of a loop of Henle.
The arrows show the direction of the movement of filtrate.

Figure 2

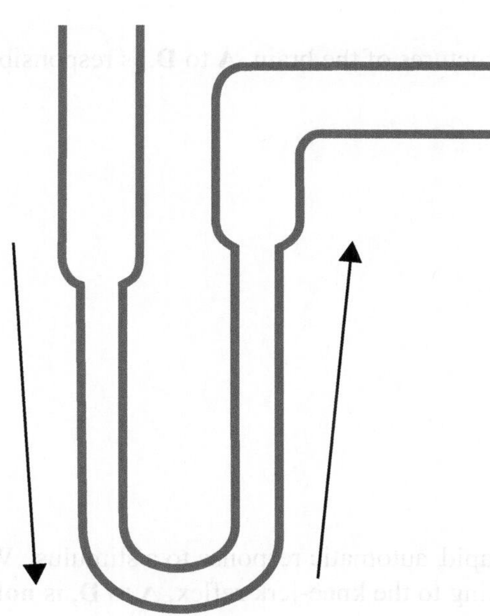

(a) (i) Draw an arrow on **Figure 2** to show where sodium and chloride ions are moved out of the loop of Henle by active transport.

(1 mark)

(ii) Explain why the active transport of ions causes the filtrate within the loop of Henle to become more concentrated.

....

....

....

....

(3 marks)

(b) Animals that live in dry, desert conditions often have loops of Henle that are longer than those in animals living in areas with more rainfall. Suggest and explain why this is the case.

....

....

....

....

(3 marks)

Take extra care when you're doing dealing with tiny units such as millimetres and micrometres. It might not be obvious whether you have a big/small enough number at the end of a calculation, so be sure not to accidentally write too many or too few zeros when doing unit conversions.

Score

24

Animal Responses — 1

Animal responses are controlled by signalling pathways that involve the nervous system and/or hormones. This is a complex topic, so make sure you take your time with these questions — I know you've got this.

For each of questions 1-3, give your answer by writing the correct letter in the box.

1 Which of the following structures of the brain, **A** to **D**, is responsible for controlling breathing rate?

A cerebellum

B pituitary gland

C hypothalamus

D medulla oblongata

Your answer ☐

(1 mark)

2 The knee-jerk reflex is a rapid, automatic response to a stimulus. Which of the following options relating to the knee-jerk reflex, **A** to **D**, is **not** correct?

A The knee-jerk reflex helps to maintain posture and balance.

B The knee-jerk reflex involves sensory and motor neurones only.

C The central nervous system is not involved in the knee-jerk reflex.

D The stimulus for the knee-jerk reflex is detected by stretch receptors in the quadriceps muscle.

Your answer ☐

(1 mark)

3 The following statements relate to the organisation of the mammalian nervous system. Which of the statements is/are **correct**?

Statement 1: The autonomic nervous system is a structural division of the nervous system, which connects the brain and spinal cord to the rest of the body.

Statement 2: The somatic nervous system controls conscious activities.

Statement 3: The sympathetic nervous system involves neurones that release noradrenaline and the parasympathetic nervous system involves neurones that release acetylcholine.

A 1, 2 and 3

B 1 and 2 only

C 2 and 3 only

D 3 only

Your answer ☐

(1 mark)

4 **Figure 1** shows a cross-section of the human brain.

Figure 1

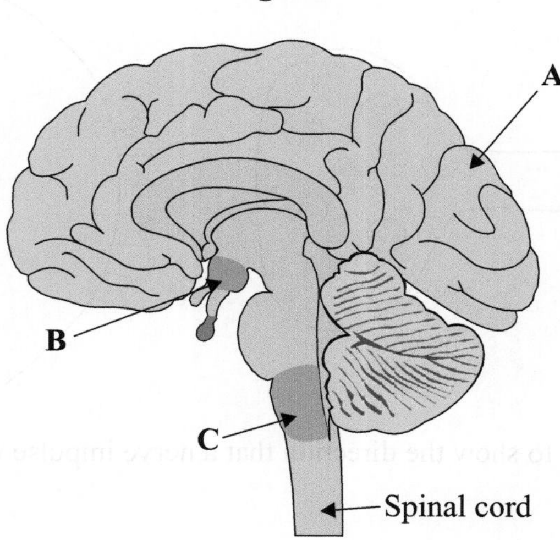

(a) (i) Name structure **A** in **Figure 1**.

....

(1 mark)

(ii) Give **two** processes that structure **A** is involved in.

1. ....

2. ....

(2 marks)

(b) Some parts of the brain labelled in **Figure 1** are involved in coordinating the 'fight or flight' response to a stimulus.

(i) Describe **one** role of structure **B** in the 'fight or flight' response.

....

....

....

(2 marks)

The 'fight or flight' response causes heart rate to increase.

(ii) Give **two** other effects that the 'fight or flight' response has on the body.

1. ....

2. ....

(2 marks)

(iii) Explain how structure **C** acts to increase heart rate.

....

....

....

....

(3 marks)

5 **Figure 2** shows a neuromuscular junction.

Figure 2

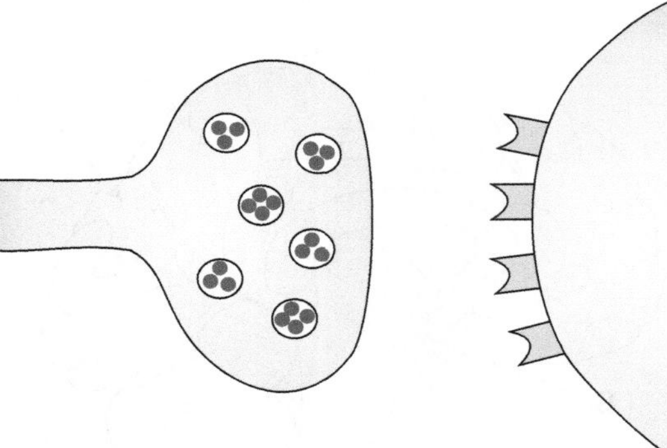

(a) Draw an arrow on **Figure 2** to show the direction that a nerve impulse would travel across this neuromuscular junction.

(1 mark)

(b) Explain why the transmission of nervous impulses only occurs in one direction across a neuromuscular junction.

....

....

(2 marks)

(c) An action potential arrives at a neuromuscular junction.
Describe how the action potential stimulates the release of calcium ions throughout the muscle fibre.

....

....

....

(3 marks)

(d) Explain **two** ways in which the release of calcium ions following an action potential is important for muscle contraction.

1. ....

....

2. ....

....

(4 marks)

(e) Curare is a poison which binds to acetylcholine receptors and inhibits them.
Suggest and explain what effect a high dose of curare would have on the contraction of muscles.

....

....

....

....

....

(4 marks)

6 **Figure 3** shows a section of muscle tissue.

Figure 3

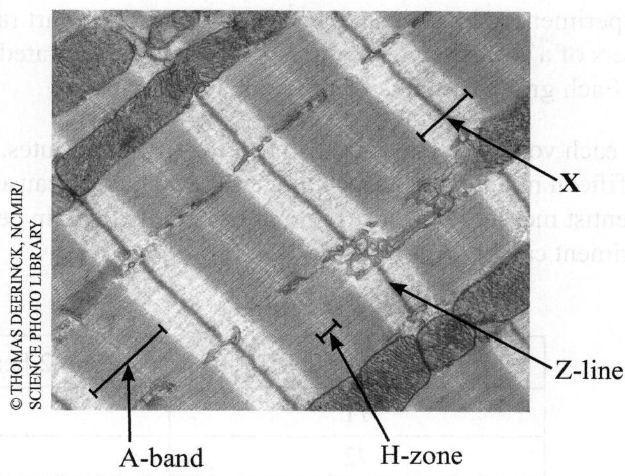

(a) Name the part of the myofibril labelled **X** on **Figure 3**.

....

(1 mark)

(b) Which part of a sarcomere labelled on **Figure 3** contains the lowest concentration of actin filaments? Give a reason for your answer.

....

....

(2 marks)

(c) (i) During muscle contraction the lengths of the sarcomeres shorten. Name the parts of the sarcomere that shorten.

....

(1 mark)

(ii) Outline how the myosin and actin filaments interact to shorten the lengths of the sarcomeres.

....

....

....

....

(3 marks)

(iii) Explain how ATP is used in shortening the lengths of the sarcomeres.

....

....

....

(2 marks)

This isn't an easy topic. Practice makes perfect though, so keep going until you can answer all of these questions correctly. There are some key things you should make sure that you know for the exam, including how nerves and hormones control the fight or flight response and heart rate. Oh, and the mechanism of muscle contraction. Right, let's keep those brain cells firing...

Score

36

Animal Responses — 2

1 A scientist set up an experiment to investigate the effect of stress on heart rate. He selected 16 volunteers of a similar age, height and weight, and separated them into two groups. Each group contained eight male participants.

The scientist instructed each volunteer in Group 1 to rest for fifteen minutes, and each volunteer in Group 2 to complete a fifteen minute public speaking task, designed to cause stress. At the end of the fifteen minutes, the scientist measured the heart rate of each individual, in beats per minute (bpm). The results of the experiment can be seen in **Table 1**.

Table 1

	Group 1 heart rates (bpm)	Group 2 heart rates (bpm)
	71	91
	72	86
	68	79
	74	89
	67	84
	65	88
	73	89
	70	90
Mean	70	87
Standard deviation	3.12	3.93

(a) The scientist used a Student's t-test to determine whether there was a significant difference between the mean heart rates of Groups 1 and 2.

(i) Calculate the value of t for the data shown in **Table 1** using the formula:

$$t = \frac{\bar{x}_1 - \bar{x}_2}{\sqrt{(s_1^2 / n_1) + (s_2^2 / n_2)}}$$

This is a complicated formula and it's easy to go wrong, so make sure you write down your working. It'll help reduce the chance of you making a mistake and if you do end up with the wrong answer, you could still get a mark for showing the correct working.

where,

$\bar{x}$ = mean $\quad$ n = number of values in a group

s = standard deviation $\quad$ $_1$ or $_2$ = the group being referred to

Give your answer to **two** decimal places.

t = ...

(2 marks)

(ii) The scientist's null hypothesis was:

'There is no significant difference between the mean heart rate of individuals who are resting, and the mean heart rate of individuals who are completing the public speaking task'.

The critical value for this test at a probability of 5% or less is **2.15**.

Using your answer to part (a)(i), explain whether the scientist should accept or reject the null hypothesis.

....

....

(1 mark)

(b) From this experiment, the scientist makes an overall conclusion about the effect of stress on heart rate.

'Stress causes heart rate to increase.'

Evaluate the validity of this conclusion.

....

....

....

....

....

....

....

(4 marks)

2* The human body consists of hundreds of muscles. These include the deltoid muscle, the muscularis externa and cardiac muscle.

The deltoid muscle is located on top of the shoulder and functions to move the arm upwards. The muscularis externa surrounds the intestines and contracts automatically to move food through them. Cardiac muscle functions to keep the heart pumping blood around the body.

Using the information above, and your own knowledge, explain how the structures or properties of the deltoid muscle, muscularis externa and cardiac muscle are related to their corresponding functions.

....

....

....

....

....

....

....

....

....

....

....

....

(6 marks)

3 Creatine is a dietary supplement often used by weightlifters — it affects the levels of creatine phosphate in the muscles. A team of scientists investigated the use of a creatine supplement. They measured the amount of creatine phosphate present in the muscles of four weightlifters at the beginning of an experiment and after taking a creatine supplement for five days. Their results are shown in **Table 2**.

Table 2

	Concentration of creatine phosphate in muscle / mmol kg^{-1} dry mass		
Individual	Before creatine supplement	After creatine supplement	Percentage difference / %
1	66	81	22.7
2	84	90.6	7.9
3	81	96	
4	69	85.8	

(a) (i) Complete **Table 2** to show the percentage difference in the concentration of creatine phosphate before and after taking a creatine supplement.

(2 marks)

(ii) Calculate the mean percentage difference in the creatine phosphate concentration of all the individuals after taking a creatine supplement.

Mean percentage difference = ...%

(1 mark)

The scientists also investigated the effect of creatine on weightlifting performance using a different group of weightlifters over a 10-day period.

Each day they recorded the maximum weight each individual could comfortably lift, and immediately after this each individual was given a supplement. Half of the individuals were given a creatine supplement and the other half of the individuals were given a placebo supplement that did not contain any creatine. Three hours later the maximum weight each individual could comfortably lift was recorded again.

(b) Explain why using creatine supplements might improve a weightlifter's performance.

....

....

....

(3 marks)

(c) The scientists found no significant difference in the performance of the weightlifters taking creatine and those taking a placebo. They concluded that the creatine supplement had no effect on the performance of a weightlifter. Suggest **two** reasons why their conclusion may be flawed. Explain your answer.

A placebo is a negative control used in drug testing.

1. ....

....

2. ....

....

(4 marks)

In the exam you might be asked to apply your knowledge to something you're unfamiliar with, like in Q2 — in this case you need to use your knowledge to link the descriptions of how these muscles function to the type of muscle that each one is, and then you can relate the properties of each muscle type to its function. These questions just require a little more thought.

Score

23

Plant Responses and Hormones

I don't think I've ever looked at a plant and thought about how it grows... it's surprising how complex plants are. In the exams, you might need to answer questions on Plant Responses and Hormones, so have a bash at these...

For each of questions 1-3, give your answer by writing the correct letter in the box.

1 Hormones have a range of important roles in controlling plant responses.

Which row, **A** to **D**, in the table below correctly identifies the plant hormones responsible for each process?

	Geotropism	Stem elongation	Stomatal closure	Leaf loss
A	Gibberellins	Auxins	Abscisic acid	Ethene
B	Auxins	Abscisic acid	Ethene	Gibberellins
C	Auxins	Gibberellins	Abscisic acid	Ethene
D	Gibberellins	Abscisic acid	Auxins	Ethene

Your answer ☐

(1 mark)

2 *Drosera rotundifolia* is a type of carnivorous plant. An insect can become trapped in the glue-like substance on the surface of the tentacles of the plant. When this happens, the movement of the insect as it struggles to escape causes adjacent tentacles to bend towards it.

What type of plant response, **A** to **D**, is this an example of?

A Thigmotropism

B Geotropism

C Hydrotropism

D Thermotropism

Your answer ☐

(1 mark)

3 The following statements relate to auxins, which are a type of plant hormone.

Statement 1: Auxins are transported around the plant in the phloem.

Statement 2: In shoots, auxins move to the more illuminated part of the plant and inhibit cell elongation, thus causing the shoot to bend towards the light.

Statement 3: In roots, auxins move to the more shaded part of the plant and stimulate cell elongation, thus causing the root to bend away from the light.

Which of the statements related to the function of auxins is/are **true**?

A 1, 2, and 3

B 1 and 2

C 2 and 3

D 1 only

Your answer ☐

(1 mark)

4 A student carries out an experiment on plant growth responses. The student grows four seedlings in identical conditions for two weeks. She then places each seedling in a separate covered box, with a light source pointed at an angle of 90° towards the seedling, as shown in **Figure 1**.

Figure 1

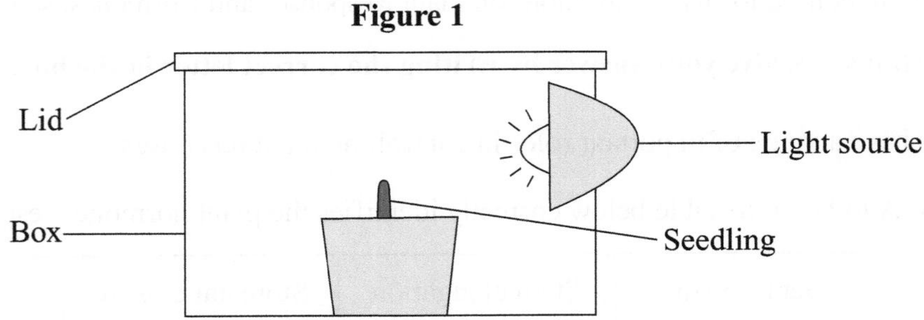

The student labels the seedlings **A** to **D**. She applies the following treatments to each seedling:

- The shoot tip of seedling **A** is covered with tin foil.
- The shoot tip of seedling **B** is cut off.
- The shoot tip of seedling **C** is cut off. The auxin indoleacetic acid (IAA) is added to the top of the shoot on the side nearest to the light source only. It is reapplied at regular intervals.
- Seedling **D** is not treated.

The degree of curvature of each seedling after one week is shown in **Table 1**.

Table 1

Seedling	Degree of curvature / °
A	0
B	0
C	40 (towards light source)
D	40 (towards light source)

(a) Name the growth response shown by seedling **D**.

....

(1 mark)

(b) What do the results of the experiment suggest about where indoleacetic acid is produced in a plant? Explain your answer.

....

....

(2 marks)

(c) Give **two** variables that should have been controlled during this experiment.

Work out which is the variable that's being changed and which is the variable that's being measured — all other variables are the ones that must be controlled.

1. ....

2. ....

(2 marks)

(d) Explain why no curvature was observed in seedlings **A** and **B**.

A: ....

....

B: ....

....

(2 marks)

(e) Explain why there was no difference in results for seedlings **C** and **D**.

....

....

(1 mark)

5 Bananas are grown on huge plantations in countries such as Uganda. Unfortunately these plantations are at risk from insects, such as the banana weevil, which feed on the banana crop.

(a) What term is used to describe plants being eaten by animals, such as banana weevils?

....

(1 mark)

(b) In response to the banana weevil, the bananas release chemicals called phenylphenalenones.

(i) Suggest **two** other types of chemical defence that plants may produce in response to being eaten by animals **and** explain how each one works.

1. ....

....

2. ....

....

(4 marks)

(ii) Bananas also release phenylphenalenones in response to abiotic stress.
Suggest **one** example of an abiotic stress that may be faced by banana plants.

....

(1 mark)

(c) Bananas that are sold abroad are picked from the plantations and transported to their destination. Once there, the bananas are treated with ethene before they go on sale.

(i) Explain the purpose of the bananas being treated with ethene.

....

....

(2 marks)

(ii) Ethene is an example of a plant hormone that is used commercially.
Outline how **one** other type of plant hormone can be used commercially.

....

....

....

(3 marks)

6 A group of scientists decided to investigate the effect of an important gibberellin, called gibberellic acid (GA_3), on seed germination. For the experiment they used seeds from a plant species that normally has a low germination success rate.

The scientists set up six beakers containing equal volumes of liquid. One beaker contained distilled water, and the remaining five beakers contained different concentrations of GA_3. The scientists then soaked 60 seeds in each beaker for 48 hours. Following this, they rinsed all the seeds in sterilised water and transferred them onto labelled Petri dishes.

The scientists set up three Petri dishes of 20 seeds for each concentration of GA_3. They then placed the Petri dishes into growth chambers, set at 15 °C. After ten days, the scientists counted the number of seeds that had germinated.

The results can be seen in **Table 2**.

Table 2

GA_3 concentration (mg dm^{-3})	Mean number of seeds germinated per Petri dish (%)
0	11.7
50	23.3
100	31.7
200	40.0
500	63.3
1000	83.3

(a) Explain the results in **Table 2**.

....

....

....

....

....

....

(3 marks)

(b) Explain why the scientists carried out repeats and recorded a mean for each concentration of GA_3.

....

....

(2 marks)

(c) Describe how the scientists could have made a 50 mg dm^{-3} solution from a 1000 mg dm^{-3} solution.

....

....

....

(2 marks)

If you're asked a question on this topic in the exam, it's likely to be about an experiment involving plant hormones. Therefore it's a good idea to get your head around what each plant hormone does, and where it acts, so that you stand a better chance of interpreting the results. Simple.

Score

29

Photosynthesis — 1

Plants have the ability to harness light energy through photosynthesis. This is a really important process that you need to know — that's why I've included plenty of exam-style questions for you to have a bash at.

For questions 1 and 2, give your answer by writing the correct letter in the box.

1 The light-dependent reaction of photosynthesis can be split into non-cyclic photophosphorylation and cyclic photophosphorylation.

Which of the following statements, **A** to **D**, regarding cyclic and non-cyclic photophosphorylation is **correct**?

A Both cyclic and non-cyclic photophosphorylation involve the use of light energy to synthesise ATP.

B Both cyclic and non-cyclic photophosphorylation involve the production of reduced NADP.

C Non-cyclic photophosphorylation involves photosystems I and II, whereas cyclic photophosphorylation involves only photosystem II.

D Both cyclic and non-cyclic photophosphorylation produce O_2.

Your answer ☐

(1 mark)

2 The image below shows a TEM micrograph of a chloroplast.

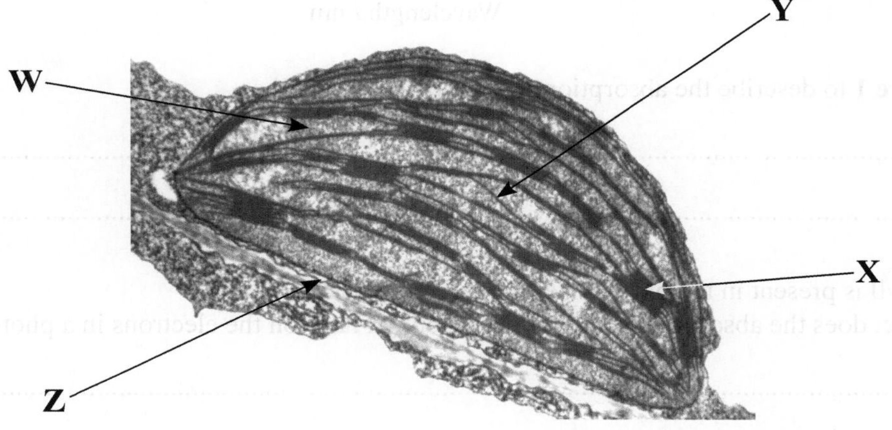

Select the row in the table, **A** to **D**, that correctly identifies the structures labelled **W**, **X**, **Y** and **Z**.

	W	X	Y	Z
A	granum	lamella	stroma	thylakoid membrane
B	stroma	granum	lamella	outer membrane of chloroplast envelope
C	granum	stroma	lamella	thylakoid membrane
D	lamella	granum	stroma	outer membrane of chloroplast envelope

Your answer ☐

(1 mark)

3 All plants contain several different photosynthetic pigments in their leaves.

Figure 1 shows the absorption spectra for the pigments chlorophyll a, chlorophyll b and carotene.

Figure 1

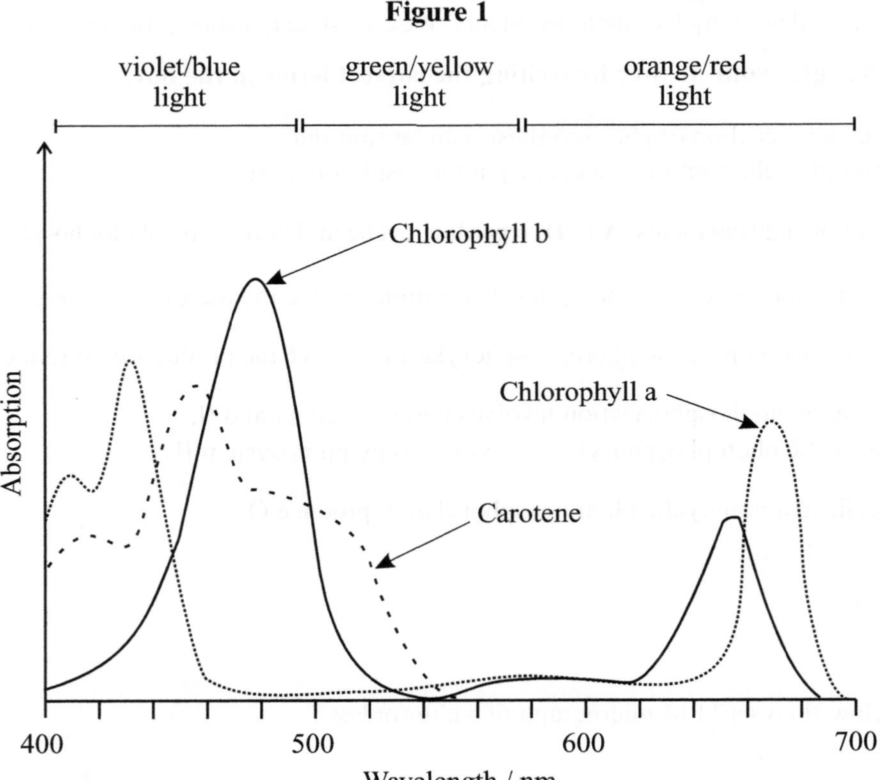

(a) Use **Figure 1** to describe the absorption of light by chlorophyll a.

....

....

(2 marks)

(b) Chlorophyll is present in the photosystems of a chloroplast.
What effect does the absorption of light by chlorophyll have on the electrons in a photosystem?

....

....

(1 mark)

(c) Describe what the light energy absorbed by the photosystems is used for.

....

....

....

....

(3 marks)

In a typical forest, smaller plant species have light as a limiting factor because larger trees restrict the amount of light that reaches the forest floor.

(d) Suggest **one** limiting factor for photosynthesis in larger trees.

....

(1 mark)

4 A scientist carried out an experiment to investigate the effect of different light intensities on the rate of photosynthesis in an aquatic plant.

The experiment was conducted under two different concentrations of carbon dioxide (low and high). Light intensity was varied by placing a lamp at different distances from a beaker which contained the aquatic plant. Temperature was controlled throughout the experiment. Photosynthetic rate was calculated by measuring the rate at which oxygen was released.

(a) Suggest **one** other way in which photosynthetic rate could have been measured.

....

(1 mark)

(b) Explain how the scientist could have made sure his results were valid.

To make sure your results are valid you need to make sure you're only testing the thing you want to.

....

....

(1 mark)

Table 1 shows the results of the experiment.

Table 1

Distance of lamp from plant / m	Rate of O_2 release with low CO_2 concentration / arbitrary units	Rate of O_2 release with high CO_2 concentration / arbitrary units
1.75	0.2	0.2
1.50	0.4	0.4
1.25	0.6	1.1
1.00	0.8	1.4
0.75	1.0	1.6
0.50	1.2	1.8
0.25	1.2	1.8

(c) Explain the results of the experiment.

....

....

....

....

....

....

(4 marks)

(d) Suggest **one** way that the scientist could improve this experiment.

....

....

(1 mark)

(e) Describe how you would present the results in **Table 1** as a graph **and** explain why you have chosen a certain type of graph.

....

....

....

(3 marks)

(f) The following equation can be used as a measure of light intensity, where d represents the distance of the light source from the plant.

$$\text{light intensity (arbitrary units)} = \frac{1}{d^2}$$

Using the results in **Table 1**, calculate the light intensity at which photosynthesis has become limited for the aquatic plant exposed to a low CO_2 concentration.

light intensity = ... arbitrary units
(1 mark)

5 ATP and reduced NADP are important molecules in photosynthesis.

(a) Explain the role of the electron transport chain in the production of ATP during the light-dependent reaction.

....

....

....

....

....

....

....

(4 marks)

(b) Explain how ATP and reduced NADP are used in the light-independent reaction of photosynthesis.

....

....

....

(3 marks)

If you're asked to interpret data from a table or graph, like in question 4, make sure you take some time to study the experiment in detail, so you know exactly what the investigation was trying to find out. Getting your head around what the results should be showing you will make the questions easier to answer. Okay folks, we haven't quite finished Photosynthesis just yet...

Score

27

Photosynthesis — 2

1 A student wanted to find out whether the leaves of two types of plant contain similar pigments.

(a) Outline how the student could carry out a chromatography experiment to determine the pigments present in the leaves of one of the types of plant.

....

....

....

....

....

....

....

(4 marks)

(b) Explain **two** safety precautions that the student should take during their experiment.

1. ....

....

2. ....

....

(2 marks)

Figure 1 shows some of the chromatography results obtained from the investigation.
Table 1 shows the reference R_f values for some common pigments.

Figure 1

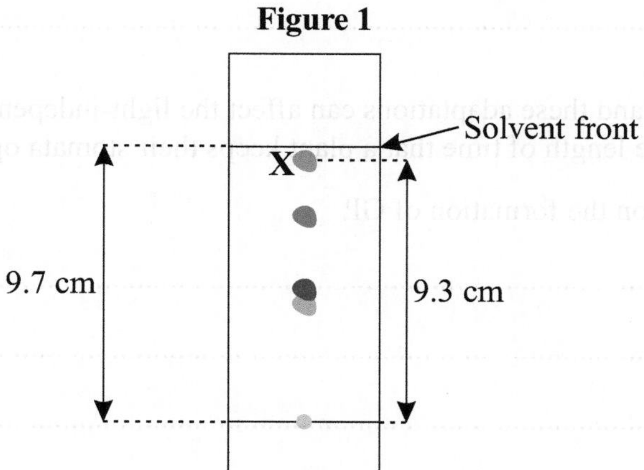

Table 1

Pigment	R_f Value
carotene	0.95
chlorophyll a	0.43
chlorophyll b	0.35
xanthophyll 1	0.30
xanthophyll 2	0.10

(c) Use the information in **Figure 1** and **Table 1** to identify pigment **X**.

Pigment X = ...

(1 mark)

(d) Explain how the chromatography experiment separates out the pigments.

....

....

....

....

(3 marks)

(e) Describe how the student could demonstrate that their results are repeatable and reproducible.

....

....

....

(2 marks)

2 The light-independent reaction is the second reaction in photosynthesis.

Ribulose bisphosphate (RuBP) is produced as a result of the light-independent reaction.

(a) Name the enzyme that catalyses the reaction of CO_2 with RuBP.

....

(1 mark)

(b) Explain why it is important that RuBP and glucose are produced as a result of the light-independent reaction.

RuBP ....

....

Glucose ....

....

(2 marks)

Some plants are adapted to reduce water loss and these adaptations can affect the light-independent reaction. One such adaptation is to reduce the length of time that a plant keeps their stomata open for.

(c) Explain what effect this adaptation will have on the formation of GP.

....

....

....

....

(3 marks)

So that's the questions on the tricky topic of Photosynthesis done with. The key with this topic is making sure you know the theory really well, and not putting off learning it just because it is tricky and a bit dull. E.g. if you know the light-independent reaction off by heart you'll be half way there with answering questions like 2b and 2c. I know you've got this...

Score

18

Respiration — 1

Ahh, now onto respiration — this topic can be a bit tricky at first, but it's a really important process that you need to know. There's no need to panic though, I've got plenty of questions for you to practise, and practice makes perfect...

For each of questions 1-3, give your answer by writing the correct letter in the box.

1 Glycolysis includes two stages, which are phosphorylation and oxidation.

Which of the following statements correspond to the molecules produced during the phosphorylation stage?

Statement 1: Two molecules of triose phosphate

Statement 2: Two molecules of ATP

Statement 3: Two molecules of reduced NAD

A 1, 2, and 3

B 2 and 3 only

C 1 and 2 only

D 1 only

Your answer ☐

(1 mark)

2 Which of the following statements about the Krebs cycle is/are true?

Statement 1: During the Krebs cycle, acetyl coenzyme A is combined with citrate to form oxaloacetate.

Statement 2: The Krebs cycle occurs in the mitochondrial matrix.

Statement 3: The Krebs cycle produces two molecules of ATP per molecule of glucose.

A 1, 2, and 3

B 1 and 2 only

C 2 and 3 only

D 1 only

Your answer ☐

(1 mark)

3 Under some circumstances, the fungus *Aspergillus niger* is known to respire tartaric acid.

The equation for the respiration of tartaric acid is shown below:

Respiration equation: $2C_4H_6O_6 + 5O_2 \rightarrow 8CO_2 + 6H_2O$

Which of the following options, **A** to **D**, is the respiratory quotient (RQ) for the respiration of tartaric acid?

A 1.6

B 0.6

C 0.8

D 1.2

Your answer ☐

(1 mark)

4 **Figure 1** shows part of aerobic respiration in animal cells.

Figure 1

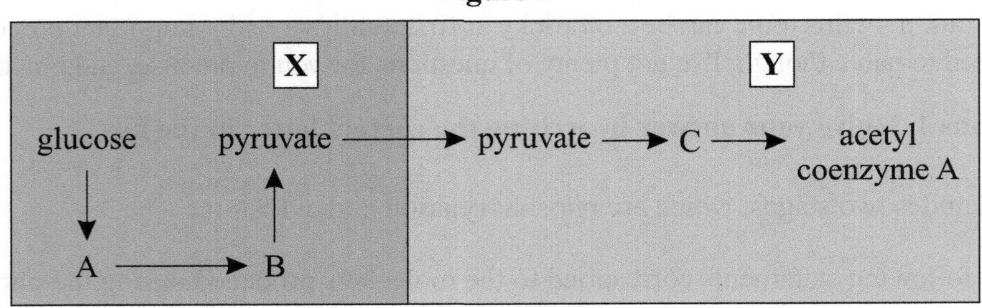

(a) Identify the locations in the cell represented by **X** and **Y** in **Figure 1**.

X .... **Y** ....

(1 mark)

(b) (i) Outline the reaction that converts glucose into substance **A**.

....

....

(3 marks)

(ii) Explain how acetyl coenzyme A is formed from pyruvate.

....

....

....

....

....

(5 marks)

(c) Animal cells can also carry out anaerobic respiration.

(i) With reference to **Figure 1**, explain how glycolysis can be maintained during anaerobic respiration.

....

....

....

....

(4 marks)

(ii) Explain why animal cells obtain a lower yield of ATP from anaerobic respiration than aerobic respiration.

....

....

....

(2 marks)

EXAM TIP

There's a lot to remember when it comes to respiration — but as long as you know your stuff, you'll get through it. The key things to take note of are where in the cell each stage takes place, which reactions occur during each stage, and which molecules are formed at each stage. That way, if you're given a diagram like in Q4, you'll know exactly what's going on.

Score

18

Respiration — 2

1 A student was investigating the effect of pH on the rate of anaerobic respiration in yeast. He set up two conical flasks — one at pH 5 and the other at pH 7. Each conical flask contained glucose solution and was attached to a gas syringe. The student added 10 g of yeast to each conical flask and measured the volume of carbon dioxide produced over time.

(a) Carbon dioxide dissolves in water to form a weakly acidic solution. Explain how this may affect the validity of the student's results.

....

....

....

(2 marks)

Figure 1 shows the results of the experiment.

Figure 1

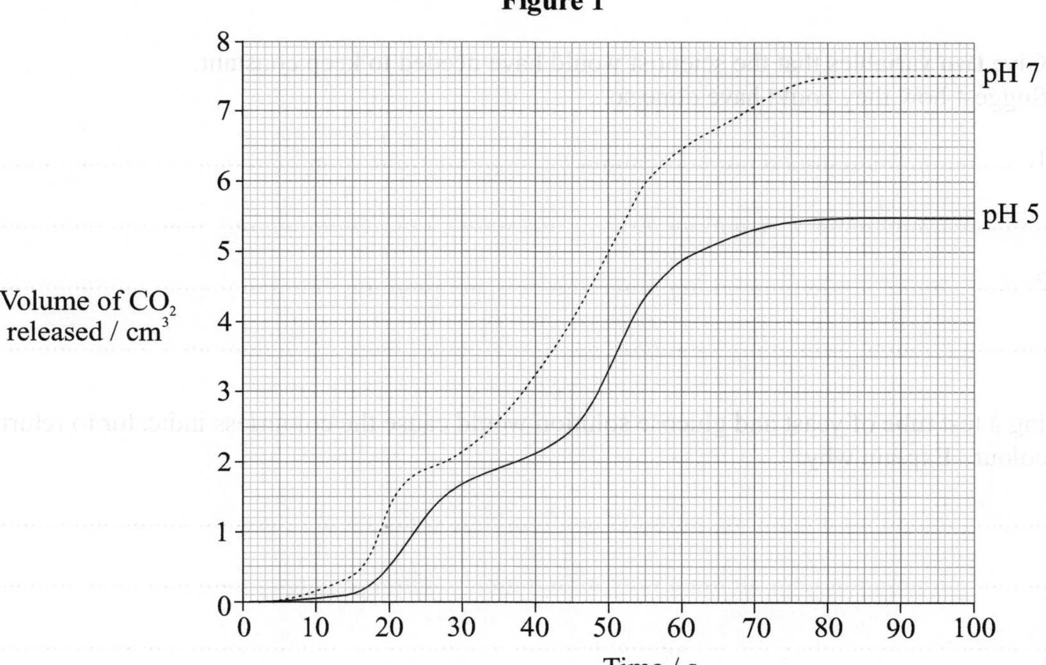

(b) Describe and explain the shape of the curves after 80 seconds.

....

....

(2 marks)

(c) Draw a tangent to the curve representing pH 5 to find the rate of reaction at 45 seconds. Show your working.

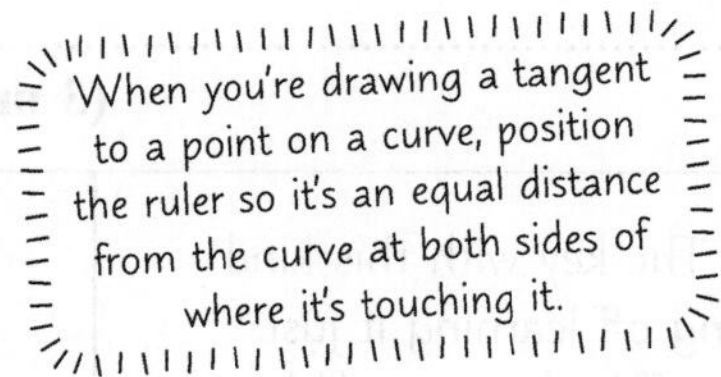

Rate = ... $cm^3 s^{-1}$

(2 marks)

2 A scientist investigated the rate of aerobic respiration in yeast cells. She set up several test tubes which each contained a mixture of yeast cells, and a different concentration of glucose solution. To each of the test tubes she added an indicator known as methylene blue, which changes from blue to colourless when it is reduced. The scientist measured how long it took for the colour change to occur.

(a) Methylene blue acts as an alternative coenzyme by accepting electrons.
Identify **two** coenzymes that it could be acting in place of.

1. ....

2. ....

(2 marks)

(b) i) Describe how the scientist could have set up a control for the experiment.

....

....

....

(2 marks)

ii) Give **two** variables that the scientist would have needed to keep constant.
Suggest how they could have done so.

1. ....

....

2. ....

....

(4 marks)

(c) Shaking a test tube of yeast and glucose solution would cause the colourless indicator to return to its blue colour. Explain why.

....

....

....

(2 marks)

(d) Methylene blue accepts electrons from the electron transport chain during oxidative phosphorylation.
Outline how the movement of electrons down the electron transport chain leads to the formation of ATP.

....

....

....

....

....

(3 marks)

EXAM TIP

So that's the questions on the topic of Respiration done with. Phew. The key with this kind of topic is making sure you know the theory really well, and not putting off learning it just because it is tricky and a bit dull. E.g. if you know aerobic respiration off by heart you'll be half way there with answering questions like 2a. Remember, practice makes perfect...

19

Cellular Control

Cells need to be in control of what's going on inside them. No doubt you want to be in control when it comes to your exams too — so make sure you know your stuff by testing yourself with these questions.

For each of questions 1-3, give your answer by writing the correct letter in the box.

1 Gene expression is controlled by regulatory mechanisms which act at the transcriptional, post-transcriptional or post-translational level.

Which of the rows, **A** to **D**, in the table below gives a correct example of a control mechanism that acts at each level?

	Transcriptional level	Post-transcriptional level	Post-translational level
A	control of *lac* operon	mRNA editing	activation of proteins by cAMP
B	mRNA editing	control of *lac* operon	activation of proteins by cAMP
C	mRNA editing	activation of proteins by cAMP	control of *lac* operon
D	control of *lac* operon	activation of proteins by cAMP	mRNA editing

Your answer ☐

(1 mark)

2 The *lac* operon in *E. coli* contains the genes for the enzymes that are required to respire lactose.

Which of the following options, **A** to **D**, is **not** found in the *lac* operon?

A a regulatory gene

B a promoter

C structural genes

D the gene for RNA polymerase

Your answer ☐

(1 mark)

3 Which of the following statements about control of the *lac* operon is/are **true**?

Statement 1: RNA polymerase must bind to the operator in order for transcription to begin.

Statement 2: The operator is a protein transcription factor.

Statement 3: The repressor binds to the operator when there is no lactose present.

A 1, 2 and 3

B 1 and 2 only

C 2 and 3 only

D 3 only

Your answer ☐

(1 mark)

4 Lactase is an enzyme which breaks down lactose — the main sugar in milk.
In humans, lactase is only produced in the cells of the small intestine.

(a) (i) Describe how mature mRNA would be produced from primary RNA in the cells of the small intestine.

....

....

(1 mark)

(ii) Explain how lactase is produced in the cells of the small intestine in humans, but not other body cells.

....

....

(1 mark)

Lactase production usually decreases after infancy, so adults in many parts of the world are unable to digest lactose. This is known as lactose intolerance. Thousands of years ago, mutations arose in European populations which led to the continued production of high levels of lactase in adulthood. This is known as lactase persistence.

One mutation that leads to lactase persistence is a substitution mutation.
It does not occur in the lactase gene, so it does not affect the function of lactase.

(b) (i) The lactase persistence mutation leads to more transcription factors being attracted to the lactase gene during adulthood. Explain how this could lead to continued high levels of lactase production.

....

....

....

(2 marks)

(ii) The lactase persistance mutation has become more common in European populations because it is a beneficial mutation. Suggest why it is a beneficial mutation.

....

....

(1 mark)

(c) (i) Give **two** reasons why a substitution mutation that occurs in a gene may have a neutral effect on protein function.

1. ....

2. ....

(2 marks)

(ii) Suggest and explain why a substitution mutation that occurs in a gene is more likely to have a neutral effect on protein function than an insertion or deletion mutation.

....

....

....

....

(4 marks)

5 Hox genes are involved in the development of the body plans of many organisms. For example, Hox genes help to control the development of limbs in vertebrates.

(a) Explain how Hox genes affect the development of body plans.

....

....

....

....

....

(3 marks)

Figure 1 shows a biological drawing of a normal vertebrate limb in a developing embryo (**A**) and a vertebrate limb in which a single Hox gene has not been expressed correctly (**B**).

Figure 1

digits

A **B**

(b) Suggest the role of the Hox gene that was expressed incorrectly in **Figure 1**.

....

....

(1 mark)

(c) In a normally developing vertebrate embryo, the digits are initially connected by webbing — a thin layer of cells that forms a membrane between the digits. The webbing is not present at birth. Suggest and explain how the webbing between digits is removed in the developing embryo.

....

....

....

....

(3 marks)

EXAM TIP

Use the number of marks the question is worth as a guide to how much to write in your answer. For example, if a question's worth 1 mark, you probably only need to write a word or a single sentence. If it's worth 4 marks, you need to write several sentences and make at least four separate points. For calculation questions, more marks indicate more steps in the calculation.

Score

21

Patterns of Inheritance — 1

Organisms pass on their genes to their offspring. There can be one or more different versions of a gene, called alleles, which are represented using letters. Hopefully this sounds familiar because I've got plenty to test you on...

For each of questions 1-3, give your answer by writing the correct letter in the box.

1 Humans can have the blood group A, B, AB or O. Blood group is determined by a single gene with multiple alleles. Humans can have any eye colour within a range. Human eye colour is determined by multiple genes. Which row in the table, **A** to **D**, correctly describes the genetics of both human blood groups and human eye colour?

	Blood group	Eye colour
A	A continuous, polygenic trait	A continuous, monogenic trait
B	A discontinuous, polygenic trait	A continuous, polygenic trait
C	A continuous, monogenic trait	A discontinuous, polygenic trait
D	A discontinuous, monogenic trait	A continuous, polygenic trait

Your answer ☐

(1 mark)

2 In fruit flies, the allele for red eyes, R, is dominant to the allele for brown eyes, r. The allele for a brown body, B, is dominant to the allele for a black body, b. Assuming the genes for eye colour and body colour are not linked and are not epistatic, which of the following options, **A** to **D**, shows the expected phenotypic ratio for the offspring of the cross RrBb × RrBb?

A 1 : 1

B 3 : 1

C 1 : 2 : 1

D 9 : 3 : 3 : 1

Your answer ☐

(1 mark)

3 Menkes disease is an X-linked recessive disorder that results in copper deficiency. A woman who is a carrier of the disease has a child with an unaffected man. Which of the following options, **A** to **D**, shows the probability of the child inheriting Menkes disease?

A 0%

B 25%

C 50%

D 100%

Your answer ☐

(1 mark)

4 **Scientists are investigating the inheritance of cuticle colour in a new species of insect.**

The scientists find that cuticle colour is controlled by a single gene with three different alleles.

- The red allele (P^R) results in the production of a red pigment.
- The purple allele (P^P) results in the production of a purple pigment.
- The yellow allele (P^y) results in the production of a yellow pigment.

The P^P and P^R alleles are codominant. The P^y allele is recessive.
The phenotypes corresponding to each possible genotype are shown in **Table 1**.

Table 1

Phenotype	Genotype
Red cuticle	P^RP^R or P^RP^y
Purple cuticle	P^PP^P or P^PP^y
Yellow cuticle	P^yP^y
Red cuticle with purple spots	P^PP^R

(a) (i) Explain why the P^P and P^R alleles can be said to be codominant.

....

....

....

(2 marks)

(ii) Describe the difference between a homozygous genotype and a heterozygous genotype, giving an example of each from **Table 1**.

....

....

....

(2 marks)

As part of the scientists' investigation, insects with the genotype P^RP^y were crossed with red and purple spotted insects.

(b) Draw a genetic diagram to show the expected phenotypic ratio in the offspring of this cross.

Expected phenotypic ratio: ....

(3 marks)

(c) The results of the scientists' cross are shown in **Table 2**.

Table 2

	Red cuticle	Purple cuticle	Red cuticle with purple spots	Total
Number of offspring	48	19	21	88

The scientists used a chi-squared test to compare the observed and expected results.

(i) This is the formula for chi-squared:

$$\chi^2 = \Sigma\frac{(O - E)^2}{E}$$

Complete **Table 3** to calculate the chi-squared statistic for the scientists' cross.

Table 3

Phenotype	Expected Result (E)	Observed Result (O)	(O – E)	$(O - E)^2$	$\frac{(O - E)^2}{E}$
Red cuticle	44	48	4	16	0.364
Purple cuticle	22				
Red cuticle with purple spots					
Total		88	–	–	

χ^2 = ...

(3 marks)

(ii) Before carrying out the test, the scientists came up with a null hypothesis.
Suggest what the null hypothesis for their investigation would have been.

....

....

....

(1 mark)

(iii) The critical value for the chi-squared test was determined to be 5.99.
Explain whether or not the null hypothesis can be rejected.

....

....

(1 mark)

(iv) The statistical test was performed at the 5% probability level.
Explain what this tells you about the results.

....

....

(1 mark)

5 In maize plants, different genes control seed colour and shape. The allele for coloured seeds (C) is dominant over the allele for colourless seeds (c). The allele for a full seed shape (S) is dominant over the allele for shrunken seeds (s).

A scientist crossed a maize plant that was heterozygous for both genes with a maize plant that was homozygous recessive for both genes.

(a) Give the phenotypes of the parent plants.

....

....

(1 mark)

The phenotypes of the offspring produced by the cross are shown in **Figure 1**.

Figure 1

(b) Explain why the results in **Figure 1** suggest that the genes that control seed colour and shape are autosomally linked.

....

....

....

....

(3 marks)

(c) The phenotypic traits of plants, like maize plants, can be caused by the environment as well as genes. Give **one** example of a phenotypic trait in plants that is determined only by the environment and explain how it is caused.

....

....

....

(2 marks)

EXAM TIP

Genetic crosses can get quite complex, especially when they involve multiple alleles. You should always label any genetic diagrams you are asked to draw in the exams. That way it'll be clear to the examiner what you're trying to show and, most importantly, what to award the marks for. Punnett squares are usually the simplest type of diagram to draw and to follow.

Score

22

Patterns of Inheritance — 2

1 Coat colour in horses is influenced by a variety of autosomal genes.

The dominant allele for the grey gene (G) results in coat colour turning progressively grey.
The recessive allele (g) results in the normal coat colour being maintained (non-grey phenotype).

(a) A non-grey female is crossed with a heterozygous male.
Draw a genetic diagram in the space below to show the expected ratio of phenotypes of the offspring.

Expected phenotypic ratio: ....

(3 marks)

The extension gene also influences coat colour. The dominant allele (E) results in the production of black pigment, while the recessive allele (e) results in the production of red pigment.

The dominant allele of the white gene (W) blocks pigment production.
A horse with the W allele will have a white coat irrespective of what extension alleles they have.

(b) (i) Name the term used to describe the interaction between the extension and white genes.

....

(1 mark)

(ii) Complete **Table 1** by filling in the pigment produced as a result of each genotype.
If no pigment is produced, write 'none'.

Table 1

Genotype	Pigment produced
EeWw	
Eeww	
eeww	

(1 mark)

(iii) If a male that is heterozygous for both the extension and white coat colour genes is crossed with a red-pigment producing female, what is the probability that their offspring will produce a black pigment? Show your working.

Probability of offspring producing black pigment = ...

(3 marks)

(iv) The white gene and extension gene are both located on chromosome 3.
Explain how this could affect the expected results of the cross described in (b) (iii).

....

....

....

(3 marks)

2 A scientist is investigating the inheritance of two genes in a particular species of flowering plant.

A single gene controls flower colour. The dominant allele (R) results in red flowers, and the recessive allele (r) results in yellow flowers.

A second gene controls the number of flowers on each stem. The dominant allele (M) results in multiple flowers on each stem, and the recessive allele (m) results in only a single flower on each stem.

The scientist initially crosses a plant that is homozygous dominant for both genes with a plant that is homozygous recessive for both genes. He then observes the phenotypes of the offspring.

(a) (i) Give the genotypes of all possible gametes that could be produced in this cross.

....

(1 mark)

(ii) Describe the expected phenotype(s) of the offspring.

....

....

(1 mark)

The offspring from the cross described above were subsequently crossed with each other and the phenotypes of the offspring in the next generation were observed and recorded. The observed and expected results of this cross are shown in **Table 2**.

Table 2

Phenotype	Expected Result (E)	Observed Result (O)			
Multiple red flowers	36	46			
Single red flower	12	11			
Multiple yellow flowers	12	7			
Single yellow flower	4	0			

(b) (i) Calculate χ^2 for the results shown in **Table 2**.
Use the blank columns in **Table 2** to show your working.
The formula for χ^2 is shown below.

$$\chi^2 = \sum \frac{(O - E)^2}{E}$$

$\chi^2 =$ ....

(3 marks)

Table 3 shows some critical values for the chi-squared test.

Table 3

	Probability level					
	0.5	0.2	0.1	0.05	0.01	0.001
Degrees of freedom	Critical values					
1	0.46	1.64	2.71	3.84	6.64	10.83
2	1.39	3.22	4.61	5.99	9.21	13.82
3	2.37	4.64	6.25	7.82	11.34	16.27
4	3.36	5.99	7.78	9.49	13.28	18.47

(ii) The scientist had expected there to be no significant difference between the expected and observed results of his cross.
Use **Table 3** and your answer to part (b) (i) to conclude whether there is a significant difference between the observed and expected results of this cross. Explain your answer.

Hint: you'll need to work out the degrees of freedom. Here, it's the number of classes minus 1.

....

....

....

(2 marks)

(iii) Explain **two** reasons why the observed results of a genetic cross could be different from the expected results.

1. ....

....

....

2. ....

....

....

(4 marks)

(c) The flowering plant species investigated by the scientist is capable of reproducing both sexually and asexually, using mitosis, depending on the environmental conditions. Explain why asexually reproducing populations of the plant will be less genetically varied than sexually reproducing populations.

....

....

....

....

(3 marks)

EXAM TIP

Unfortunately you need to understand a bit about the chi-squared test for this section. It can be tricky to get your head around, but just take your time when working through the questions. If you're not given a table to fill in when working out chi-squared in the exam, it might help to quickly sketch yourself one so you can keep track of your working out.

Score

25

Evolution — 1

Evolution is responsible for the huge diversity of species on Earth. There are some complex processes involved, so the next few pages won't be easy — but you'll be glad you've done them if this topic comes up in your exams.

For each of questions 1-3, give your answer by writing the correct letter in the box.

1 Two separate squirrel species live on either side of the Grand Canyon. The two species are thought to be descended from a single species present in the area before the Grand Canyon was formed.

Which of the following options, **A** to **D**, is this scenario an example of?

A sympatric speciation

B allopatric speciation

C genetic drift

D founder effect

Your answer ☐

(1 mark)

2 In a population of rabbits, fur colour varies from very pale grey to very dark grey.

Which of the following statements, **A** to **D**, would be an example of **stabilising selection** in this population?

A Rabbits with darker fur are more likely to be eaten by predators, so paler fur becomes more common over time.

B Fur colour has no impact on chances of survival and reproduction, so the full range of variation in fur colour is maintained.

C Very pale and very dark rabbits are more likely to be eaten by predators, so the alleles for these fur colours become less common over time.

D Very pale and very dark rabbits are more likely to find a mate, so the alleles for these fur colours become more common over time.

Your answer ☐

(1 mark)

3 Which of the following statements related to evolution is/are **correct**?

Statement 1: Evolution only occurs when a selection pressure means that some individuals are better adapted to the environmental conditions than others.

Statement 2: In order for evolution to occur, there has to be a change in the environment that causes directional selection.

Statement 3: Evolution may occur because certain alleles are passed on to the next generation by chance, rather than because they provide a selective advantage.

A 1, 2 and 3 **B** 1 only

C 2 and 3 only **D** 3 only

Your answer ☐

(1 mark)

4 **Figure 1** shows the distributions of three populations of a species of flightless bird. The species cannot survive in a mountain habitat so the populations are distributed in a ring around the base of a mountain range. The arrows show gene flow between them.

Figure 1

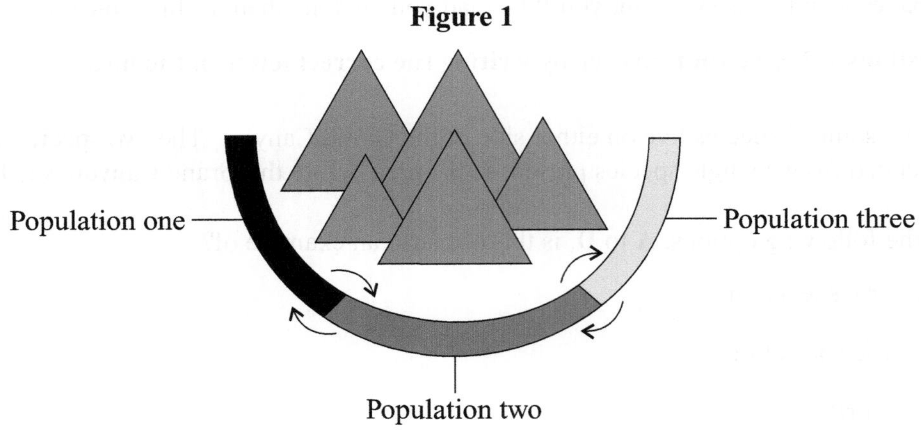

(a) The Hardy-Weinberg principle does **not** apply to these populations. Using **Figure 1**, suggest **one** reason why.

....

....

(1 mark)

(b) Population **one** and population **three** are geographically isolated from one another by the mountain range. Explain why this could lead to speciation of these two populations.

....

....

....

....

....

(4 marks)

(c) The scientist observed that population **two** was beginning to show different courtship behaviours to population **one**. Suggest what may happen to the gene flow between these two populations as a result. Explain your answer.

....

....

....

(3 marks)

5 In a species of small rodent, fur colour is controlled by a single gene with two alleles. The dominant 'W' allele results in a white fur phenotype. Two copies of the recessive 'w' allele result in a brown fur phenotype. Fur colour provides the rodents with camouflage from predators.

Scientists measured the frequency of these two alleles in populations of the rodent and recorded this against the latitude at which the populations were found. When measured in degrees north (° N), latitude is a measure of how far north a location is from the equator. The higher the number, the further north it is.

Table 1 shows the frequencies of the two fur colour alleles in populations living at different latitudes.

Table 1

Latitude / ° N	Allele frequency 'W'	Allele frequency 'w'
64	0.62	
66		0.33
68		0.17
70	0.92	0.08

(a) The Hardy-Weinberg principle states that:

$$p + q = 1$$
$$p^2 + 2pq + q^2 = 1$$

Where: p = the frequency of the dominant allele
q = the frequency of the recessive allele

(i) Complete **Table 1** by calculating the missing allele frequencies.

(1 mark)

(ii) Calculate the frequency of the white fur phenotype at latitude 70° N. Show your working.

frequency = ...

(2 marks)

(b) As the latitude increases, the frequency of snowy weather increases. Using this information, explain how natural selection has led to the differences in allele frequencies between the populations in **Table 1**.

....

....

....

....

....

....

(4 marks)

(c) Another group of scientists studied a population of the same rodent species at 62° N. They found the allele frequency of 'W' to be 0.58 and the allele frequency of 'w' to be 0.35. The scientists hypothesised that this population showed a mutation, resulting in a third allele for fur colour. Suggest why they made this hypothesis.

....

....

(1 mark)

You'll be provided with the Hardy-Weinberg equations in the exam, but that doesn't mean you don't need to practise using them. You should know that p^2 means the frequency of the homozygous dominant genotype, $2pq$ means the frequency of the heterozygous genotype and q^2 means the frequency of the homozygous recessive genotype.

Score

19

Evolution — 2

1 Commercially grown tomato plants produce a large number of tomatoes. These plants have been through several years of artificial selection.

(a) Explain why artificial selection may have made commercially grown tomato plants susceptible to new diseases.

....

....

....

(2 marks)

(b) *Solanum pimpinellifolium* is the wild ancestor of all tomatoes grown for food today. It is still found in the wild in South America. Seeds from *Solanum pimpinellifolium* have been collected and stored in seed banks. Explain how this could be beneficial for commercial growers of tomato plants in the future.

....

....

....

(2 marks)

(c) Artificial selection is also carried out with animals.
Describe **one** ethical problem that can arise as a result of artificial selection in animals.

....

....

(1 mark)

2 A team of scientists discovered a new species of tree frog in a forest. The species showed two different colour phenotypes, green and yellow. The green allele is dominant and the yellow allele is recessive. The scientists recorded the phenotype frequencies present in the frog population over several years.

The scientists' results are shown in **Figure 1**.

Figure 1

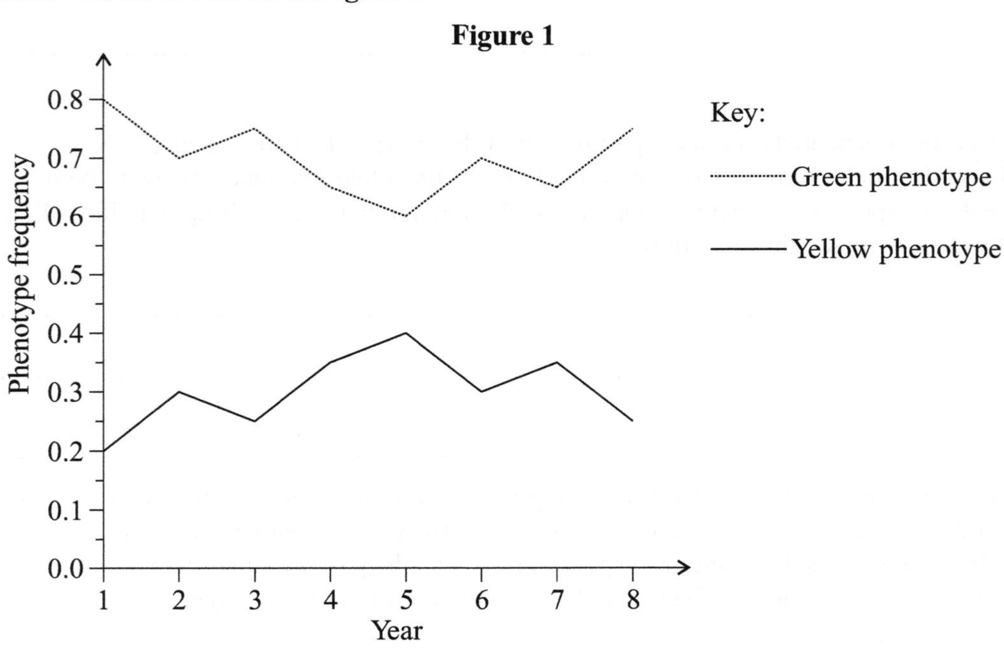

(a) The Hardy-Weinberg principle states that:

$$p + q = 1$$
$$p^2 + 2pq + q^2 = 1$$

Where: p = the frequency of the dominant allele
q = the frequency of the recessive allele

Using **Figure 1**, calculate the expected frequency of heterozygous individuals in the population in **Year 3**. Show your working.

frequency = ...

(3 marks)

(b) Using **Figure 1**, explain how you know selection is not acting on this phenotypic trait.

....

....

....

(3 marks)

(c) Suggest **one** reason why the phenotype frequencies are changing over time.

....

(1 mark)

3 The Galapagos Islands are a group of small islands lying about 1000 km west of South America. Several different species of finch live there. Each species has a different size and shape of beak, which relates to their diet. For example, finches with larger beaks are better at feeding on large, tough seeds. *Geospiza fortis* is a medium-sized ground finch with a medium-sized beak, which can feed on a broader range of seed sizes than other ground finch species on the Galapagos.

(a) In 2004, a severe drought caused a reduction in the number of large seeds produced. The year following the drought, scientists observed that not only had the population size of *Geospiza fortis* fallen, but the average beak size for this species was now significantly smaller. Explain how this change in average beak size would have occurred.

....

....

....

....

(3 marks)

(b) Suggest **one** reason why genetic drift may have a greater effect on a population of Galapagos finches than a population on the South American mainland.

....

....

(1 mark)

EXAM TIP

If you have to give the frequency of a phenotype or genotype in a Hardy-Weinberg question, your answer will always be something between 0 and 1. If you get something else, take a look back through your working to find where you went wrong. Remember, '$p^2 + 2pq + q^2 = 1$' is for genotype frequencies and '$p + q = 1$' is for allele frequencies.

Score

16

Manipulating Genomes — 1

The questions in this section have all kinds of examples of how scientists can manipulate genomes to help out in the real world — it's very impressive. Have a go at them and see how much you know.

For each of questions 1-3, give your answer by writing the correct letter in the box.

1 The polymerase chain reaction (PCR) is a technique that is commonly used to amplify fragments of DNA. Which of the following enzymes are required for PCR?

1: DNA polymerase

2: restriction endonuclease

3: DNA ligase

A 1, 2 and 3 **B** 1 and 2 only

C 2 and 3 only **D** 1 only

Your answer ☐

(1 mark)

2 Gel electrophoresis can be used to separate DNA fragments. Which of the following statements, **A-D**, correctly describes how this occurs?

A The DNA migrates towards the positive electrode, with smaller DNA fragments travelling faster

B The DNA migrates towards the negative electrode, with smaller DNA fragments travelling faster.

C The DNA migrates towards the positive electrode, with larger DNA fragments travelling faster.

D The DNA migrates towards the negative electrode, with larger DNA fragments travelling faster

Your answer ☐

(1 mark)

3 This question is about modern methods of biological research. Which of the following statements related to these methods is/are **correct**?

Statement 1: Computational biology means developing computer software to analyse biological data.

Statement 2: Synthetic biology involves building biological systems from artificially made molecules.

Statement 3: Gene sequencing allows scientists to predict polypeptide structures.

A 1, 2 and 3

B 1 and 3 only

C 2 and 3 only

D 1 only

Your answer ☐

(1 mark)

4 Blood has been found at a crime scene. A forensic scientist has been asked to confirm who the blood is from. The forensic scientist takes a sample of the blood, extracts the DNA and then uses the polymerase chain reaction (PCR) to amplify it. A DNA profile of the sample is then produced, alongside DNA profiles of the samples of DNA from the victim of the crime and three potential suspects.

(a) Suggest why it is necessary to amplify the DNA sample using PCR before producing a DNA profile.

....

....

....

(2 marks)

(b) Explain the role of complementary base pairing in the PCR process.

....

....

....

(2 marks)

(c) The forensic scientist produced the DNA profiles shown in **Figure 1** using gel electrophoresis.

Figure 1

(i) Outline how gel electrophoresis of the DNA samples is carried out.

....

....

....

(3 marks)

(ii) Explain why DNA samples from different individuals produce different patterns of bands when DNA profiles are produced.

....

....

....

....

....

....

(4 marks)

(iii) On the basis of the results shown in **Figure 1**, what conclusion can be drawn regarding the blood from the crime scene?

....

....

(1 mark)

(iv) Gel electrophoresis can also be used to separate proteins. Explain **one** way in which the process of gel electrophoresis differs when it is carried out on proteins rather than DNA.

....

....

....

(2 marks)

5 Severe combined immunodeficiency (SCID) is a genetic disorder that affects the functioning of white blood cells. There are a number of different genetic defects that can cause SCID, one of which is a mutation in the IL2RG gene.

In the future, it is hoped that gene therapy could be used to treat individuals with an IL2RG mutation. One way this could be achieved is to take a sample of white blood cells from the patient, infect the cells with a virus containing a functional copy of the IL2RG gene, and then inject the cells back into the patient.

(a) Is the method described above an example of somatic cell gene therapy or germ line cell gene therapy? Explain your answer.

....

....

(1 mark)

(b) (i) Explain how a functional copy of the IL2RG gene could be inserted into a virus.

....

....

....

....

....

....

....

(4 marks)

(ii) Explain the role of the virus in gene therapy to treat an IL2RG mutation.

....

....

....

(2 marks)

(c) Is the IL2RG mutation likely to be recessive or dominant? Explain your answer.

....

....

(1 mark)

(d) Suggest **two** potential disadvantages of using this form of gene therapy to treat a patient with SCID.

1. ....

....

2. ....

....

(2 marks)

6 *Cryptosporidium* is the pathogen that causes cryptosporidiosis, a diarrhoeal disease. There is no vaccine for cryptosporidiosis, and there is only one drug used to treat it, which is unsuitable for some patients. The pathogen is difficult to detect, but scientists have genetically modified it to make it easier to study.

(a) Suggest **one positive** and **one negative** ethical issue that may be associated with the genetic modification of *Cryptosporidium* for scientific research.

Postive: ....

....

Negative: ....

....

(2 marks)

(b) *Cryptosporidium* can be genetically modified for research using synthetic biology rather than traditional methods of genetic engineering. Suggest how the modification of *Cryptosporidium* using genetic engineering would be different to the modification of *Cryptosporidium* using synthetic biology.

....

....

....

....

(2 marks)

(c) Suggest how animal 'pharming' could play a role in the treatment of cryptosporidosis.

....

....

(1 mark)

You might have to interpret the results of gel electrophoresis (the technique used to separate DNA fragments, RNA fragments or proteins) in your exams. Luckily, it's quite straightforward — fragments are separated by size, and fragments of the same size (indicating a match) travel exactly the same distance in the gel. Use a ruler to compare where bands are located if it helps.

Score

32

Manipulating Genomes — 2

1 A group of scientists is experimenting with an enzyme produced by a rare species of plant. In order to produce large amounts of this enzyme quickly and easily, they decide to clone the gene for the enzyme and then produce a strain of *E. coli* that is capable of making the enzyme in large quantities. The process used by the scientists is outlined in **Figure 1**.

Figure 1

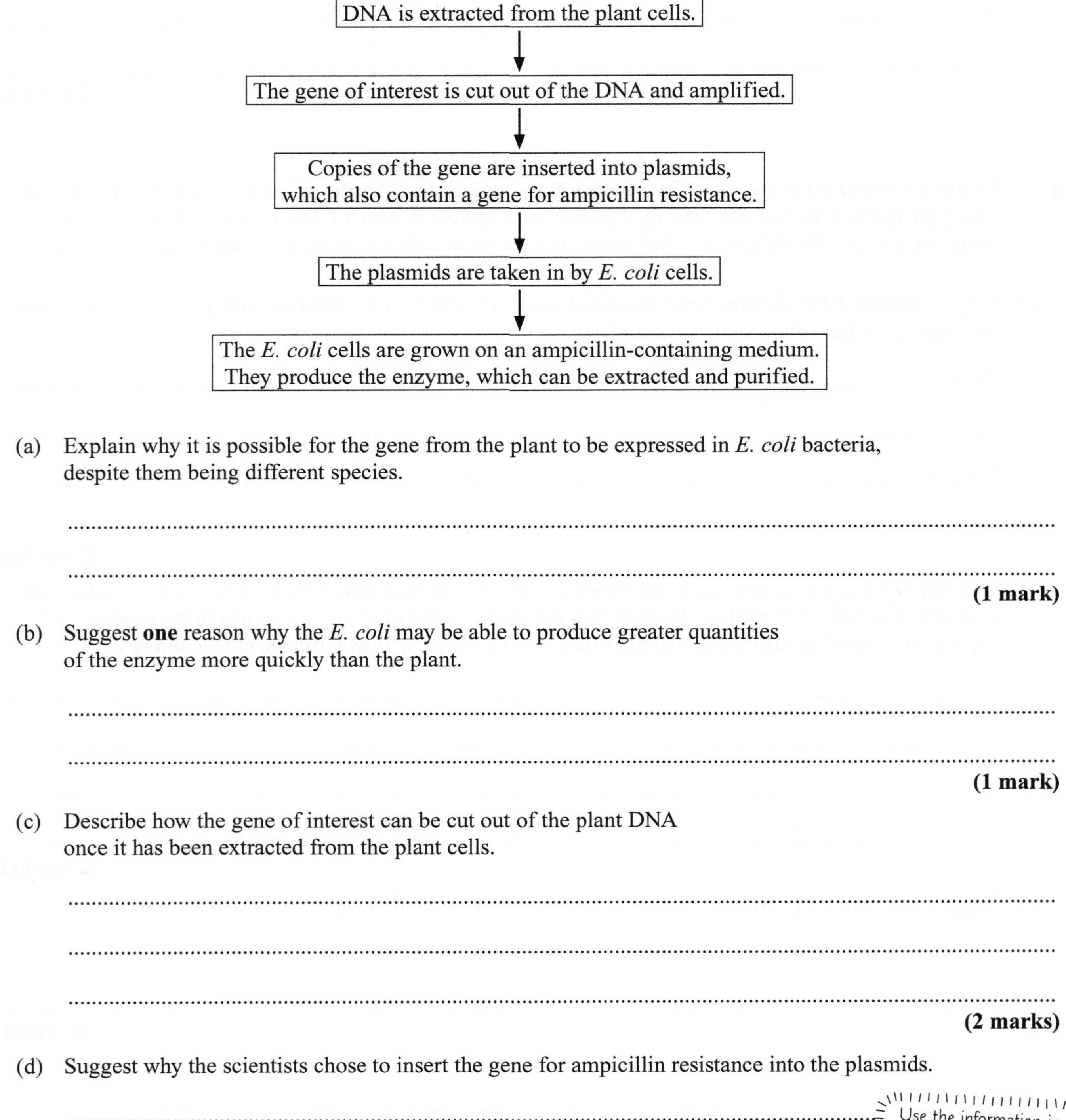

(a) Explain why it is possible for the gene from the plant to be expressed in *E. coli* bacteria, despite them being different species.

....

....

(1 mark)

(b) Suggest **one** reason why the *E. coli* may be able to produce greater quantities of the enzyme more quickly than the plant.

....

....

(1 mark)

(c) Describe how the gene of interest can be cut out of the plant DNA once it has been extracted from the plant cells.

....

....

....

(2 marks)

(d) Suggest why the scientists chose to insert the gene for ampicillin resistance into the plasmids.

....

....

....

Use the information in Figure 1 to help you answer this question.

(2 marks)

(e) Explain how the scientists may have used electroporation as part of the process shown in **Figure 1**.

....

....

....

(3 marks)

2 A group of scientists identifies a new strain of bacteria that lives in Antarctic lakes. The scientists sequence the genome of the bacteria. Having done so, they identify a novel version of a gene that codes for an anti-freeze protein. Anti-freeze proteins prevent ice crystals from forming in the cells of organisms that live in sub-freezing conditions.

(a) (i) The genome of the bacteria is 240 000 base pairs in length. The scientists sequenced the entire genome 6 times in order to ensure that their sequence was accurate. They used a sequencing technique capable of reading 12 000 base pairs per minute. Calculate how many hours the team spent sequencing the genome in total.

.... hours

(2 marks)

(ii) The scientists used a high-throughput sequencing technique. Explain why high-throughput sequencing is an improvement on older genome sequencing techniques.

....

....

....

(2 marks)

(b) A second group of scientists decides to investigate whether the novel anti-freeze gene could be inserted into maize plants. They hope this will increase the maize plants' resistance to cold. Discuss the advantages and disadvantages for society of using genetic engineering to produce a cold-resistant strain of maize.

....

....

....

....

....

....

....

....

(4 marks)

If a question asks you for two things, e.g. 'advantages and disadvantages', you need to write about them both. Even if you've described loads of advantages, you wouldn't get full marks unless you've also written something to balance out the argument on the other side.

Score

17

Cloning and Biotechnology — 1

Cloning is all about producing genetically identical cells, or whole organisms, from the cells of an existing organism — this can be a natural or artificial process. Don't you just wish you had a clone to sit your exams for you...

For each of questions 1-3, give your answer by writing the correct letter in the box.

1 Which of the following statements describe a disadvantage of using fungi as a source of single-cell protein for meat substitutes?

1. The substrates that are required to grow microorganisms are often expensive and difficult to obtain.
2. The consumption of high quantities of single-cell protein can cause health problems due to the uric acid released when it is broken down.
3. Single-cell protein doesn't have the same texture or flavour as real meat.
4. The culture conditions have to be carefully controlled to avoid contamination by unwanted bacteria.

A 1, 2, 3 and 4 **B** 2, 3 and 4

C 1, 3 and 4 **D** 3 and 4

Your answer ☐

(1 mark)

2 Which statement correctly describes a difference between tissue culture and micropropagation?

A In micropropagation, cells are taken from the leaves, whereas in tissue culture, cells are taken from the stem or root tips.

B Micropropagation is usually performed on a small scale, whereas tissue culture is more suitable for large-scale applications.

C Micropropagation involves the sub-culturing of cells taken from the developing plant clones, whereas tissue culture does not.

D Micropropagation is a technique used to create artificial clones of plants, whereas tissue culture is a technique used to create natural clones.

Your answer ☐

(1 mark)

3 Species A is a fungal species that can be grown and used industrially.
Its optimum conditions for growth are a temperature of 25 °C and a starting pH of 4.

The growth curve for Species A grown at 28 °C, with an initial pH of 6 is shown as curve **X**.

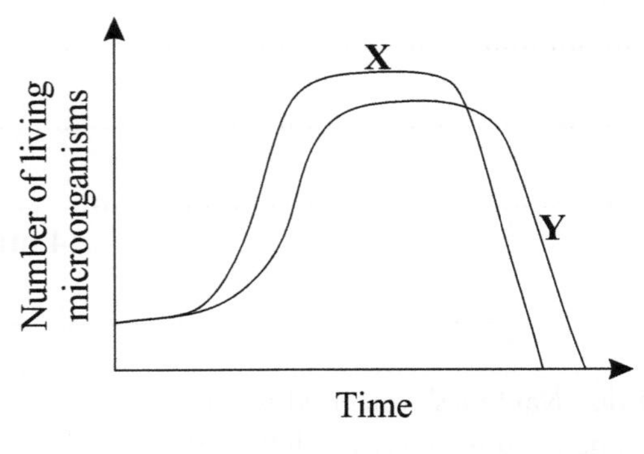

Which of the following conditions could result in curve **Y**?

A A temperature of 30 °C and an initial pH of 7.

B A temperature of 26 °C and an initial pH of 5.

C A temperature of 28 °C and an initial pH of 6, with a greater supply of nutrients.

D A temperature of 25 °C and an initial pH of 4, with a greater supply of nutrients.

Your answer ☐

(1 mark)

4 **Vegetative propagation can be used by horticulturists to reproduce plants with desirable characteristics.**

A horticulturist that runs a garden centre has found a plant with a very striking pattern of colours on the petals. She wants to produce a large number of plants with the same coloured petals to sell in her shop.

(a) Outline how the horticulturist could use the stem of the desired plant to carry out vegetative propagation to reproduce it.

....

....

....

....

....

(4 marks)

(b) Explain why, in this case, vegetative propagation is a more suitable method for reproducing the plant than simply collecting seeds from it.

....

....

....

(2 marks)

One of the horticulturist's colleagues suggests that she should consider using tissue culture instead of vegetative propagation to reproduce the plant. The process of tissue culture is illustrated in **Figure 1**.

Figure 1

1. Cells are removed from the stem/root tip of the plant to be cloned.
2. Cells are sterilised and grown on a culture medium.
3. Cells grow and divide into a small plant.
4. The small plant is moved into soil to grow.

(c) (i) Explain why the plant cells in **Figure 1** must be taken from the stem or root tips of the plant, and not from another part of the plant, such as the leaves.

....

....

(1 mark)

(ii) Explain why the sterilisation step in **Figure 1** is important for the process of tissue culture.

....

....

....

(2 marks)

(iii) Discuss the use of tissue culture, versus vegetative propagation, for the horticulturist in this case.

....

....

....

....

....

....

(4 marks)

5 Methicillin-resistant *Staphylococcus aureus* (MRSA) is a type of bacteria that is resistant to methicillin and other antibiotics.

When outbreaks of MRSA occur in hospitals, the staff at the hospital may be screened to determine whether they are a carrier of MRSA. This can be achieved by taking a nasal swab from the member of staff, and then culturing any microorganisms present in the swab on an agar plate, containing methicillin or other antibiotics. When performing this test, it is important that the laboratory technician uses aseptic techniques.

(a) (i) Describe the result you would expect to observe in this test if the individual were a carrier of MRSA.

....

(1 mark)

(ii) Explain why it is important for the laboratory technician to use aseptic techniques when performing this diagnostic test.

....

....

....

(2 marks)

(iii) Controls are used to make sure that the test is working properly. What could be used as a negative control for this test?

....

....

(1 mark)

A group of scientists have discovered a new antibiotic that they think may be effective in treating MRSA. To determine what concentration of the antibiotic would be most effective in inhibiting the growth of MRSA they culture MRSA in broth and then grow samples of it on agar plates that contain different concentrations of the new antibiotic. For each agar plate, the number of MRSA colonies are counted.

(b) On some plates there may be too many MRSA colonies to count. Describe a technique that could be used to overcome this problem.

....

(1 mark)

EXAM TIP

In your exam, it's likely that you'll be given a question which tests you on the scientific process of an experiment. It's really important to learn what a negative control is and what a positive control is, what control variables are, and the reasons why certain techniques must be used. Well, that's enough from me, there are still plenty of questions left for you to have a bash at...

Score

21

Cloning and Biotechnology — 2

1 Lactose-free dairy products are produced using the enzyme lactase, which breaks lactose down. Lactase is produced industrially from the fermentation of certain fungal species, including *Aspergillus niger*.

(a) Describe the advantages of using microorganisms like *Aspergillus niger* in industry.

....

....

....

(2 marks)

Aspergillus niger is usually grown in a fermentation vessel like the one shown in **Figure 1**.

Figure 1

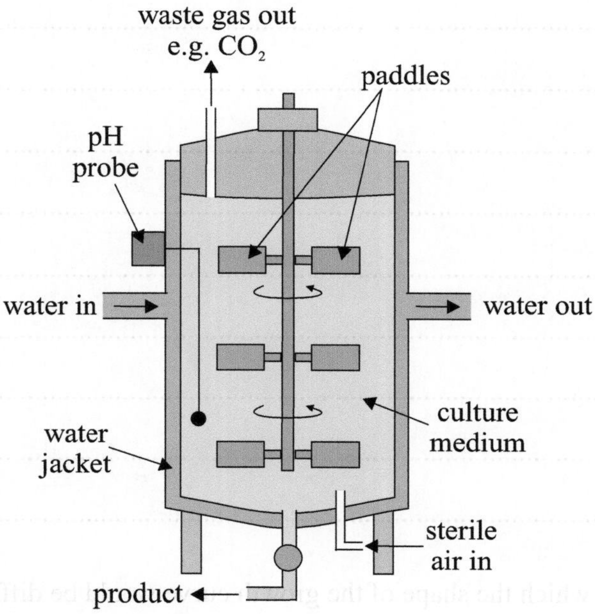

(b) (i) Explain **two** ways that the fermentation vessel shown in **Figure 1** is adapted to ensure that the maximum yield of lactase is produced.

1. ....

....

2. ....

....

(2 marks)

(ii) *Aspergillus niger* naturally secretes lactase.
Suggest and explain why this is advantageous for industrial lactase production.

....

....

....

(2 marks)

When *Aspergillus niger* is grown using a batch fermentation process, it exhibits a growth curve similar to that shown in **Figure 2**.

Figure 2

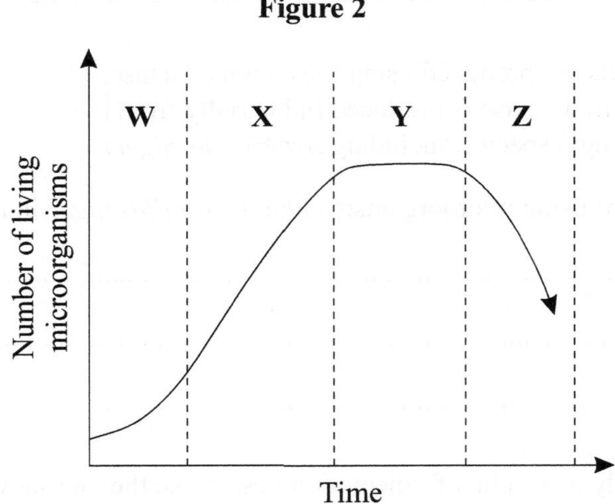

(c) (i) Explain the stages **W-Z** on the growth curve shown in **Figure 2**.

....

....

....

....

....

....

....

....

....

(4 marks)

(ii) Explain **one** way in which the shape of the growth curve would be different if *Aspergillus niger* were grown using a continuous fermentation process.

....

....

....

(2 marks)

The lactase produced from the fermentation of *Aspergillus niger* can be immobilised and used in the production of lactose-free milk.

(d) (i) Outline **three** ways that lactase could be immobilised.

....

....

....

....

(3 marks)

(ii) Give **two** disadvantages of using immobilised enzymes in industry.

1. ....

....

2. ....

....

(2 marks)

(iii) Other than lactase, describe **one** other example of an immobilised enzyme used in industry.

....

....

(1 mark)

2 In 2009, scientists successfully cloned an extinct subspecies of wild goat known as the Pyrenean ibex. To achieve this, the scientists used fibroblast cells obtained from the last living Pyrenean ibex, before it died in 2000, and oocytes collected from a closely related species of domesticated goat.

(a)* Outline the process used by the scientists to clone the extinct Pyrenean ibex, and discuss the disadvantages of using this process.

....

....

....

....

....

....

....

....

....

(6 marks)

Animals can also be cloned by the process of artificial embryo twinning. It would not have been possible to use artificial embryo twinning to clone the extinct Pyrenean ibex, but artificial embryo twinning is often used in research to create populations of cloned animals for testing new drugs.

(b) (i) Explain why it would not have been possible to use artificial embryo twinning to clone the extinct Pyrenean ibex.

....

....

....

(1 mark)

(ii) What is the main advantage of using cloned animals in drug testing?

....

....

(1 mark)

(iii) Other than drug testing, suggest **one** potential use of artificial embryo twinning.

....

(1 mark)

3 A student was investigating the growth of bacteria and its use in the biotechnology industry.

The student grew a bacterial culture in a flask of liquid broth. She measured the amount of light being absorbed by the broth culture every hour over a period of 24 hours, and used the measurements to calculate the number of bacteria present. **Figure 2** shows the growth of the population of bacteria.

Figure 2

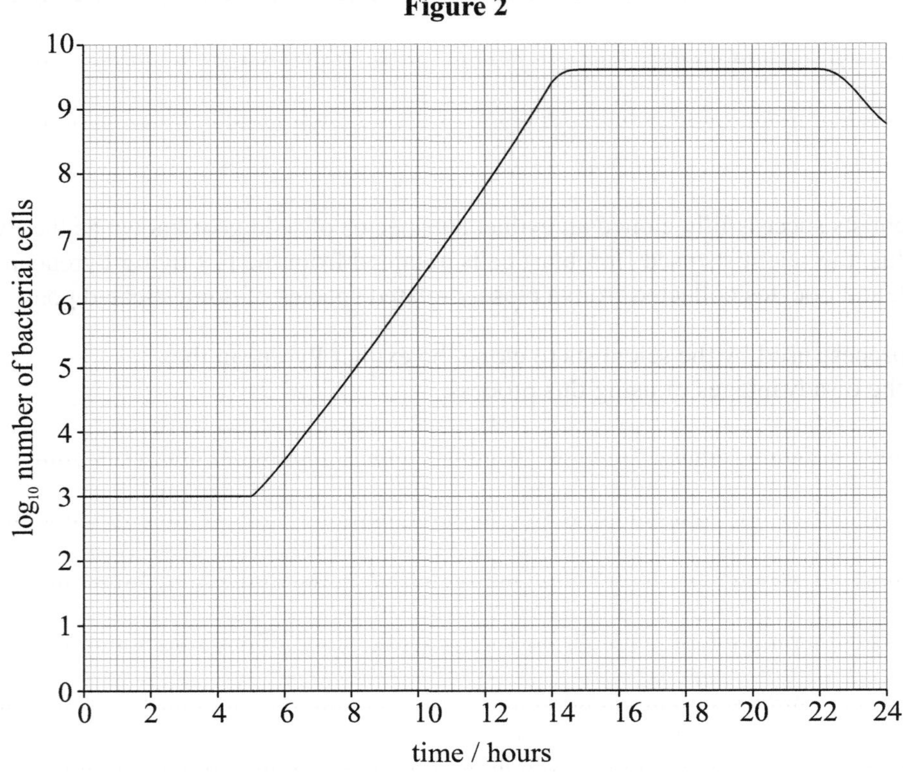

(a) Calculate the rate of bacterial population growth between 5 hours and 12 hours. Show your working. Give your answer to **two** significant figures.

rate = ...cells hour^{-1}

(2 marks)

(b) Explain **two** ways in which bacteria are used in the biotechnology industry.

1. ....

....

2. ....

....

(2 marks)

In the exam, you could be asked to apply your knowledge to explain a graph or table of results. First, try to think about what knowledge the question is testing you on. Then take a moment to study the graph or table, and pick out the relevant bits of information, before forming an answer. It's all too easy to waffle on about the wrong bits of data, but I know you've got this...

Score

31

Ecosystems — 1

All ecosystems, no matter how small, have got a lot going on. There are a few tricky ideas in this section, like biomass transfers and the recycling of nitrogen and carbon, so I suggest you take some time to try these questions.

For questions 1-3, give your answer by writing the correct letter in the box.

1 *Rhizobium*, *Nitrosomonas*, *Nitrobacter* and *Azotobacter* are all types of bacteria with roles in the nitrogen cycle. Which row, **A** to **D**, in the table below correctly identifies the process in which each type of bacteria is involved?

	Rhizobium	*Nitrosomonas*	*Nitrobacter*	*Azotobacter*
A	Nitrification	Nitrogen fixation	Nitrogen fixation	Nitrification
B	Ammonification	Nitrogen fixation	Ammonification	Nitrification
C	Ammonification	Denitrification	Nitrogen fixation	Nitrogen fixation
D	Nitrogen fixation	Nitrification	Nitrification	Nitrogen fixation

Your answer ☐

(1 mark)

2 Which of the following is an example of primary succession?

Statement 1: The colonisation of a coastal rock face following a drop in sea level.
Statement 2: The colonisation of an area of grassland following a bush fire.
Statement 3: The colonisation of an area of concrete after a building is demolished.

A 1, 2 and 3
B 1 and 3 only
C 2 and 3 only
D 1 only

Your answer ☐

(1 mark)

3 In a particular food chain, the producer stores 18 000 kJ m^{-2} yr^{-1} of energy in its biomass. The primary consumer stores 2.4×10^6 J m^{-2} yr^{-1} of energy in its biomass. Which of the following, **A-D**, shows the percentage efficiency of energy transfer from the producer to the primary consumer?

A 0.75%
B 10.0%
C 13.3%
D 14.2%

Your answer ☐

(1 mark)

4 **Figure 1** shows the types of vegetation present at each stage of primary succession in a sand dune ecosystem.

Figure 1

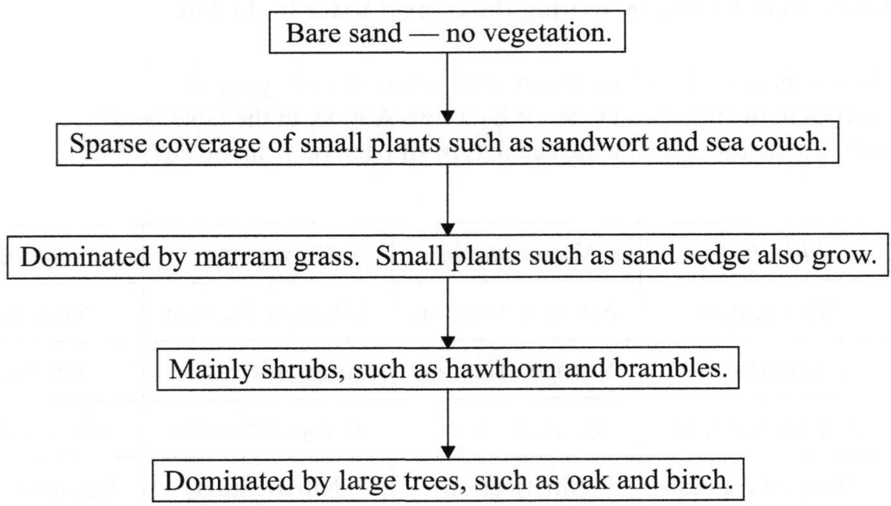

(a) (i) Which **two** of the species named in **Figure 1** are pioneer species?

....

(1 mark)

(ii) Describe the role of pioneer species in primary succession.

....

....

....

(2 marks)

(b) Woodland is the climax community for the ecosystem in **Figure 1**. Explain what this means.

....

....

(1 mark)

(c) Suggest why marram grass was only dominant in the third stage in **Figure 1**.

....

....

....

....

....

....

....

(4 marks)

(d) Explain how succession would be affected if a herd of grazing cattle was introduced to the sand dunes.

....

....

....

(2 marks)

5 Farmers aim to maximise crop yields. To do this, they need to consider both the biotic and abiotic factors that could affect their crops.

(a) Describe **one** biotic factor that might reduce the amount of biomass a farmer can harvest from a crop field.

....

....

(1 mark)

Soil nutrient availability is an abiotic factor that affects crop yield.

(b) To improve nutrient availability, farmers often apply fertilisers to their fields after the crops have been harvested. Some fertilisers are made of dead plant material, such as composted vegetables or crop residues. Explain how nitrogen in dead plant material is made available to growing plants in the soil.

....

....

....

....

....

....

....

(4 marks)

(c) A farmer's field was flooded and became waterlogged.
Waterlogging creates anaerobic conditions in the soil.
Using your knowledge of the nitrogen cycle, explain how this could affect crop yield.

....

....

....

....

....

(3 marks)

If you're having a hard time remembering the nitrogen cycle, try drawing it out... again and again, until it sticks and you can draw it all off by heart. Then when you get a question on the nitrogen cycle in the exam, you can always quickly sketch it out — that way it's easier to pinpoint the part of the cycle that the question is asking about. It's as easy as that.

Score

21

Ecosystems — 2

1 A student was investigating a forest ecosystem. He noticed that different areas of the forest had varying amounts of ground vegetation. He decided to investigate whether the amount of ground vegetation was affected by the amount of light reaching the forest floor.

(a) Apart from light, suggest **one** other abiotic factor that might affect the distribution of ground vegetation within a forest.

....

(1 mark)

The student used a random number generator to produce coordinates. He then used these coordinates to place a quadrat at different locations in the forest. The quadrat was divided into 100 squares. Each time the student placed the quadrat, he counted the number of squares that contained plants in order to calculate the percentage cover of ground vegetation. He also used a light meter to record the light intensity.

(b) Suggest **one** other method that the student could have used to place the quadrats.

....

....

(1 mark)

(c) **Table 1** shows the student's results.

Table 1

Quadrat number	Ground vegetation cover / %	Light intensity / lux
1	0	160
2	18	100
3	50	300
4	23	280
5	0	50
6	10	230
7	85	500
8	3	90
9	0	260
10	34	490

(i) State the type of graph the student should use to present the data in **Table 1**. Explain your answer.

....

....

....

(2 marks)

(ii) Suggest **one** reason the student's data might not be valid.

....

....

(1 mark)

2 A scientist investigated the effect of artificial fertiliser on the biomass of a crop field. The scientist divided the field into small plots and applied different masses of fertiliser to each one. After several months, the crops were harvested and dried out. The dry mass of crop plants in each plot was then measured. The scientist's results are shown in **Table 2**.

Table 2

Mass of fertiliser added to plot / kg ha^{-1}	Dry mass of crop yield / tonnes ha^{-1}
0	4.5
40	5.4
80	6.3
120	6.9
160	7.3
200	6.6
240	5.9
280	5.6

(a) Describe the results shown in **Table 2**.

....

....

....

(2 marks)

(b) Calculate the maximum percentage increase in dry mass of crop yield seen when fertiliser is added, compared to when no fertiliser is added.

.... %

(1 mark)

(c) Explain why dry mass is a more accurate measure of biomass than the mass of the freshly harvested crop.

....

....

(1 mark)

(d) The scientist hopes to use this experiment to advise all farmers on the optimum amount of fertiliser to use. Suggest **one** change the scientist would need to make to the experiment in order to be able to do this.

....

....

(1 mark)

(e) Using fertilisers is one example of a method used by farmers to increase the amount of biomass produced by crops. Explain **one** other way in which farmers manipulate the transfer of biomass in their fields.

....

....

....

(2 marks)

3* **Figure 1** shows how carbon moves between different parts of an ocean ecosystem. The arrows indicate the direction in which carbon moves.

Figure 1

With reference to **Figure 1**, explain how biological, chemical and physical processes cycle carbon through an ocean ecosystem.

....

....

....

....

....

....

....

....

....

....

....

....

....

(9 marks)

Make sure you know your stuff when it comes to processing and presenting data. You might have to name or draw a suitable graph type for a data set in the exam, so make sure you learn what the different types are for, e.g. scatter graphs, bar charts and histograms.

Score

21

Populations and Sustainability

You've nearly got through every section of your A-level biology course now — by the time you've had a go at these Populations and Sustainability questions, you'll have covered the bulk of what might come up in your exams.

For questions 1 and 2, give your answer by writing the correct letter in the box.

1 The graph below shows how the populations of two species change over time.

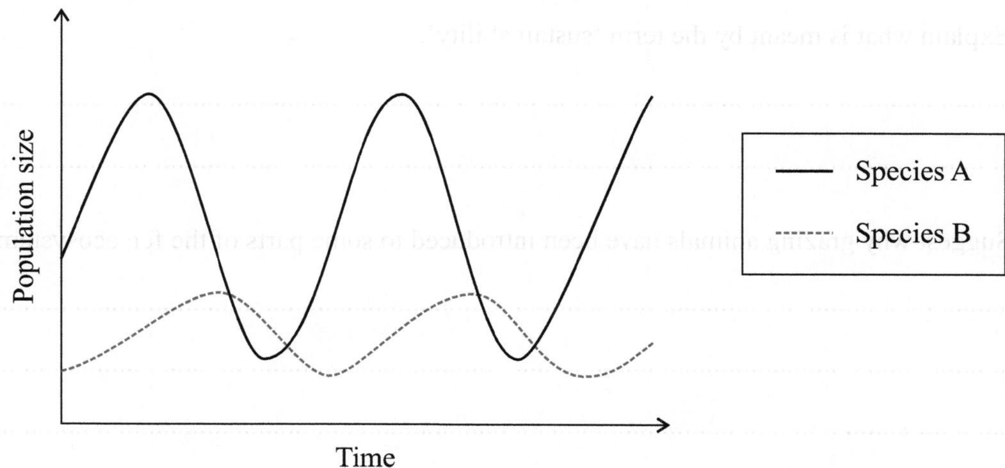

Which of the following statements, **A-D**, correctly explains the shape of this graph?

A Species A is a predator of Species B, and their population sizes are interlinked by positive feedback.

B Species B is a predator of Species A, and their population sizes are interlinked by positive feedback.

C Species A is a predator of Species B, and their population sizes are interlinked by negative feedback.

D Species B is a predator of Species A, and their population sizes are interlinked by negative feedback.

Your answer ☐

(1 mark)

2 Conservation of ecosystems is important to ensure that natural resources will be available for future generations. Which of the following statements related to conservation is/are **correct**?

Statement 1: Conservation is the protection of ecosystems so that they are kept exactly as they are.

Statement 2: Using fishing quotas to limit the amount of certain species of fish that fishermen can catch is an example of conservation.

Statement 3: There are ethical reasons for the conservation of biological resources but it is not economically viable.

A 1, 2 and 3

B 1 and 2 only

C 2 and 3 only

D 2 only

Your answer ☐

(1 mark)

3 Fens are low-lying, marshy areas of land that are dominated by reeds, rushes and sedge. Over time, they can naturally develop into an ecosystem known as carr woodland, which is dominated by shrubs and trees.

There are large areas of fen in the east of England, which form the habitat of many rare species of plant, insect and bird. Many tourists visit the area every year to enjoy the scenery and wildlife, and to go boating on a network of waterways that run through the fens.

These fens are carefully managed to maintain the sustainability of the natural resources they provide. As a conservation strategy, grazing ponies and cattle have been introduced to some of these fens.

(a) Explain what is meant by the term 'sustainability'.

....

....

(1 mark)

(b) Suggest why grazing animals have been introduced to some parts of the fen ecosystem.

....

....

....

(2 marks)

(c) (i) Give **one** social reason for the conservation of the fens in the east of England.

....

....

(1 mark)

(ii) Suggest **one** reason why there might be conflicts between human needs and conservation in the fens.

....

....

(1 mark)

4 The Lake District is a national park in the north west of England. Around 15.8 million people visit the park each year. The region is known for its scenery, including its hills, lakes and forests. These make it popular for walking and other outdoor activities, such as running, cycling and water sports.

(a) (i) Explain **one** example of a negative impact on animal and plant populations that could arise from tourism in UK national parks such as the Lake District.

....

....

....

(2 marks)

(ii) Describe how the negative impact you gave in part **(a) (i)** could be controlled.

....

....

(1 mark)

(b) As well as providing income from tourism, areas of forest in the Lake District are used for timber production. The woodland is cleared in small patches, and new trees are planted to replace the ones that are cut down.

(i) Suggest **one** reason why clearing the trees in small patches is more sustainable than clearing one large area. Explain your answer.

....

....

....

(2 marks)

(ii) Suggest **one** other way that timber production could be managed to make it sustainable.

....

....

(1 mark)

5 **Figure 1** shows how the size of a population of crabs on a sandy beach changed over time.

Figure 1

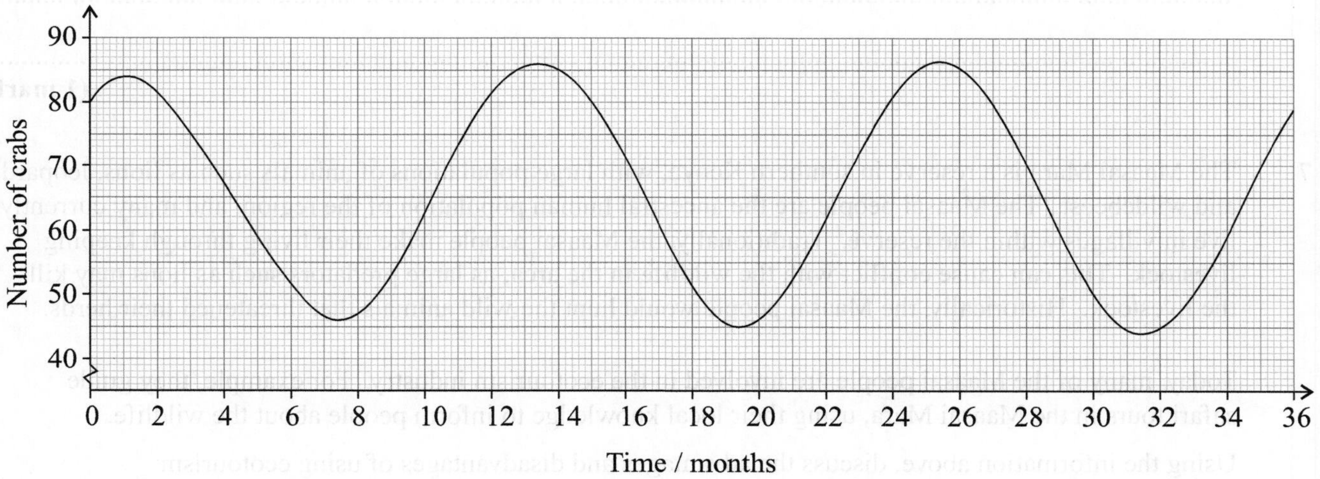

(a) Explain how intraspecific competition could have caused the shape of the curve in **Figure 1**.

....

....

....

....

....

(3 marks)

(b) Using **Figure 1**, estimate the carrying capacity of the crab population.

carrying capacity = ...

(1 mark)

6 The Galapagos Islands in the Pacific Ocean have many native species that do not occur elsewhere. Many people have migrated to the islands over the last century and the human population there continues to grow. This has affected the animal and plant populations of the Galapagos Islands.

(a) Fishing around the Galapagos Islands has increased in order to feed the growing human population and to provide residents with a source of income. This has reduced the populations of many aquatic organisms, including species that are not caught for food.

(i) Suggest **two** reasons why an increase in fishing has reduced the populations of non-food species in the seas around the Galapagos Islands.

1. ....

2. ....

(2 marks)

(ii) State **two** ways that fishing could managed to be more sustainable around the Galapagos Islands.

1. ....

2. ....

(2 marks)

(b) The Galapagos Islands are also popular with tourists.
There are restrictions on visitors bringing plants and animals to the islands. Suggest **one** reason why.

....

....

(1 mark)

7 The Maasai Mara is a reserve in southern Kenya, with large populations of animals such as lions, leopards and wildebeest. The Maasai people are the ancestral human population of the region, and many currently live in villages within the reserve. Traditionally, the Maasai people make their living through keeping livestock. This can cause conflict with the wildlife in the area, as large predators such as lions may kill the livestock. Historically, the Maasai people would hunt the wild animals that threatened their herds.

Today, many of the Maasai people are involved in the ecotourism industry. For example, they guide safari tours in the Maasai Mara, using their local knowledge to inform people about the wildlife.

Using the information above, discuss the advantages and disadvantages of using ecotourism to manage the conflicts between human needs and conservation in the Maasai Mara.

....

....

....

....

....

....

(4 marks)

EXAM TIP

If an exam question looks like it's on something you don't remember studying, don't just assume you've forgotten about something you're supposed to know. Examiners often write questions with unfamiliar contexts — you just need to work out which bit of the course it relates to. All of the information you need will be given in the question, so read it carefully.

Score

26

Mixed Questions — 1

Here we go: a section of juicy Mixed Questions to get your teeth into. These questions draw together different bits of biology from across the entire A-level course, so they should really get those brain cells firing.

For each of questions 1-5, give your answer by writing the correct letter in the box.

1 Below are four statements about the circulatory system of a fish.

Which of the statements, **A** to **D**, is **false**?

A A fish's circulatory system is closed.

B Blood passes through a fish's heart once per circuit.

C The right side of a fish's heart pumps blood to the gills, and the left side pumps blood to the rest of the body.

D A fish's veins take its blood back to the heart.

Your answer ☐

(1 mark)

2 The structural formulae of four biological molecules are displayed below.

Which of the molecules, **A** to **D**, is a pyrimidine base?

A

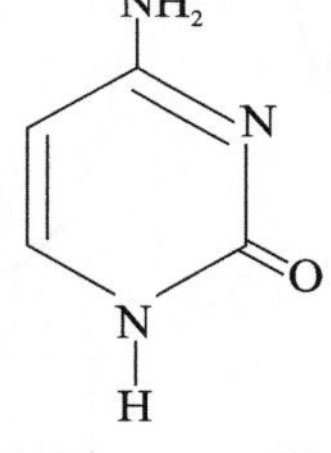

B

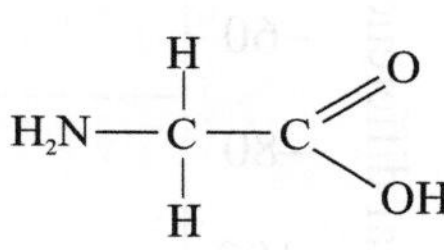

C

D

Your answer ☐

(1 mark)

3 The image below shows two xylem vessels.

Identify which type of microscope, **A** to **D**, was used to produce the image.

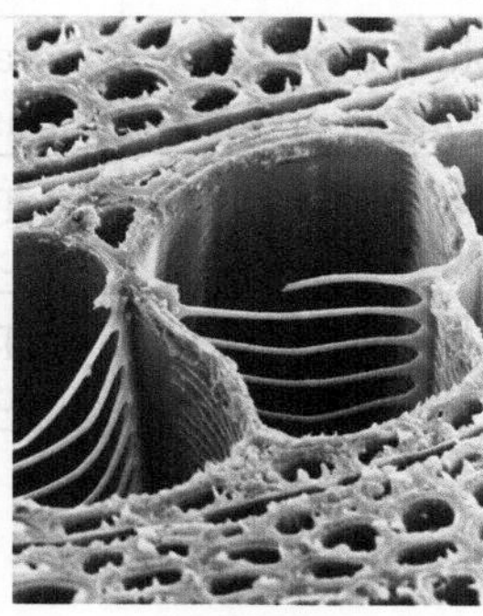

A scanning electron microscope

B light microscope

C laser scanning confocal microscope

D transmission electron microscope

Your answer ☐

(1 mark)

4 In the primrose plant, flowers are blue if the pigment malvidin is produced. There is a gene that codes for malvidin synthesis and a gene that codes for the suppression of malvidin synthesis. If a primrose plant has a dominant allele for the malvidin synthesis gene and two recessive alleles for the suppression of synthesis gene, then the flowers are blue. However, a plant with a dominant allele for malvidin synthesis will not produce blue flowers if it also has a dominant allele for suppression of synthesis.

Which of the terms **A-D** is used to describe the relationship between these two genes?

A epistasis

B codominance

C autosomal linkage

D sex linkage

Your answer ☐

(1 mark)

5 The graph below shows the changes in the potential difference across a neurone cell membrane during an action potential.

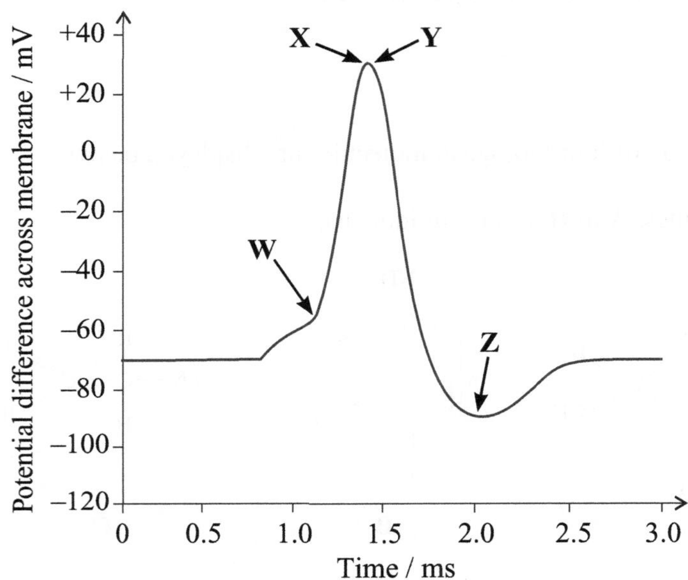

Which row, **A-D**, in the table below gives the correct description of what is happening at the points on the graph labelled **W**, **X**, **Y** and **Z**?

	W	**X**	**Y**	**Z**
A	potassium ion channels open	potassium ion channels close	voltage-gated sodium ion channels open	voltage-gated sodium ions channels close
B	voltage-gated sodium ion channels open	potassium ion channels open	voltage-gated sodium ions channels close	potassium ion channels close
C	potassium ion channels open	voltage-gated sodium ion channels open	potassium ion channels close	voltage-gated sodium channels close
D	voltage-gated sodium ion channels open	voltage-gated sodium ion channels close	potassium ion channels open	potassium ion channels close

Your answer ☐

(1 mark)

Having to choose the correct row of a table, like in Q5, is a common type of multiple choice question. It might look complicated, but if you know the right answer for just one of the columns, you can instantly narrow down your options.

Score ☐ / 5

Mixed Questions — 2

1 Lactase is an enzyme that catalyses the breakdown of lactose into glucose and galactose. This helps us to digest milk.

A student investigated the effect of pH on the activity of lactase, using the following method:

1. Add 2 ml of lactose solution and 2 ml of a pH buffer solution to a test tube.
   Swirl the contents of the tube gently for 10 seconds.
2. Add 2 ml of lactase solution to the test tube.
   Swirl the contents of the tube gently for 10 seconds.
3. After 8 minutes, dip a fresh glucose test strip into the solution in the test tube.
   Leave for 2 seconds and then remove.
4. After 1 minute, observe and record the colour of the test strip.
   Any shade of green indicates that glucose is present.
   If the paper remains yellow, no glucose is present.
5. The student repeated steps 1-4 using buffer solutions of pH 2, 4, 6, 7, 8, 10 and 12.

Table 1 shows the results of the investigation.

Table 1

pH	Glucose test result
2	Green
4	Green
6	Green
7	Green
8	Yellow
10	Yellow
12	Yellow

(a) What type of biological molecule is lactose?

....

(1 mark)

(b) (i) The solution in the test tubes contains water. Explain **one** reason why water may be needed for the reaction occurring in some of the test tubes to take place.

....

....

....

(2 marks)

(ii) The student's method specified that all volumes and timings should have been controlled as part of her investigation. Give **two** other variables that the student should have controlled.

1. ....

2. ....

(2 marks)

(c) (i) What can you conclude about the effect of pH on lactase activity from the results shown in **Table 1**? Explain your answer.

....

....

....

(2 marks)

(ii) Describe how enzyme structure is affected by pH.

....

....

....

....

(3 marks)

(iii) Suggest how the student could continue her investigation to determine a more accurate estimate for the pH at which lactase denatures. Explain your answer.

....

....

(2 marks)

(d) Despite producing functional lactase, some people are unable to consume milk products. This is due to a milk allergy, which results in an immune response against the proteins found in milk. Describe how phagocytes could cause an immune response against milk proteins.

....

....

....

....

....

(4 marks)

2 Mitosis and meiosis are both types of cell division.
Reproduction via meiosis increases genetic diversity in a population.

Figure 1 represents two cells. One cell is undergoing mitosis. The other is undergoing meiosis I.

Figure 1

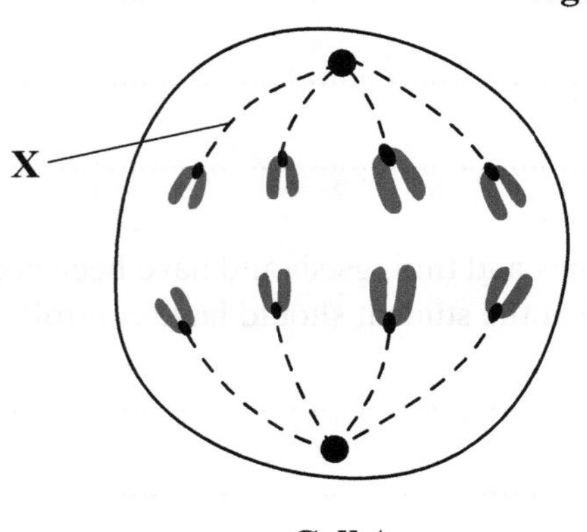

Cell A

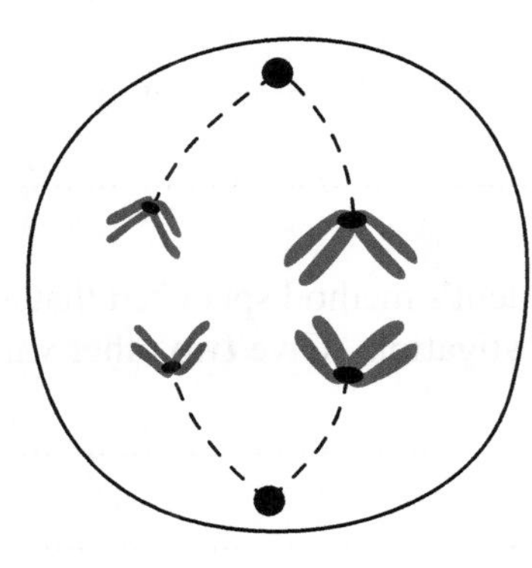

Cell B

(a) (i) Identify the structure labelled **X** in **Figure 1**.

....

(1 mark)

(ii) Which of the cells in **Figure 1** (**A** or **B**) is undergoing meiosis I? Give a reason for your answer.

....

....

(1 mark)

Figure 2 shows the life cycle of a type of plant called a liverwort. During the life cycle there are haploid (n) and diploid (2n) phases. Four stages of cell division are labelled.

Figure 2

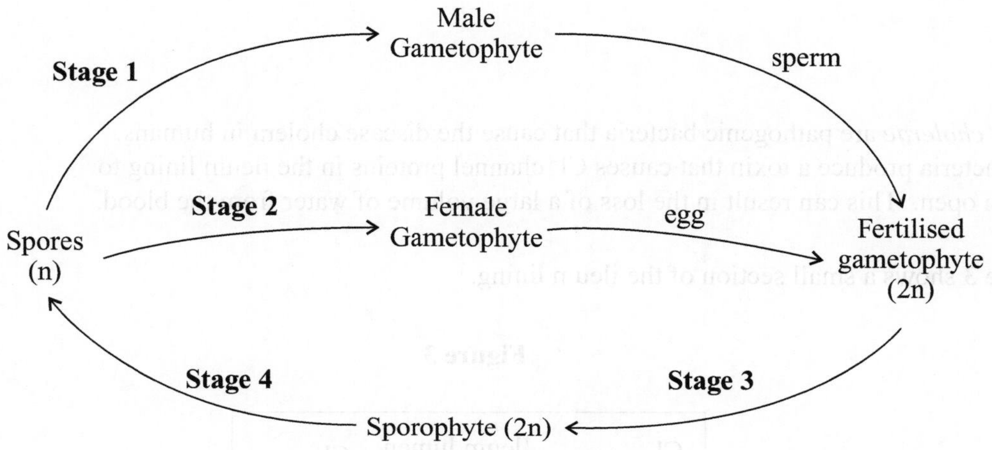

(b) The diploid number of this liverwort is 40.
How many chromosomes are present in the spore?

Number of chromosomes = ...

(1 mark)

(c) (i) Name the type of cell division occurring at **Stage 4** on **Figure 2**. Give a reason for your answer.

....

....

(1 mark)

(ii) Spores develop into male or female gametophytes (**Stages 1 and 2**).
A sperm from a male gametophyte then fertilises an egg inside a female gametophyte.

Using this information, explain why **Stages 1** and **2** on **Figure 2** must represent mitosis.

....

....

....

....

(3 marks)

(d) A scientist wants to study the DNA of liverwort species in two different areas of Scotland in order to determine how genetically diverse the two populations are.

(i) The scientist chooses to use stratified sampling to sample the liverwort populations. Suggest and explain **one** reason why she may have chosen to use this type of sampling.

....

....

....

(2 mark)

(ii) Suggest **one** way in which the scientist could reduce the effect of random error on her results.

....

....

(1 mark)

3 *Vibrio cholerae* are pathogenic bacteria that cause the disease cholera in humans. The bacteria produce a toxin that causes Cl^- channel proteins in the ileum lining to remain open. This can result in the loss of a large volume of water from the blood.

Figure 3 shows a small section of the ileum lining.

Figure 3

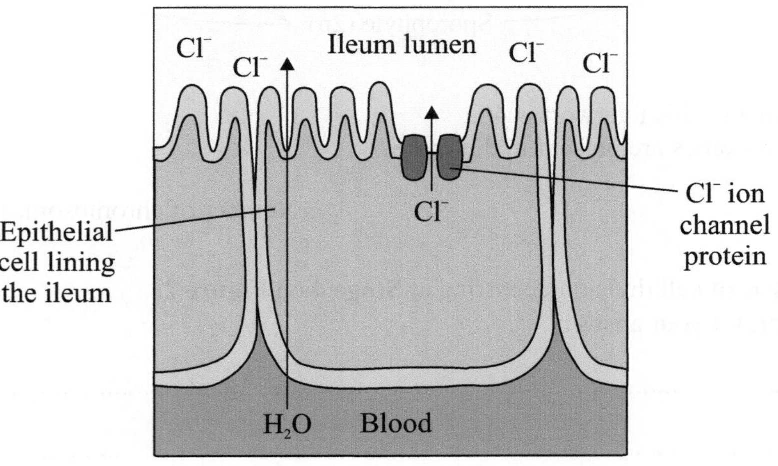

(a) Use **Figure 3** to explain how cholera causes water to be lost from the blood.

....

....

....

....

....

....

(4 marks)

(b) (i) Suggest **one** structural difference between *V. cholerae* and an ileum epithelial cell.

....

....

(1 mark)

(ii) *V. cholerae* absorbs its nutrients directly across its outer surface.
Explain why humans need a specialised exchange surface to absorb their nutrients.

....

....

....

....

....

....

(4 marks)

(c) Cholera outbreaks are common in areas where the treatment of sewage and drinking water is inadequate. The disease is spread by ingesting food or water that has been contaminated with the bacteria. The source of the contamination is usually faeces from an infected individual.

Suggest **two** ways that the spread of cholera could be reduced.

1. ....

....

2. ....

....

(2 marks)

(d) Antibiotics are used to treat severe cases of cholera.
Some strains of *V. cholerae* are now resistant to particular antibiotics.

Explain how directional selection could have led to the evolution of an antibiotic-resistant strain of *V. cholerae*.

....

....

....

....

....

....

(4 marks)

Examiners like to put questions in contexts you've not seen before. Don't let it throw you. You need to link what the question's asking you to the facts you've learnt as part of your course. Use the information in the question to help you. For example, Figure 3 in Q3 should have helped you to link the movement of Cl^- ions to the movement of water by osmosis.

Score

41

Mixed Questions — 3

1 The light-independent reaction is essential for producing useful organic substances in a plant. It involves the enzyme RuBisCo.

Figure 1 shows the light-independent reaction of photosynthesis.

Figure 1

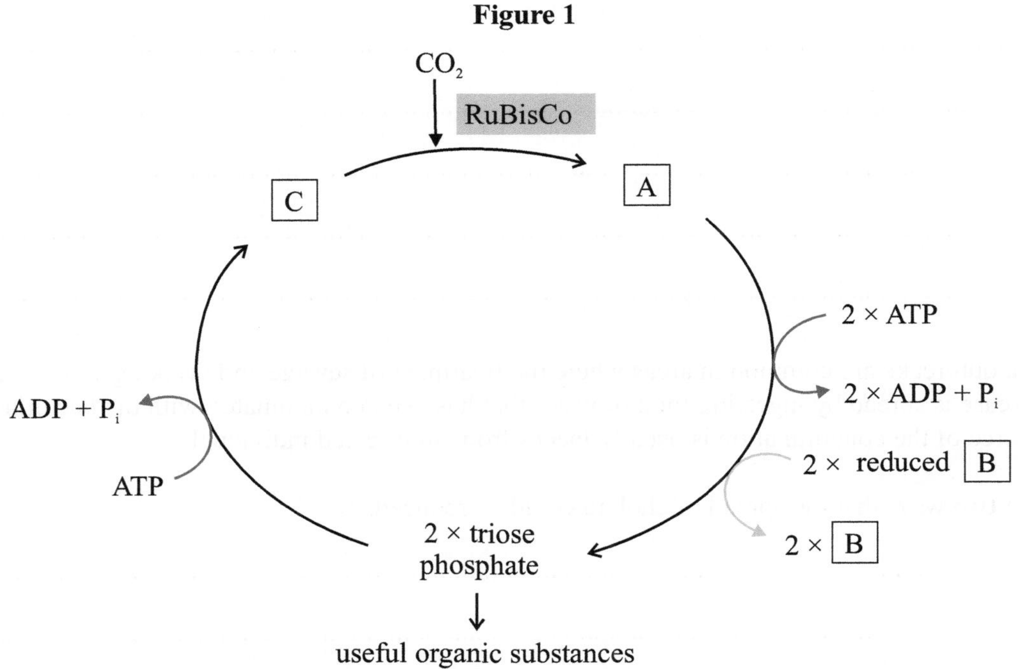

(a) Name the molecules **A-C** in **Figure 1**.

A ....

B ....

C ....

(3 marks)

(b) Plant growth can be reduced if the rate of the light-independent reaction is limited. Explain **one** reason why.

....

....

....

(2 marks)

(c) Scientists have investigated how substitution mutations in the gene that codes for RuBisCo affect the rate of the light-independent reaction.

(i) What is meant by the term 'substitution mutation'?

....

....

(1 mark)

(ii) Explain how a substitution mutation in the RuBisCo gene could lead to an **increase** in the rate of the light-independent reaction.

....

....

....

....

(3 marks)

(d) Carbon is recycled through ecosystems in the carbon cycle.
Explain the importance of RuBisCo in the carbon cycle.

....

....

....

(2 marks)

2 The human body acts to keep the blood glucose concentration at around 90 mg per 100 cm^3 of blood. People with Type 1 diabetes inject insulin to help control their blood glucose concentration.

(a) Describe **two** insulin-controlled processes that happen in the liver when blood glucose concentration gets too high.

1. ....

2. ....

(2 marks)

(b) Gene technology has allowed human insulin to be produced by *E. coli* bacteria.
Outline how *E. coli* could be made to produce human insulin.

....

....

....

....

....

(4 marks)

(c) A potential treatment for Type 1 diabetes in the future might involve the use of stem cells.
Explain how stem cells could be used to treat Type 1 diabetes.

....

....

....

(2 marks)

Each of these Mixed Questions requires you to apply your knowledge of several different areas of the specification. It shouldn't come as a surprise that you'll get exam questions that require you to do the same thing. What it boils down to is this — you need to know your stuff inside out and back to front. So if you haven't started already, you'd better get revising.

Score

19

Mixed Questions — 4

1 **Figure 1** shows a single cycle of contraction and relaxation in a muscle fibre.

Figure 1

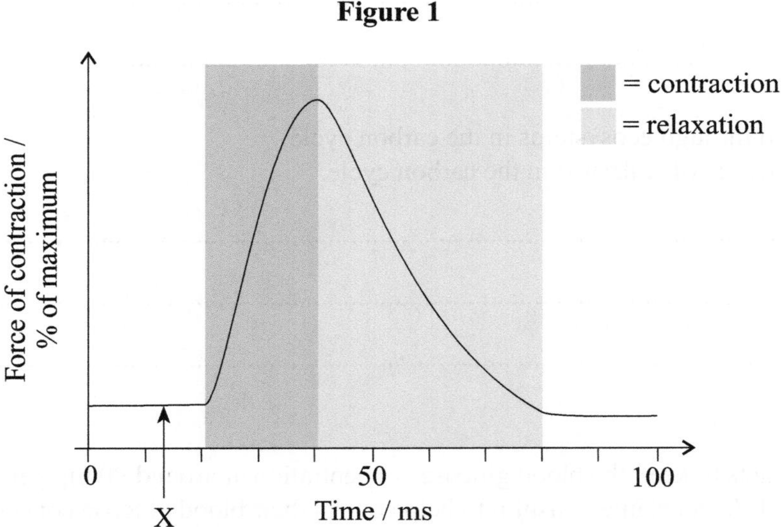

(a) The muscle fibre is stimulated by an action potential at the point in time marked **X** on **Figure 1**.

(i) What type of neurone produces an action potential that stimulates a muscle fibre?

....

(1 mark)

(ii) Suggest **two** reasons for the delay between receiving the stimulus and contraction of the fibre.

1. ....

....

2. ....

....

(2 marks)

(b) Explain what is happening to the muscle fibre during the period of relaxation shown on **Figure 1**.

....

....

....

....

....

(3 marks)

(c) (i) A scientist investigating muscle contraction calculates that the muscle she is studying has a respiratory quotient >1.0. What does this tell you about the muscle fibre?

....

....

(1 mark)

(ii) The muscle fibre releases most of the energy it needs to contract through aerobic respiration. Outline the role of the link reaction of aerobic respiration in providing the muscle fibre with energy for contraction.

....

....

....

....

....

(4 marks)

2 Petite mutants of the yeast species *Saccharomyces cerevisiae* carry mutations in their nuclear or mitochondrial DNA that result in their mitochondria being inactive. Although petite mutants are able to grow on a substrate containing glucose, they form much smaller colonies than normal cells.

(a) Using your knowledge of respiration, explain why:

- Petite mutants are able to grow on a substrate containing glucose, despite lacking functional mitochondria.
- Petite mutants form smaller colonies than normal cells.

....

....

....

....

....

....

(4 marks)

(b) Colonies of *Saccharomyces cerevisiae* petite mutants are rarely found in the wild. Suggest and explain why this is the case.

....

....

....

(2 marks)

(c) Laboratory-generated petite mutants are useful for studying the proteins needed for mitochondrial function. One example of a nuclear-encoded protein that is important for mitochondrial function is NRF-1. NRF-1 is a transcription factor that activates the expression of other proteins involved in mitochondrial function. Describe how the NRF-1 transcription factor works.

....

....

....

(2 marks)

3 Read the following statements:

A species of flightless beetle shows variation in colour. The beetles are either red, black or green.

A century ago, a small group of these beetles were accidentally carried on a ship to an island where this species did not naturally occur.

The group was released on the island and formed a new population.

The group contained beetles of all colours.

There are now noticeable differences between the original population and the island population. For example, almost all of the island population is black. The two populations are now thought to be separate species.

(a)* Using the information above and your own knowledge, explain how the founder effect may have led to the speciation of this flightless beetle.

....

....

....

....

....

....

....

....

....

....

....

....

....

(6 marks)

(b) Explain how the evolutionary relationship between two species can be determined through bioinformatics.

....

....

....

(2 marks)

If you're given some information to read in a question, make sure you do so carefully. Under exam pressure, it's easy to quickly skim over something and think you've got it, but you need to make sure you're not missing an important detail that will help you with your answer.

Score

27

Answers

Module 2 : Section 1 — Cell Structure

Pages 3-5: Cell Structure — 1

1 B *[1 mark]*

The image shows a mitochondrion. The letter X is pointing to a fold in its inner membrane called a crista.

2 C *[1 mark]*

3 D *[1 mark]*

4 a) E.g. it controls the cell's activities by controlling the transcription of DNA *[1 mark]*.

b) E.g. eosin Y stains the cytoplasm so this allowed the scientist to see the cells against the background *[1 mark]*. Methylene blue and azure B stain the nucleus so this allowed the scientist to differentiate between white blood cells and red blood cells *[1 mark]*.

c) Any four from: she could have selected the lowest-powered objective lens *[1 mark]*. Then used the coarse adjustment knob to bring the stage up to just below the objective lens *[1 mark]*. Then looked down the eyepiece and used the coarse adjustment knob to move the stage down until the image is roughly in focus *[1 mark]*. Then adjusted the focus with the fine adjustment knob until she got a clear image of what's on the slide *[1 mark]*. If a greater magnification was required, she could have refocused the microscope using a higher-powered objective lens *[1 mark]*.
[Maximum of 4 marks available]

d) i) object size = 12 µm ÷ 1000
= 0.012 mm
magnification = image size ÷ object size
= 15 mm ÷ 0.012 mm
= **× 1250**
[accept values between × 1167 and × 1333, 2 marks for the correct answer, otherwise 1 mark for the correct working]

ii) percentage error = (uncertainty ÷ reading) × 100
uncertainty = (percentage error ÷ 100) × reading
= (0.4 ÷ 100) × 12
= **± 0.05 µm** (to 1 s.f.)
[2 marks for the correct answer, otherwise 1 mark for (0.4 ÷ 100) × 12]

5 a) Similarities: any one from: e.g. a sperm cell and a bacterial cell can both have a flagellum *[1 mark]*. / A sperm cell and a bacterial cell both have a cell membrane *[1 mark]*.
Differences: any one from: e.g. a sperm cell has a nucleus but a bacterial cell has DNA that floats freely in the cytoplasm *[1 mark]*. / A bacterial cell has a cell wall but a sperm cell only has a cell membrane *[1 mark]*.
[Maximum 2 marks available]

b) i) The flagellum requires ATP to move, which is generated by mitochondria *[1 mark]*.

ii) Electron microscope/TEM/SEM *[1 mark]* because these have a higher resolution than light microscopes, which would be needed to study the internal structures of the mitochondria *[1 mark]*.

c) E.g. microtubules are responsible for the movement of the flagellum that moves the sperm cell *[1 mark]*. The *DNAH1* mutation would result in the flagellum no longer moving/ not moving properly, so the sperm cell will be unable to reach the egg and deliver genetic material *[1 mark]*.

Pages 6-8: Cell Structure — 2

1 a) E.g. each cell would only contain one nucleus. / Each nucleus would contain the same amount of genetic material. *[1 mark]*

b) The role of cell type A is to ingest invading pathogens because a greater percentage of the cell contains lysosomes than cell type B *[1 mark]*. Lysosomes are necessary to digest invading cells *[1 mark]*. The role of cell type B is to secrete enzymes because a greater percentage of the cell contains rough endoplasmic reticulum than cell type A *[1 mark]*. This organelle is covered with ribosomes which synthesise proteins, such as enzymes / is responsible for folding and processing proteins, such as enzymes *[1 mark]*.

c) E.g. chloroplasts contain thylakoid membranes/grana, whereas mitochondria contain a folded membrane that form structures called cristae *[1 mark]*. / Chloroplasts are the site of photosynthesis, whereas mitochondria are the site of aerobic respiration *[1 mark]*.

2 a) i) Put a drop of stain next to one edge of the cover slip and a piece of paper towel next to the opposite edge *[1 mark]*. The paper towel will draw the stain under the slip, across the specimen *[1 mark]*.

ii) Any one from: e.g. worn goggles/gloves / taken care not to break glass beakers/slides/cover slips / taken care with sharp tools. *[1 mark]*

b) i) One division of the stage micrometer is the same as four eyepiece divisions.
0.1 mm ÷ 4 = 0.025 mm
0.025 mm × 1000 = **25 µm**
[2 marks for the correct answer, otherwise 1 mark for the correct working]

ii) The stage micrometer will appear larger, so each eyepiece division will be a smaller measurement *[1 mark]*.

c) E.g. length of cell = 36 mm
36 mm × 1000 = 36 000 µm
object size = image size ÷ magnification
= 36 000 µm ÷ 100
= **360 µm**
[accept values between 350 µm and 370 µm, 2 marks for the correct answer, otherwise 1 mark for using the correct rearrangement of the magnification formula]

3 a) i) It is a cilium/flagellum *[1 mark]*, because the microtubules are in the 9 + 2 formation / there is an outer ring of nine microtubule pairs with two in the middle *[1 mark]*.

ii) It is involved with the separation of chromosomes during cell division *[1 mark]*.

Organelle B is a centriole.

b) i) E.g. it may cause nerve cells to lose strength/stability, causing them to break down. It may prevent vesicles from being transported through the cell to the cell surface/plasma membrane to secrete their contents. *[1 mark each]*

ii) E.g. abnormal function of mitochondria in nerve cells may result in the cell not receiving enough energy, causing them to die/preventing them from carrying out their normal function *[1 mark]*.

Module 2 : Section 2 — Biological Molecules

Pages 9-12: Biological Molecules — 1

1 D ***[1 mark]***

The formula for a phosphate ion is PO_4^{3-}. It has a negative charge, so it's an anion.

2 C ***[1 mark]***

The protein backbone will have peptide bonds between the amino acids and the carbohydrate branches will have glycosidic bonds between the monosaccharides.

3 A ***[1 mark]***

4 a) A molecule made from many monomers bonded together ***[1 mark]***.

b) i) E.g.

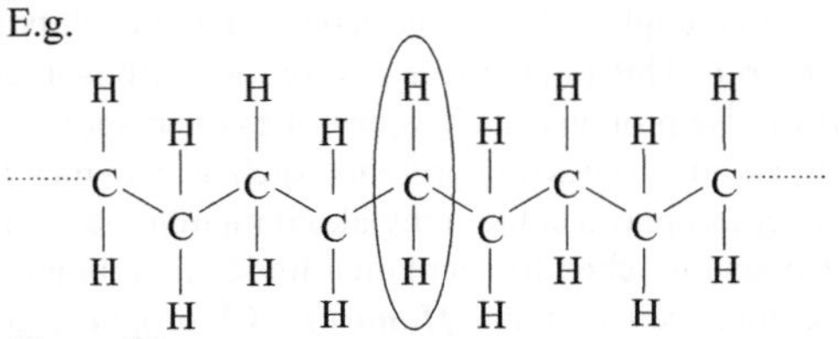

[1 mark]

ii) E.g. monosaccharides and amino acids ***[1 mark]***.

5 a) i) alpha-glucose/α-glucose ***[1 mark]***

You must have specified alpha-glucose to get the mark here. Make sure you know the difference between alpha- and beta-glucose.

ii) maltose ***[1 mark]***

iii) Number of carbon atoms = **12** ***[1 mark]***

Each alpha-glucose contains 6 carbon atoms (it's a hexose sugar).

b) A water molecule is used ***[1 mark]*** to break/hydrolyse the glycosidic bond in the disaccharide/maltose ***[1 mark]***. This produces the two monomers/alpha-glucose molecules ***[1 mark]***.

6 a) E.g. add a few drops of sodium hydroxide to a solution of the sample, then a few drops of copper (II) sulfate solution / add a few drops of biuret reagent to the sample ***[1 mark]***. A colour change from blue to purple/lilac is a positive result ***[1 mark]***.

b) i) E.g. haemoglobin ***[1 mark]***

ii) So that it can be transported in the blood to the tissues where it acts ***[1 mark]***.

Insulin is a hormone. Hormones are secreted by glands and transported to their target cells by the blood, so they must be soluble.

iii) Hydrophobic R groups on the amino acids of the insulin molecule clump together ***[1 mark]***. This causes hydrophilic R groups to be pushed to the outside of the molecule, making the molecule soluble ***[1 mark]***.

iv) E.g. insolubility ***[1 mark]*** and strength ***[1 mark]***.

7 a) A lot of energy is removed from the kangaroo's body when the water in the saliva evaporates from its forearms ***[1 mark]***. This reduces the kangaroo's body temperature ***[1 mark]***.

b) i) Water has a high specific heat capacity / it takes a lot of energy to break the hydrogen bonds in water ***[1 mark]***, which means it doesn't heat up as quickly as the air ***[1 mark]***.

ii) The water molecules are polar ***[1 mark]***, which means that hydrogen bonds form between them ***[1 mark]***. This means the water molecules are cohesive, which allows them to travel up a tree trunk ***[1 mark]***.

8 a) i)

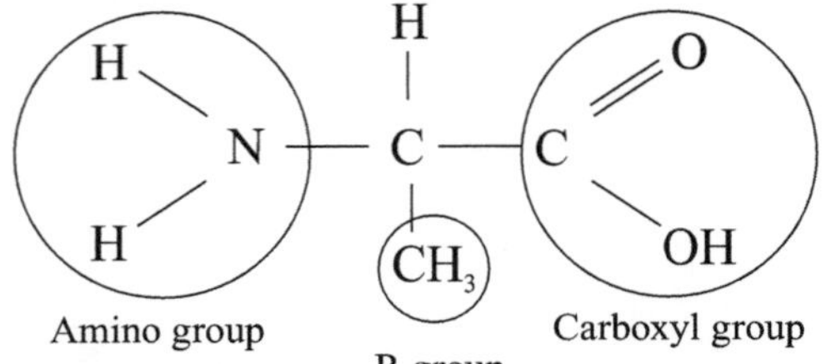

[1 mark each]

ii) It has a different R group ***[1 mark]***.

b) i) water ***[1 mark]***

ii) E.g.

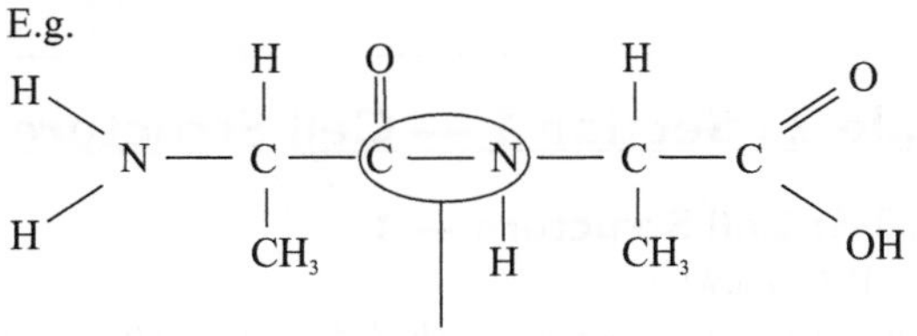

Peptide bond

[1 mark for the correct diagram, 1 mark for correctly labelling the peptide bond]

Pages 13-16: Biological Molecules — 2

1 a) i) alpha-helix/α-helix ***[1 mark]***

ii) Both secondary and tertiary structures contain hydrogen bonds ***[1 mark]***. Tertiary structures also contain ionic bonds / disulfide bridges / hydrophobic and hydrophilic interactions ***[1 mark]***.

b)* How to grade your answer:

Level 0: There is no relevant information. ***[No marks]***

Level 1: The answer briefly explains the structure of catalase. The answer has no clear structure. The information given is basic and lacking in detail. It may not all be relevant. ***[1 to 2 marks]***

Level 2: The answer explains the structure of catalase and makes at least one suggestion about how the structure of catalase helps it to carry out its function. The answer has some structure. Most of the information given is relevant and there is some detail involved. ***[3 to 4 marks]***

Level 3: The answer fully explains the structure of catalase, given the information provided, and makes several suggestions about how this helps the enzyme to carry out its function. The answer has a clear and logical structure. The information given is relevant and detailed. ***[5 to 6 marks]***

Indicative scientific content may include:

<u>The structure of catalase</u>

Catalase is a globular protein, so it is round and compact.
Its hydrophilic R groups are pushed to the outside of the protein.
Catalase is conjugated, so it contains (a) non-protein/prosthetic group(s).
Catalase has a quaternary structure, so it is made up of more than one polypeptide chain.
The polypeptide chains are held together by bonds.

<u>How the structure helps catalase carry out its function</u>

Its compact size allows catalase to act in the peroxisome, which is relatively small.
The hydrophilic R groups on the outside of the protein make the enzyme soluble, so it can be easily transported from where it is made in the cytoplasm to where it acts.
The non-protein / prosthetic group(s) may help catalase to bind to hydrogen peroxide.
The bonds holding the polypeptide chains together give catalase's active site a specific shape, which allows the substrate/hydrogen peroxide to bind.

2 a) i) Add Benedict's reagent to the sample and heat in a water bath that has been brought to the boil ***[1 mark]***. A positive result gives a coloured, e.g. yellow/orange/brick-red, precipitate ***[1 mark]***.

ii)

Sample	Type of carbohydrate present		
	Reducing sugar	Non-reducing sugar	Starch
A		✓	
B			✓
C	✓		

[2 marks for all three correct, otherwise 1 mark for one or two correct answers]

b) i) A fresh test strip is dipped in a solution of each sample and changes colour in the presence of glucose ***[1 mark]***. This colour can be compared to a chart to give an indication of glucose concentration ***[1 mark]***.

ii) E.g. colorimetry / a glucose biosensor ***[1 mark]***

3 a) phospholipid ***[1 mark]***

b) i) The phospholipid head is hydrophilic ***[1 mark]***, but the phospholipid tail is hydrophobic ***[1 mark]***. The molecules arrange themselves in this way to shield the hydrophobic tails from water ***[1 mark]***.

ii) E.g. they make up cell membranes ***[1 mark]***. The hydrophobic regions act as a barrier to water-soluble substances ***[1 mark]***.

4 a) i) Fatty acid 2 has a double bond between two carbon atoms, whereas fatty acid 1 does not ***[1 mark]***. This means that fatty acid 1 is saturated and fatty acid 2 is unsaturated ***[1 mark]***.

ii) Three fatty acids combine with one glycerol molecule ***[1 mark]*** in a series of three condensation reactions / a process known as esterification ***[1 mark]***. Ester bonds are formed between the glycerol and fatty acids ***[1 mark]***.

iii) E.g. triglycerides are used for storage of energy ***[1 mark]*** because they have a high energy content / they're insoluble ***[1 mark]***.

b) i) Shake some of the sample to be tested with ethanol until it dissolves, then pour into a test tube of water ***[1 mark]***. If a lipid is present, a white emulsion will form ***[1 mark]***.

ii) Lipids cannot dissolve in water so if they are present, they form an emulsion ***[1 mark]***.

Pages 17-19: Biological Molecules — 3

1 a) i) Alpha-glucose molecules join together in a chain via a serious of condensation reactions ***[1 mark]***, which form glycosidic bonds between the molecules ***[1 mark]***.

ii) E.g.

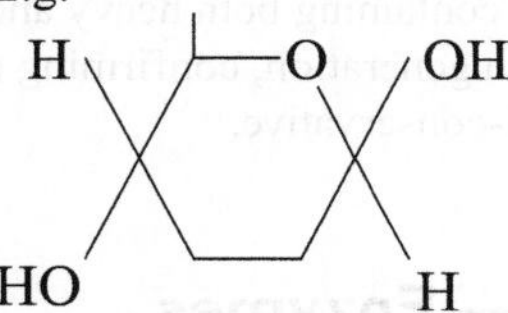

[1 mark]

In alpha-glucose the OH/hydroxyl group and the H/hydrogen on the right-hand side are reversed ***[1 mark]***.

You could have drawn the full skeletal formula for beta-glucose here instead.

iii) It allows cellulose molecules to form strong fibres/microfibrils ***[1 mark]***, which provide structural support/support the cell wall ***[1 mark]***.

b) Advantage: e.g. it is more compact, which allows more of it to be stored in a cell ***[1 mark]***.
Disadvantage: e.g. it can't be broken down as quickly, so the glucose it stores is less readily available ***[1 mark]***.

2 a) i) To stop the solvent evaporating ***[1 mark]***.

ii) To act as the mobile phase, through which the molecules that are being separated can move ***[1 mark]***.

iii) Water is also a polar molecule ***[1 mark]***. This means that the glucose molecules are attracted to the water molecules / can form hydrogen bonds with the water molecules and will dissolve in water ***[1 mark]***.

b) i) $R_f = \frac{\text{distance travelled by solute}}{\text{distance travelled by solvent}}$

Distance travelled by solvent = 50 mm
R_f value for A = 13 ÷ 50 = 0.26
R_f value for B = 16 ÷ 50 = 0.32
R_f value for C = 9 ÷ 50 = 0.18
Glucose = **C**

[2 marks for all three R_f values correctly calculated and a correct answer of C, otherwise 1 mark for two R_f values calculated correctly]

ii) To make the spots of colourless sugars visible ***[1 mark]***.

3 a)

Final concentration of glucose /mM	Volume of distilled water / cm^3	Volume of glucose solution / cm^3
4.0	0.0	10.0
2.0	5.0	5.0
1.0	7.5	2.5
0.5	8.75	1.25

[1 mark for three correct glucose concentrations]

b) Any four from: the student could carry out the Benedict's test on each known glucose solution ***[1 mark]***. He could then use the colorimeter to measure the absorbance values of the solutions resulting from each Benedict's test ***[1 mark]***. These absorbance values could then be used to plot a calibration curve ***[1 mark]***. A Benedict's test could then be carried out on a sample of each energy drink and a colorimeter measurement taken ***[1 mark]***. The absorbance value for each energy drink sample would then be read off the calibration curve to find the associated glucose concentration ***[1 mark]***. ***[Maximum of 4 marks available]***

c) i) E.g. 10 cm^3/the same volume of distilled water only ***[1 mark]***.

ii) To demonstrate that only the colour of the solution/the presence of glucose is affecting the readings ***[1 mark]***.

d) E.g. the colour of the drinks may have increased the absorbance readings ***[1 mark]***, and therefore the estimates of glucose concentration for these drinks will be too low ***[1 mark]***.

Module 2 : Section 3 — Nucleotides and Nucleic Acids

Pages 20-22: Nucleotides and Nucleic Acids — 1

1 C ***[1 mark]***

2 D ***[1 mark]***

3 D ***[1 mark]***

*First work out what the DNA mutation is: TAC/**CTA**/GCT has become TAC/**CTC**/GCT during replication. Now work out the change to the mRNA sequence: the complementary mRNA codon for CTA is GAU, and the complementary mRNA codon for CTC is GAG. Then you can use the table to find that GAU codes for Asp (aspartate), and GAG codes for Glu (glutamate).*

4 a) i) Ribose ***[1 mark]***

ii) Phosphodiester bond ***[1 mark]***

b) i) The molecule contains uracil/U bases (in place of thymine/T bases) ***[1 mark]***.

ii) Complementary base pairing ***[1 mark]*** means that hydrogen bonds will form between the base pairs A and U, and C and G ***[1 mark]***. Because the two halves of the RNA sequence are complementary, it causes the RNA strand to fold into a stem-loop structure ***[1 mark]***.

iii) Number of purines (A and G) = 12
Total bases = 23
(12 ÷ 23) × 100 = **52.2%** ***[1 mark]***

5 a) i) DNA helicase separates the nucleotide strands / causes the DNA helix to unwind ***[1 mark]*** by breaking the hydrogen bonds between bases ***[1 mark]***. DNA polymerase joins the nucleotides in the new DNA strand together ***[1 mark]***.

ii) To ensure genetic information is conserved/stays the same/is not changed ***[1 mark]***. Changes to the DNA sequence could alter the sequence of amino acids in a protein ***[1 mark]***, which may result in the protein no longer functioning properly ***[1 mark]***.

b) i) The results show that DNA replication has not occurred in the absence of ATP or when ATP hydrolase is inactive ***[1 mark]***.

ii) E.g. the results suggest that the breakdown of ATP (by ATP hydrolase) is essential for DNA replication ***[1 mark]***. This could be because DNA replication requires energy and/ or inorganic phosphate released by the breakdown of ATP ***[1 mark]***.

Pages 23-25: Nucleotides and Nucleic Acids — 2

1 a) E.g. valine is coded for by four DNA codons ***[1 mark]***.
'Degenerate' means that multiple DNA codons can code for one amino acid, so any evidence that shows this from the table could gain a mark.

b) i) An A will be swapped for a C / the mRNA codon GAC will become GCC ***[1 mark]***.

ii) The fifth amino acid in this part of the sequence will be arginine instead of a leucine ***[1 mark]***.

c) The mRNA attaches to a ribosome. tRNA molecules carry **amino acids** ***[1 mark]*** to the ribosome. tRNA molecules attach to the mRNA via **complementary base pairing** ***[1 mark]***. rRNA in the ribosome catalyses the formation of a **peptide bond** ***[1 mark]*** between two **amino acids** ***[1 mark]***. The ribosome moves along the mRNA, producing a polypeptide chain. The process continues until a **stop codon** ***[1 mark]*** on the mRNA is reached.

2 a) Any four from: e.g. after the DNA has been unwound ***[1 mark]***, RNA polymerase lines up free RNA nucleotides along the template strand ***[1 mark]*** according to the rules of complementary base pairing ***[1 mark]***. RNA polymerase then joins the RNA nucleotides together as it moves along the DNA template strand ***[1 mark]***. Once RNA polymerase reaches a stop codon, it detaches and the mRNA is released ***[1 mark]***. ***[Maximum of 4 marks available]***

b) i) The levels of mRNAs 2 and 3 were only slightly affected by the drug ***[1 mark]***. If RNA polymerase was inhibited, the levels of all of the mRNAs would have decreased by a large amount ***[1 mark]***.

ii) Only the level of mRNA 1 has been significantly reduced ***[1 mark]***. This indicates that mRNA 1 contains the particular sequence destroyed by the drug ***[1 mark]***.

3 How to grade your answer:

Level 0: There is no relevant information. ***[No marks]***

Level 1: There is a brief description of semi-conservative replication or an attempt to explain how the experiment provides evidence that DNA replication is a semi-conservative process. The answer has no clear structure. The information given may be basic and lacking in detail. It may not all be relevant. ***[1 to 2 marks]***

Level 2: There is a description of semi-conservative replication and some explanation of how the experiment provides evidence that DNA replication is a semi-conservative process. The answer has some structure. Most of the information given is relevant and there is some detail involved. ***[3 to 4 marks]***

Level 3: There is a description of semi-conservative replication and a full explanation of how the experiment provides evidence that DNA replication is a semi-conservative process. The answer has a clear and logical structure. The information given is relevant and detailed. ***[5 to 6 marks]***

Indicative scientific content may include:

<u>Knowledge of semi-conservative replication</u>

Original DNA molecule unwinds.

Each strand acts as a template for a new DNA strand, which is made from free-floating DNA nucleotides.

Each new DNA molecule contains one original (template) strand and one new strand.

<u>Explanation of results as evidence for semi-conservative replication</u>

100% of the DNA molecules in bacterial generation 0 contained heavy nitrogen. This is because the *E. coli* were originally grown in a heavy nitrogen nutrient broth.

100% of the DNA molecules in bacterial generation 1 contained both heavy nitrogen and light nitrogen.

This suggests that DNA replication could be semi-conservative, with each DNA molecule in generation 1 containing one heavy nitrogen template strand (from bacterial generation 0) and one new strand made up of light nitrogen nucleotides that were synthesised from the surrounding broth.

In bacterial generation 2, 50% of the DNA contained both heavy and light nitrogen and 50% contained only light nitrogen.

This means that DNA replication must be semi-conservative because any DNA molecules synthesised from a template strand containing heavy nitrogen will contain both heavy and light nitrogen.

Also, any DNA molecules synthesised from a template strand that only contains light nitrogen will themselves only contain light nitrogen.

The percentage of DNA containing both heavy and light nitrogen halves with each generation, confirming that DNA replication must be semi-conservative.

<u>Module 2 : Section 4 — Enzymes</u>

Pages 26-27: Enzymes — 1

1 C ***[1 mark]***
At temperatures below the optimum, a Q_{10} value of 2 means the reaction rate doubles when the temperature is raised by 10 °C.
0.8 × 2 = 1.6.

2 B ***[1 mark]***
Competitive inhibitors compete with the substrate for an enzyme's active site. This means the rate of reaction is slower at lower substrate concentrations than it would have been without the inhibitor. The maximum rate of reaction is still reached, but it takes a greater concentration of substrate than is needed without the inhibitor.

3 a) At low temperatures, the rate of the reaction is slow because the kinetic energy of the enzyme and substrate molecules is low ***[1 mark]***. As temperature increases to the optimum, the rate increases as there are more successful collisions between enzymes and substrate molecules ***[1 mark]***. At temperatures higher than the optimum, the rate decreases as the enzyme is denatured ***[1 mark]***.

b) Enzyme B because it has the higher optimum temperature ***[1 mark]***, which will allow it to function at the higher temperatures found in a tropical climate ***[1 mark]***.

c) The insecticide molecule is a similar shape to enzyme A's substrate ***[1 mark]***. The insecticide molecule occupies enzyme A's active site ***[1 mark]*** so the substrate cannot fit and the respiration reaction cannot be catalysed ***[1 mark]***. This interrupts the respiration process and kills the insect ***[1 mark]***.

Pages 28-30: Enzymes — 2

1 a) Pepsin is found in the body, so 40 °C is likely to be within the optimal range for pepsin action ***[1 mark]***.

b) The reaction is fastest at pH 2 ***[1 mark]***, which suggests pepsin has an optimum pH between those values found in the stomach (pH 1.5 to pH 3.5) ***[1 mark]***. At pH values similar to those found in the small intestine (pH 5 and pH 8), the reaction is much slower ***[1 mark]***, suggesting that pepsin would denature in the small intestine ***[1 mark]***.

2 a) i) Extracellular enzymes work outside cells, whereas intracellular enzymes work within cells ***[1 mark]***.

ii) E.g. amylase / trypsin ***[1 mark]***.

b) The independent variable is enzyme concentration and the dependent variable is the volume of oxygen produced ***[1 mark]***.

c) ± 0.5 cm^3 ***[1 mark]***

d) E.g. collected the gas in a measuring cylinder with a smaller resolution ***[1 mark]***.

e) i) Rate = $\frac{17}{20}$

$= \mathbf{0.85\ cm^3\ s^{-1}}$

[1 mark for 0.85, 1 mark for the correct units]

ii)

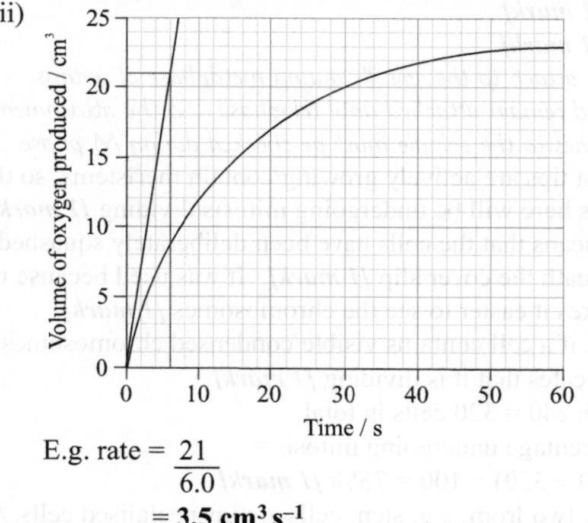

E.g. rate = $\frac{21}{6.0}$

$= \mathbf{3.5\ cm^3\ s^{-1}}$

[1 mark for a tangent drawn to the curve at time = 0 s, 1 mark for an answer between 3.2 cm³ s⁻¹ and 3.8 cm³ s⁻¹]

Tangents can be tricky things to draw accurately so the examiners will usually accept answers that are a bit below or a bit above what they got themselves — even so, try to draw your line as carefully as you can.

f) E.g.

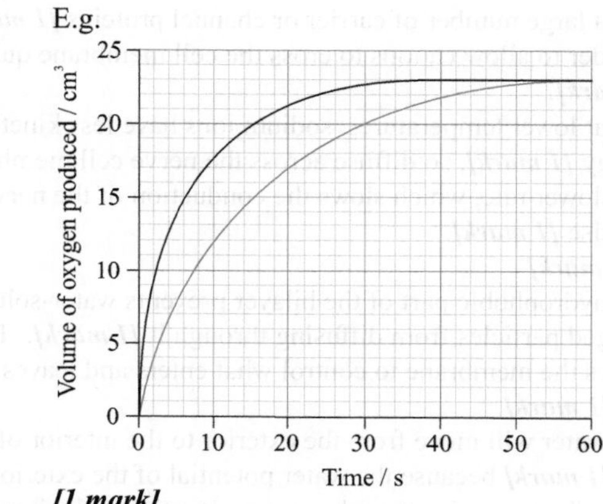

[1 mark]

Don't worry if your line's not exactly like this. You just need to make sure it's steeper than the original but still starts and plateaus at the same values.

3 a) Vitamin KO binds to the active site of vitamin KO reductase ***[1 mark]***. As it does so, vitamin KO makes the active site change shape slightly to fit more closely around it ***[1 mark]***. Reduced vitamin K is not able to make vitamin KO reductase's active site change shape in the right way, so vitamin KO reductase won't catalyse its conversion back to vitamin KO ***[1 mark]***.

b) It is an organic, non-protein molecule ***[1 mark]***, that binds to an enzyme and helps it to function ***[1 mark]***.

c) By inhibiting the action of vitamin KO reductase, warfarin prevents the production of the coenzyme reduced vitamin K ***[1 mark]***. Without reduced vitamin K, carboxylase is unable function properly and can't catalyse the conversion of precursor prothrombin into prothrombin ***[1 mark]***. This means that thrombin and fibrin can't be made ***[1 mark]*** and the lack of fibrin prevents a blood clot from forming ***[1 mark]***.

Module 2 : Section 5 — Biological Membranes

Pages 31-34: Biological Membranes — 1

1 C ***[1 mark]***

2 B ***[1 mark]***

Hypotonic means the solution has a higher water potential than the cells. Water moves from areas of higher water potential to areas of lower water potential, so water will move from the solution into the cells. The cells swell and become turgid.

3 D ***[1 mark]***

Ammonia will diffuse fastest when the surface area to volume ratio of the cube is highest and its concentration gradient is steepest. Smaller cubes have a higher surface area to volume ratio and the more concentrated ammonia solution will provide the steepest concentration gradient (i.e. the biggest difference in ammonia concentration).

4 a) i) Proteins are scattered amongst the phospholipids, like tiles in a mosaic ***[1 mark]***. The phospholipids are constantly moving, so the structure is fluid ***[1 mark]***.

ii) The cholesterol molecules would restrict the movement of the phospholipids ***[1 mark]***, making the structure less fluid and more rigid ***[1 mark]***.

iii) Any two from: e.g. they stabilise the membrane by forming hydrogen bonds with surrounding water molecules. / They bind to drugs/hormones/antibodies. / They act as receptors for cell signalling. / They act as antigens. ***[2 marks]***

iv) Any two from: e.g. phospholipids would be packed more closely together. / The channel proteins and carrier proteins would deform. / Ice crystals may form and pierce the membrane. ***[2 marks]***

b) i) E.g. a large number of carrier or channel proteins *[1 mark]* in order to allow cations to cross the cell membrane quickly *[1 mark]*.

ii) E.g. at lower temperatures, sodium ions have less kinetic energy *[1 mark]*, so diffuse across the nerve cell membrane at a slower rate, which slows the conduction of the nerve impulse *[1 mark]*.

5 a) B *[1 mark]*

b) The hydrophobic part of the bilayer prevents water-soluble/charged particles from diffusing through it *[1 mark]*. This allows the membrane to control what enters and leaves the cell *[1 mark]*.

c) The water will move from the exterior to the interior of the cell *[1 mark]* because the water potential of the exterior is higher/less negative than the water potential of the interior *[1 mark]*.

6 a) Liver and skeletal muscle cells have different types of receptors on their surface, each with a specific shape *[1 mark]*. Glucagon has a complementary shape to a liver cell receptor but not a skeletal muscle cell receptor, so it is able to bind to liver cells, and not to skeletal muscle cells *[1 mark]*.

b) It is a similar shape to glucagon, so it may bind to glucagon-specific receptors in the place of glucagon *[1 mark]*. This will prevent glucagon from activating the conversion of glycogen into glucose and increasing the blood sugar level *[1 mark]*.

7 a) To make sure any betalains/pigments released by the cutting of the beetroot were washed away *[1 mark]*.

b) Colorimetry analysis of distilled water *[1 mark]*.

c) Any four from: e.g. increasing the temperature from 20 °C to 40 °C increases the fluidity of the phospholipids in the beetroot cell membranes *[1 mark]*. At temperatures above 40 °C, the membrane starts to break down / proteins in the membrane start to denature *[1 mark]*. The membrane surrounding the vacuole therefore becomes more permeable with increasing temperature *[1 mark]*, meaning that betalains/pigments leak out into the distilled water *[1 mark]*. The more pigments released, the higher the absorbance reading *[1 mark]*.

d) Cell membranes contain channel proteins and carrier proteins *[1 mark]*. Proteins are denatured by extremes of pH / extremes of pH interfere with the bonding in proteins, causing them to change shape *[1 mark]*. If the proteins are not able to function and control what goes in or out of the cell, membrane permeability will increase *[1 mark]*.

Pages 35-36: Biological Membranes — 2

1 a) E.g. histamine is too big / it's charged/polar *[1 mark]*.

You're not expected to know the characteristics of histamine, just to apply your knowledge of why molecules are usually unable to diffuse directly through cell membranes.

b) Exocytosis *[1 mark]*. The granules containing histamine fuse with the plasma membrane and release their contents outside of the cell *[1 mark]*.

2 a)

Concentration of sucrose solution to be made up / mol dm^{-3}	Volume of 1 mol dm^{-3} sucrose solution used / cm^3	Volume of water used / cm^3	Final volume of solution to be made up / cm^3
1	20	0	20
0.75	15	**5**	20
0.5	**10**	**10**	20
0.25	**5**	**15**	20
0	**0**	**20**	20

[2 marks for all four rows correct, otherwise 1 mark for three rows correct]

b) Any two from: e.g. the temperature the potato samples were incubated at / the length of time the potato samples were incubated for / the volume of sucrose solution used / the variety of potato used / the age of potato used. *[2 marks]*

c) The line of best fit crosses the x-axis of Figure 1 halfway between 0.25 and 0.50, so the sucrose concentration of potato cells = approximately 0.375 mol dm^{-3}.
A 0.3 mol dm^{-3} sucrose solution has a water potential of −850 kPa. A 0.4 mol dm^{-3} sucrose solution has a water potential of −1130 kPa.
So a 0.375 mol dm^{-3} sucrose solution has a water potential of approximately:
(−1130) − (−850) = 280 × 0.75 = 210
−850 − 210 = **−1060 kPa**
[2 marks for an answer > −850 and < −1130 kPa, otherwise 1 mark for estimating the sucrose concentration of the potato cells to be between 0.3 and 0.4 mol dm^{-3}]

d) The sweet potato tissue is likely to have a lower water potential than that of the white potato *[1 mark]* because it is likely to have a higher sucrose concentration *[1 mark]*.

The extra sucrose (with some other sugars too) is what makes the sweet potato sweet.

e) No, the cells in pure water increased in mass, so they gained water *[1 mark]*. Cells become plasmolysed when they lose water, not when they gain it *[1 mark]*.

Module 2 : Section 6 — Cell Division and Cellular Organisation

Pages 37-40: Cell Division and Cellular Organisation

1 B *[1 mark]*

2 C *[1 mark]*

3 A *[1 mark]*

Chromosomes attach to the spindle during metaphase of mitosis (M phase) and remain attached until telophase. So the attachment of the chromosomes to the spindle must be checked during M phase.

4 a) Root tips are actively growing/contain meristems, so the cells here will be undergoing mitosis/dividing *[1 mark]*.

b) It means that the cells have been deliberately squashed beneath the cover slip *[1 mark]*. It was used because it makes it easier to see the chromosomes *[1 mark]*.

c) i) E.g. if a cell contains visible/condensed chromosomes this indicates that it is dividing *[1 mark]*.

ii) 80 + 240 = 320 cells in total
percentage undergoing mitosis =
(240 ÷ 320) × 100 = **75%** *[1 mark]*

d) i) Any two from: e.g. stem cells are unspecialised cells. / Stem cells are capable of differentiating to form other types of cell. / Stem cells are capable of self-renewing. *[2 marks]*

ii) E.g. xylem / phloem *[1 mark]*

5 a) i) S phase *[1 mark]*. Blocking the formation of nucleotides will stop DNA from replicating *[1 mark]*.

ii) The cells will be unable to pass through the checkpoint that checks DNA has been successfully replicated/the next checkpoint/the G_2 checkpoint *[1 mark]*.

b) E.g. red blood cells are produced from stem cells in the bone marrow *[1 mark]*. Methotrexate stops the cell cycle, so it may prevent stem cells from dividing to produce more red blood cells (leading to a low red blood cell count) *[1 mark]*.

6 a) i) In anaphase II, the sister chromatids are separated *[1 mark]*, whereas in anaphase I the pairs of homologous chromosomes are separated *[1 mark]*.

ii) Telophase II occurs / the nuclear envelope forms around the separate sets of chromatids *[1 mark]*. Cytokinesis then occurs / the cytoplasm divides (to produce four daughter cells) *[1 mark]*.

b) A pollen grain is a gamete and therefore a haploid cell ***[1 mark]***. Meiosis is needed to halve the chromosome number and produce a haploid cell from a diploid cell ***[1 mark]***.

c) The crossing over of homologous chromosomes in meiosis I ***[1 mark]*** leads to the four daughter cells containing different combinations of alleles ***[1 mark]***. Independent assortment in meiosis I ***[1 mark]*** leads to the daughter cells containing any combination of maternal and paternal chromosomes ***[1 mark]***.

7 a) Prophase ***[1 mark]***. The chromosomes have condensed but have not started to divide ***[1 mark]***.

b) A peak in the concentration of cyclin E occurs when the mass of DNA starts to increase ***[1 mark]***. This suggests that cyclin E may trigger DNA replication in the cell / entry into the S stage of interphase ***[1 mark]***. The peak in the concentration of cyclin B is followed by a decrease/halving in the mass of DNA ***[1 mark]***. This suggests that cyclin B may trigger the cell to enter mitosis/M phase ***[1 mark]***.

Module 3 : Section 1 — Exchange and Transport

Pages 41-43: Exchange and Transport — 1

1 B ***[1 mark]***

2 C ***[1 mark]***

Tidal volume is the volume of air in an ordinary breath in or out — so in this graph, it's the height of one of the small peaks.

3 A ***[1 mark]***

4 a) E.g. dissecting scissors ***[1 mark]***

b) i) A: spiracle ***[1 mark]***
B: tracheae ***[1 mark]***

ii) E.g. pipette a drop of water onto a slide ***[1 mark]***. Use tweezers to place a section of structures B/the tracheae onto the drop of water ***[1 mark]***. Stand a cover slip upright on the slide, next to the water drop, then carefully tilt and lower it so it covers the specimen ***[1 mark]***.

c) It changes the volume of its body with rhythmic abdominal movements ***[1 mark]***. This changes the pressure in its body so that air is drawn in and out through the spiracles ***[1 mark]***.

d) E.g. oxygen from the air dissolves in the (tracheal) fluid, then diffuses from the fluid into the body cells ***[1 mark]***. Carbon dioxide diffuses into the fluid in the opposite direction ***[1 mark]***.

5 a) i) gill plate/(secondary) lamella ***[1 mark]***

ii) An arrow drawn across structure X in the opposite direction to the arrow showing water flow across the gill filament, e.g.

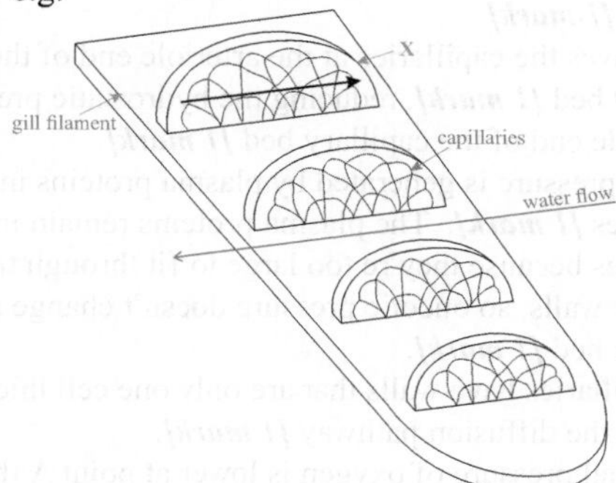

[1 mark]

Fish gills have a counter-current system, meaning the blood flows in the opposite direction to the water.

iii) E.g.

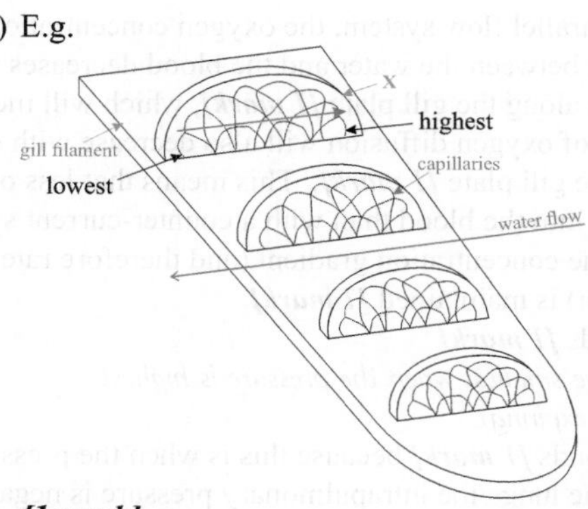

[1 mark]

Blood enters the gill plate with a low oxygen concentration. Because a steep concentration gradient is maintained between the water and the blood, a lot of oxygen has diffused into the blood by the time it leaves the gill plate.

b) E.g. the many gill plates/(secondary) lamellae give the gill filament a large surface area ***[1 mark]***, increasing the rate of diffusion of gases ***[1 mark]***.

c) E.g. when the fish opens its mouth, the floor of the buccal cavity is lowered, increasing the cavity's volume ***[1 mark]***. This decreases the pressure in the buccal cavity, so water is drawn into it ***[1 mark]***. When the fish closes its mouth, the floor of the buccal cavity is raised, decreasing the volume of the buccal cavity ***[1 mark]***. This increases the pressure in the cavity, so water is forced out across the gill filaments ***[1 mark]***.

Pages 44-46: Exchange and Transport — 2

1 a) E.g.
Bacterium A: 5 : 1
Bacterium B: 84 ÷ 22 = 3.8181..., so 84 : 22 = 3.81 : 1
Bacterium C: 15.75 ÷ 3.5 = 4.5, so 15.75 : 3.5 = 4.5 : 1
Bacterium with fastest gas exchange: Bacterium **A**
[1 mark for bacterium A, 1 mark for 3.81 or 4.5]

Converting all the ratios into the form n : 1 makes it easier to see that Bacterium A has a bigger surface area compared to its volume, which means there is a larger surface for gases to diffuse across. This means the rate of gas exchange can be faster.

b) Any two from: e.g. it would take too long for substances to travel from the outer surface to the cells deep within the body ***[1 mark]***. / Not enough substances would be exchanged across the outer surface, which is small relative to the volume of a multicellular organism ***[1 mark]***. / Multicellular organisms have a higher metabolic rate than single-celled organisms, so diffusion across the outer surface would be too slow to keep up with metabolic demand ***[1 mark]***.

2 a)

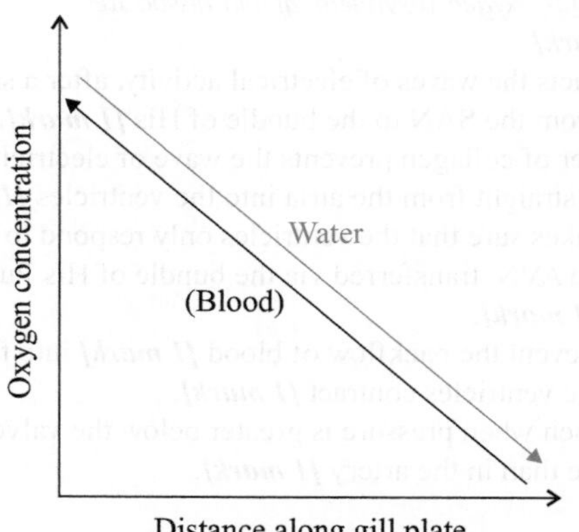

[1 mark]

b) In the parallel flow system, the oxygen concentration gradient between the water and the blood decreases with distance along the gill plate ***[1 mark]***, which will mean that the rate of oxygen diffusion will also decrease with distance along the gill plate ***[1 mark]***. This means that less oxygen diffuses into the blood than with a counter-current system, where the concentration gradient (and therefore rate of diffusion) is maintained ***[1 mark]***.

3 a) 3 seconds ***[1 mark]***

Lung volume will be smallest when the pressure is highest (and the person is expiring).

b) 0-2 seconds ***[1 mark]*** because this is when the pressure inside the lungs/the intrapulmonary pressure is negative ***[1 mark]***. Air travels from an area of higher pressure to an area of lower pressure, so air must be being taken into the lungs at this point ***[1 mark]***.

c) $60 \div 4 = 15$

15 breaths min^{-1} ***[1 mark]***

The graph shows one full breath (inspiration and expiration) which takes 4 seconds to complete.

4 a) Any three from: e.g. less oxygen is able to reach the alveoli because the bronchi are swollen/filled with mucus ***[1 mark]***. This reduces the concentration gradient of oxygen in the alveoli ***[1 mark]***, which reduces the rate at which oxygen diffuses into the blood ***[1 mark]***. This may result in shortness of breath, because the person with bronchitis may feel like they have to breathe faster/harder as the body tries to make up for a lack of oxygen reaching the cells ***[1 mark]***.

b) The alveoli are surrounded by a capillary network, so blood constantly takes oxygen away from the alveoli and brings carbon dioxide ***[1 mark]***. The alveoli are ventilated, so the air in them is constantly being replaced, with oxygen being brought in and carbon dioxide being removed ***[1 mark]***.

c) The breakdown of the alveoli walls would mean the loss of elastic fibres from the alveoli ***[1 mark]***. This would make it harder for the lungs to recoil and expel air ***[1 mark]***.

Module 3 : Section 2 — Transport in Animals

Pages 47-49: Transport in Animals — 1

1 A ***[1 mark]***

The ECG shows a very irregular heartbeat, which is fibrillation. Tachycardia is when the heartbeat is too fast (over 100 beats per minute), an ectopic heartbeat is when there's an 'extra' heartbeat (an early contraction of the atria or ventricles) and bradycardia is when the heartbeat is too slow (under 60 beats per minute).

2 C ***[1 mark]***

Statement 1 is incorrect — at low partial pressures of oxygen, haemoglobin unloads oxygen (oxyhaemoglobin dissociates).

3 D ***[1 mark]***

4 a) It conducts the waves of electrical activity, after a short delay, from the SAN to the bundle of His ***[1 mark]***.

b) The layer of collagen prevents the wave of electricity passing straight from the atria into the ventricles ***[1 mark]***. This makes sure that the ventricles only respond to signals from the AVN, transferred via the bundle of His/Purkyne tissue ***[1 mark]***.

5 a) They prevent the backflow of blood ***[1 mark]*** into the atria when the ventricles contract ***[1 mark]***.

b) They open when pressure is greater below the valve / in the ventricle than in the artery ***[1 mark]***.

c) i)

	Standing up	Lying down
Mean heart rate (bpm)	74	57
Mean cardiac output (cm^3 min^{-1})	4700	4700
Mean stroke volume (cm^3)	**63.5** (3 s.f.)	**82.5** (3 s.f.)

[2 marks for both correct answers, otherwise 1 mark for evidence of 4700 ÷ 74 or 4700 ÷ 57]

Cardiac output = heart rate × stroke volume, so stroke volume = cardiac output ÷ heart rate. So when standing up, stroke volume is 4700 ÷ 74 = 63.5, and when lying down it's 4700 ÷ 57 = 82.5.

ii) E.g. it gives the heart rate time to stabilise, as the act of changing position could cause it to increase ***[1 mark]***.

iii) E.g. heart rate is lower when lying down as blood does not have to be pumped above the level of the heart / against gravity ***[1 mark]***.

The heart has to work harder when a person is standing up, because blood has to flow against gravity. When you're lying down, the force of gravity is evenly distributed across the body.

iv) Taking multiple measurements and calculating the mean reduces the effect of random error, so makes the results more precise ***[1 mark]***.

Pages 50-53: Transport in Animals — 2

1 a) i) X = aorta ***[1 mark]***

Y = pulmonary artery ***[1 mark]***

ii) E.g. the artery walls would have felt much thicker than the vein walls ***[1 mark]***.

b)

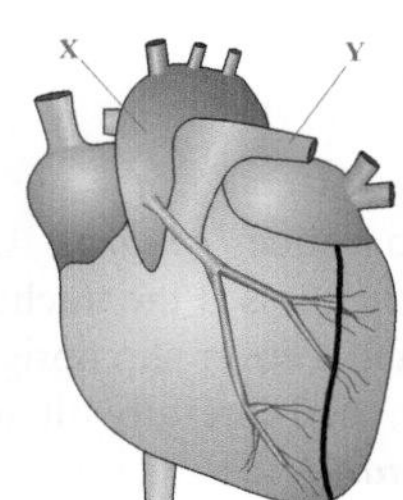

[1 mark]

c) coronary artery ***[1 mark]***

d) Any one from: e.g. use clear, continuous lines/no overlaps in lines ***[1 mark]*** / no shading ***[1 mark]*** / draw different components in proportion ***[1 mark]*** / include a scale ***[1 mark]*** / include relevant labels ***[1 mark]***.

2 a) i) E.g. there is a build-up of tissue fluid because excess fluid is not being returned to the blood via the lymphatic system ***[1 mark]***.

ii) Any two from: e.g. lymph has no red blood cells ***[1 mark]***. / Lymph has no platelets ***[1 mark]***. / Lymph has fewer proteins ***[1 mark]***.

b) i) Fluid leaves the capillaries at the arteriole end of the capillary bed ***[1 mark]***, reducing the hydrostatic pressure at the venule end of the capillary bed ***[1 mark]***.

ii) Oncotic pressure is generated by plasma proteins in the capillaries ***[1 mark]***. The plasma proteins remain in the capillaries because they're too large to fit through the capillary walls, so oncotic pressure doesn't change along the capillary bed ***[1 mark]***.

c) E.g. capillaries have walls that are only one cell thick, which shortens the diffusion pathway ***[1 mark]***.

3 a) The partial pressure of oxygen is lower at point A than at point B ***[1 mark]***. The lower the partial pressure of oxygen, the lower the affinity haemoglobin has for oxygen, and so the percentage saturation of haemoglobin will be lower at point A than point B ***[1 mark]***.

b) i) The respiration rate increases during exercise, which increases the partial pressure of carbon dioxide in the blood ***[1 mark]***. Higher partial pressures of carbon dioxide increase the rate of oxygen unloading (the Bohr effect) and the saturation of blood with oxygen is lower for a given partial pressure of O_2 ***[1 mark]***.

ii) Carbonic anhydrase catalyses the reaction between carbon dioxide and water in red blood cells to form carbonic acid ***[1 mark]***. Carbonic acid then dissociates to form HCO_3^- and H^+ ions ***[1 mark]***. The increase in H^+ ions causes haemoglobin to unload its oxygen ***[1 mark]***.

4 a) 60 ÷ 0.55 = 109.0909...
109 beats per minute ***[1 mark]***

b) 0.13 seconds ***[1 mark]***

The left atrium contracts before the left ventricle in the cardiac cycle, so you need to find a point on the graph where the pressure of the atrium increases before the pressure of the ventricle increases.

c) How to grade your answer:

Level 0: There is no relevant information. ***[No marks]***

Level 1: The answer covers one or two of the points A to D. The answer has no clear structure. The information given is basic and lacking in detail. It may not all be relevant. ***[1 to 2 marks]***

Level 2: The answer covers at least three of the points A to D. The answer has some structure. Most of the information given is relevant and there is some detail involved. ***[3 to 4 marks]***

Level 3: The answer covers all four of the points A to D in detail. The answer has a clear and logical structure. The information given is relevant and detailed. ***[5 to 6 marks]***

Indicative scientific content may include:

Point A
Pressure in the left ventricle exceeds pressure in the left atrium, because the left ventricle is contracting and the left atrium is relaxing. This causes the atrioventricular valve/the valve between the left atrium and left ventricle to close, preventing the backflow of blood into the left atrium.

Point B
Pressure increases in the left ventricle to above that of the aorta, which forces the semi-lunar valve/the valve between the left ventricle and aorta open.

Point C
The left ventricular pressure falls below that of the aorta, because blood has moved into the aorta from the ventricle and the left ventricle is relaxing. As a result, the semi-lunar valve/the valve between the left ventricle and the aorta closes.

Point D
Pressure has been increasing in the left atrium as blood has been returning to the atrium from the body. As the atrial pressure exceeds ventricular pressure, the atrioventricular valve/valve between the left atrium and left ventricle opens, allowing blood to flow into the left ventricle.

d) The left ventricle has a higher maximum pressure than the left atrium because it has a thicker muscle wall and so is able to generate more force when it contracts ***[1 mark]***.

e) The wall of the aorta is thick and muscular / the wall of the aorta contains elastic tissue to stretch and recoil / the inner lining of the aorta is folded so it can stretch ***[1 mark]***, which helps to maintain the high pressure of the blood coming out of the left ventricle ***[1 mark]***.

Module 3 : Section 3 — Transport in Plants

Pages 54-57: Transport in Plants

1 B ***[1 mark]***

2 D ***[1 mark]***

Water travelling via the symplast pathway travels through plasmodesmata (channels in the cells walls). Water travelling via the apoplast pathway travels through the cell walls themselves.

3 C ***[1 mark]***

Statement 1 is incorrect. Sunken stomata and a thick waxy epidermis are xerophytic adaptations — they help a plant to conserve water. Hydrophytes live in water, so they don't need help conserving it. Instead they need adaptations to help them get enough oxygen.

4 a) Water on the leaves would reduce the water potential gradient between inside the leaf and outside ***[1 mark]***, reducing water loss/transpiration ***[1 mark]***.

b) E.g. cut the shoot underwater / set the apparatus up underwater / check the apparatus is watertight ***[1 mark]***.

c) E.g. it is a measurement of the rate of water uptake only, which is not exactly the same as transpiration rate/the rate of water loss from the leaves ***[1 mark]***. This is because some of the water taken up by the plant is used for support/turgidity/photosynthesis ***[1 mark]***.

d) At higher temperatures, water molecules have more kinetic energy so they evaporate more quickly from the cells inside the leaf ***[1 mark]***. This increases the water potential/concentration gradient between the inside and outside of the leaf ***[1 mark]***, so water diffuses out of the leaf faster and the rate of transpiration is faster ***[1 mark]***.

5 a) Light intensity is higher at 12:00, so more stomata are open ***[1 mark]***, which increases the transpiration rate ***[1 mark]***. This draws water molecules up the xylem at a quicker rate, due to cohesion and tension ***[1 mark]***.

At 00:00, it would be dark, whereas there is sunlight at 12:00.

b) i) To prevent the plant tissue from drying out ***[1 mark]***.

ii) E.g. dyeing the tissue with a stain/named stain ***[1 mark]***.

iii) E.g. in a root, the xylem is arranged in the centre, whereas in a stem, the xylem is near the outside. / In a root, the xylem is grouped together in a cross shape, whereas in a stem, it is arranged in individual bundles that form a ring around the stem. ***[1 mark]***

6 a) Translocation requires energy/ATP ***[1 mark]***. If metabolism stops, respiration cannot occur so ATP is not produced / energy is not released ***[1 mark]***.

b) E.g. at point A, the water potential is being lowered by solutes being actively loaded from the companion cell into the sieve tube ***[1 mark]***. This causes water to enter from the xylem and companion cell, and raises the pressure ***[1 mark]***. At point B, the pressure is lower because water is leaving the sieve tube by osmosis ***[1 mark]***. This is occurring because solutes are being removed from the sieve tube and so the water potential is higher ***[1 mark]***.

Module 4 : Section 1 — Disease and the Immune System

Pages 58-60: Disease and the Immune System — 1

1 B *[1 mark]*

2 D *[1 mark]*

3 a) i) It agglutinates pathogens/causes pathogens to clump together *[1 mark]*.

ii) B lymphocytes / plasma cells / memory B cells *[1 mark]*

iii) Any two from: e.g. its variable region is complementary to a particular antigen, allowing it to bind to that antigen. / The hinge region allows flexibility when the antibody binds to the antigen. / The constant region allows the antibody to bind to receptors on immune system cells. *[2 marks]*

b) E.g. it allows the antibody to bind to more antigens at once *[1 mark]*, so there is a greater chance of agglutination occurring / more pathogens can be phagocytosed at once *[1 mark]*.

c) $2000 \times 60 \times 60 = 7200000$ *[1 mark]*

$= \mathbf{7.2 \times 10^6}$ *[1 mark]*

There are 60 seconds in a minute and 60 minutes in an hour. So, to work out how many molecules could be produced in an hour, multiply the number that can be produced in one second by 60, and then by 60 again.

4 a) Indirect transmission, because the disease is transmitted via an intermediate (contaminated water) *[1 mark]*.

b) i) E.g. there is a positive correlation between the number of deaths from the disease and monthly rainfall in this country *[1 mark]*.

ii) E.g. higher rainfall may increase flooding, making it more likely for infected human faeces to get into sources of drinking water *[1 mark]*. This could increase the transmission of the pathogen between people, resulting in a greater number of deaths from the disease *[1 mark]*.

c) E.g. each strain of the pathogen will have different, specific antigens on its surface *[1 mark]*. A specific antigen must be bound by an antibody with a complementary shape *[1 mark]*, so the vaccine will need to stimulate the body to produce different antibodies for the antigens on each strain *[1 mark]*.

Pages 61-64: Disease and the Immune System — 2

1 a) E.g. it would reduce damage caused by caterpillars to the outer surfaces of the plant, which would reduce the number of sites through which pathogens could enter the plant. / If the caterpillars are vectors for a disease, it could reduce the likelihood of them transmitting the pathogen they carry to the corn plant. *[1 mark]*

b) E.g. its cells are surrounded by cell walls, which would form a physical barrier against entry by the pathogen. / It may produce callose depositions (between its cell walls and its cell membranes) that make it harder for the pathogen to enter its cells. *[1 mark]*

2 a) i) They move in response to signals from cytokines *[1 mark]*, which are released by damaged cells/tissue at the site of the wound *[1 mark]*.

ii) E.g. it means that any pathogens entering the body through the wound can be phagocytosed/destroyed before they are able to spread *[1 mark]*.

b) Any three from: e.g. the phagocyte recognises the antigens on the pathogen as foreign *[1 mark]*. The cytoplasm of the phagocyte moves around the pathogen, engulfing it *[1 mark]*. This results in the formation of a phagosome, containing the pathogen *[1 mark]*. A lysosome fuses with the phagosome, releasing digestive enzymes to break down the pathogen / the enzymes in a lysosome break down the pathogen *[1 mark]*. The phagocyte then presents the pathogen's antigens on its surface *[1 mark]*.

c) E.g. phagocytosis may be less effective *[1 mark]* as opsonins/IgG bind(s) to foreign antigens to aid phagocytosis / allow the phagocyte to get closer to the pathogen in order to engulf it *[1 mark]*.

3 a) i) E.g. the antibody concentration remains low for several days after exposure to the antigen, while clonal selection and clonal expansion of B lymphocytes occurs *[1 mark]*. Antibody concentration increases as plasma cells (produced as a result of clonal expansion) start to rapidly produce antibodies that are complementary to the antigen *[1 mark]*. Antibody concentration reaches a gradual peak and then falls as plasma cells die off *[1 mark]*. It doesn't fall back to pre-exposure levels because memory B lymphocytes (produced by clonal expansion) remain in the body *[1 mark]*.

ii) E.g. the secondary immune response is faster/stronger than the primary immune response / the concentration of the complementary antibody increases rapidly *[1 mark]* allowing the pathogen to be destroyed before the person experiences any symptoms *[1 mark]*.

b) Anti-toxins bind to complementary toxins that are produced by the bacteria *[1 mark]*. This neutralises the toxins and prevents them from causing muscle spasms *[1 mark]*. However, anti-toxins don't bind to the antigens on the *C. tetani* bacteria themselves, so the bacteria would remain in the body if the patient was only treated with anti-toxins *[1 mark]*.

4 a) i) E.g. so that the woman produces antibodies against the bacteria, which would be transferred to her baby (via the placenta) before it is born *[1 mark]*.

ii) Any four from: e.g. the vaccine contains GBS antigens *[1 mark]*. Neutrophils/phagocytes/antigen-presenting cells present these antigens to T helper cells *[1 mark]*. When the antigens bind to receptors on T helper cell membranes, the T helper cells are activated *[1 mark]*. The activated T helper cells then release interleukins/cytokines/chemical messengers to activate B lymphocytes *[1 mark]*. Both B lymphocytes and T helper cells undergo clonal expansion to produce memory cells *[1 mark]*.

b) Any two from: e.g. the immunity the baby receives from its mother is immediate, whereas immunity from a vaccine takes time to develop. / A vaccine involves exposing the baby to an antigen, whereas breastfeeding provides immunity without needing to expose the baby to an antigen. / The baby does not produce memory cells as a result of breastfeeding, but memory cells are produced as a result of a vaccine. / The immunity the baby gets from breastfeeding only lasts for a short time, whereas the immunity from a vaccine lasts much longer. *[2 marks]*

c) i) E.g. the GBS bacteria damage the protective layers around the brain causing the tissue to release messenger molecules *[1 mark]*. The messenger molecules increase the permeability of nearby blood vessels/cause vasodilation *[1 mark]*. This causes fluid to leak into the area, resulting in swelling/this increases blood flow to the area, making it hot *[1 mark]*.

ii) E.g. the bacteria that cause meningitis may become resistant to the antibiotics used to kill them, making it harder to treat the disease *[1 mark]*.

5 a) How to grade your answer:

Level 0: There is no relevant information. *[No marks]*

Level 1: The answer briefly describes/explains something that would happen if a person with blood type A received a transfusion of blood type B. The answer has no clear structure. The information given is basic and lacking in detail. It may not all be relevant. *[1 to 2 marks]*

Level 2: The answer describes and explains most of what would happen if a person with blood type A received a transfusion of blood type B. The answer has some structure. Most of the information given is relevant and there is some detail involved. ***[3 to 4 marks]***

Level 3: The answer fully describes and explains what would happen if a person with blood type A received a transfusion of blood type B. The answer has a clear and logical structure. The information given is relevant and detailed. ***[5 to 6 marks]***

Indicative scientific content may include:
The antigens on type B red blood cells are different/a different shape to the antigens on type A red blood cells.
As a result, the type A person's phagocytes will not recognise the antigens on the type B red blood cells / will recognise that the type B antigens are foreign.
This will cause a phagocyte that encounters a type B red blood cell to engulf the cell.
The type B red blood cell is broken down by the phagocyte and its antigens are presented on the phagocyte's surface.
T lymphocytes with complementary receptors bind to the presented antigens. This causes the T lymphocytes to undergo clonal selection.
The selected T lymphocytes then undergo clonal expansion. Some of these T lymphocytes become T helper cells.
B lymphocytes with complementary receptors also bind to the presented antigens.
This binding, along with substances released by T helper cells, causes the B lymphocytes to undergo clonal selection.
Selected B lymphocytes divide/undergo clonal expansion to produce plasma cells.
The plasma cells secrete antibodies against the antigens on the type B red blood cells.
The antibodies bind to the type B antigens causing the type B red blood cells to clump together/agglutinate.
The agglutinated type B red blood cells are destroyed by phagocytosis.

b) Blood type O has no antigens, so no immune response will be triggered ***[1 mark]***.

c) E.g. agglutinins for type A and type B antigens could be added to a sample of the person's blood ***[1 mark]***. If no agglutination/clumping is observed, then the person must have type O blood ***[1 mark]***.

Module 4 : Section 2 — Biodiversity

Pages 65-68: Biodiversity

1 B ***[1 mark]***

2 B ***[1 mark]***

Statements 1 and 2 are both correct. Statement 3 is incorrect because marine conservation zones involve protecting species in their natural habitat, whereas ex situ conservation means removing organisms from their habitat and placing them in a new location.

3 C ***[1 mark]***

Statement 1 might be true but you can't tell from this data alone because Simpson's Index takes into account both species richness and species evenness. Statement 2 is definitely false because the closer the value of Simpson's Index to O, the less diverse the habitat — so Habitat B actually has the lowest biodiversity. The closer the value is to 1, the more diverse the habitat, so Habitat C is more diverse than Habitat D and statement 3 is the only statement that you can say is definitely true.

4 a) i)

Species	Number of individual plants counted in different quadrats					Mean number counted
Rapeseed	24	46	32	28	32	**32.4**
Common sunflower	1	0	2	1	1	**1**
Common poppy	8	12	6	10	8	**8.8**
Creeping thistle	13	14	7	15	13	**12.4**

[1 mark]

ii) $N = 32.4 + 1 + 8.8 + 12.4 = 54.6$

$$D = 1 - \left(\left(\frac{32.4}{54.6}\right)^2 + \left(\frac{1}{54.6}\right)^2 + \left(\frac{8.8}{54.6}\right)^2 + \left(\frac{12.4}{54.6}\right)^2\right)$$

$D = \mathbf{0.570}$ (to 3 s.f.)

[2 marks for the correct answer, otherwise 1 mark for correct working. Allow full marks if incorrect answers to 4 a) i) used correctly here.]

b) E.g. the field could have been divided into a grid and a random number generator could have been used to select coordinates at which to place the quadrats ***[1 mark]***.

c) The scientists could have used a Student's t-test ***[1 mark]*** as this would have allowed them to compare two mean values ***[1 mark]***.

d) E.g. animal grazing prevents some plants from growing, reducing plant diversity ***[1 mark]***. This would mean there are fewer habitats and food resources to support other organisms, further reducing species diversity ***[1 mark]***.

5 a) Because an index of diversity takes into account both species richness and species evenness ***[1 mark]***, which means that it takes into account species that are only present in small numbers, which species richness does not ***[1 mark]***.

b) Any three from: e.g. there were fewer ladybird species on the conventional farm than on the organic farm. / The standard deviation bars do not overlap, so the difference was significant/the standard deviation bars are short, showing that the data is precise. / However, there is no indication of how many samples were taken, so the data may not be representative of all organic/conventional farms. / There may be factors other than the way in which the fields were farmed, which influenced the number of ladybird species present. / The scientists' conclusion is correct for this data, but further investigation is needed to ensure that these results are valid ***[1 mark for each correct answer]***.

c) i) E.g. habitat diversity is lost because large areas of land need to be cleared to make way for monoculture. / Species diversity is lost because only one type of crop is grown and naturally occurring plants and animals are removed using pesticides. ***[1 mark]***

ii) E.g. continuous monoculture causes soil depletion ***[1 mark]***. This means a lot of money needs to be spent on fertilisers to artificially replace soil nutrients / yields can decrease in the long run, reducing the profit that can be made from the land ***[1 mark]***.

6 a) i) E.g. the proportion of polymorphic gene loci indicates the genetic diversity of the population / genetic diversity is likely to be low in a population of animals bred in captivity ***[1 mark]***. Monitoring it will help the breeding programme to be managed so that genetic diversity is maximised ***[1 mark]***.

ii) number of polymorphic gene loci = 165 − 132 = 33
proportion of polymorphic gene loci =
number of polymorphic ÷ total number of loci =
33 ÷ 165 = **0.2**

[2 marks for correct answer, otherwise 1 mark for using the correct formula]

Polymorphism is when a locus has more than one allele.

b) Any one from: e.g. without beavers the ecosystem would be dramatically different. / Many organisms depend on the habitats created and maintained by beavers. ***[1 mark]***

c) Any one from: e.g. habitats near rivers may have been cleared to make way for more housing/road developments/ farmland. / River habitats may have been polluted by increased use of pesticides/fertilisers. / River habitats may have been over-exploited/over-fished to meet an increasing demand for food. ***[1 mark]***

Human population growth has also contributed to climate change, so you could have written about that too.

d) E.g. the Convention on International Trade in Endangered Species (CITES) regulates the international trade in wild animal and plant specimens ***[1 mark]***. The countries that signed it agreed to make it illegal to kill endangered species/ban the trade of products made from endangered species ***[1 mark]***.

You could have written about another agreement here instead, e.g. the Rio Convention on Biological Diversity (CBD) or the Countryside Stewardship Scheme (CSS).

Module 4 : Section 3 — Classification and Evolution

Pages 69-70: Classification and Evolution — 1

1 B ***[1 mark]***

2 D ***[1 mark]***

Statement 2 is false because the most recent common ancestor of the blind snakes, pythons and boas is the same as the most recent common ancestor of the blind snakes and vipers, so blind snakes are equally related to either group. Statement 3 is also false, because elapids, Atractaspis *and colubrids diverged at the same point.*

3 a) four ***[1 mark]***

The genera shown on the phylogenetic tree are Panthera, Meles, Lutra *and* Canis*. You know that these are the genera because the binomial name for a species is made up of two parts, e.g.* Panthera leo*, and the first part is always the genus.*

b) *Canis aureus* and *Canis lupus* because they both belong to the same genus ***[1 mark]***.

c) family ***[1 mark]***

d) Molecular evidence showed that the kingdom of Prokaryotae could be split into the domains of Archaea and Bacteria ***[1 mark]***, e.g. the enzyme RNA polymerase was found to be different in Bacteria and Archaea ***[1 mark]***.

Pages 71-73: Classification and Evolution — 2

1 a) Concentrating their urine allows them to conserve water, which means they are less likely to become dehydrated in their hot desert habitat ***[1 mark]***.

b) Some mice had an allele/alleles for golden-brown fur ***[1 mark]***. This would have been beneficial because it would have been harder for predators to see these mice ***[1 mark]***, so they would have been more likely to survive long enough to reproduce and pass on their beneficial alleles to the next generation ***[1 mark]***. After many generations, the frequency of the allele/alleles for golden-brown fur would have increased in the population ***[1 mark]***.

c) Every species has a Latin/binomial name ***[1 mark]***, which avoids confusion, as there might be other common names than 'golden spiny mice'/because binomial names are internationally recognised ***[1 mark]***.

d) i) The variation in mass could have been caused by genetic factors, as these individuals could have inherited alleles that caused them to have a greater mass ***[1 mark]***. It could also have been caused by environmental factors, such as these mice having more food available to them, causing them to become heavier ***[1 mark]***.

ii) $\bar{x} = \dfrac{43.9 + 39.9 + 42.6 + 43.1 + 37.4}{5} = 41.38$

$$\sum(x-\bar{x})^2 = (43.9-41.38)^2 + (39.9-41.38)^2 + (42.6-41.38)^2 + (43.1-41.38)^2 + (37.4-41.38)^2 = 28.828$$

$$s = \sqrt{\frac{28.828}{5-1}} = 2.68458... = \mathbf{2.68\ (3\ s.f.)}$$

[2 marks for correct answer, otherwise 1 mark for correct working]

iii) By carrying out a Student's t-test ***[1 mark]***.

Student's t-tests are for comparing the means of two sets of data.

2 a) E.g. Wallace came up with the idea of natural selection as a mechanism for evolution at the same time as Darwin ***[1 mark]***, and provided evidence to support it, e.g. he wrote about advantageous adaptations that had evolved by natural selection, such as warning colours to deter predators ***[1 mark]***.

b) The *Archaeopteryx* fossils show that there could have been evolution from land dinosaurs into birds ***[1 mark]***, because the *Archaeopteryx* had some of the features of the land dinosaurs they may have evolved from, but also some of the features of birds, which they could have evolved into over time ***[1 mark]***.

c) E.g. scientists can compare molecules (e.g. proteins) in different organisms to find similarities and differences ***[1 mark]***. Those organisms that have diverged away from each other more recently and are more closely related will have more similar molecules ***[1 mark]***.

3 How to grade your answer:

Level 0: There is no relevant information. ***[No marks]***

Level 1: The answer covers how refuge areas reduce the spread of Bt corn resistance or the implications of reducing the spread of Bt resistance for human populations. The answer has no clear structure. The information given is basic and lacking in detail. It may not all be relevant. ***[1 to 2 marks]***

Level 2: The answer covers how refuge areas reduce the spread of Bt corn resistance and some of the implications of reducing the spread of Bt resistance for human populations. The answer has some structure. Most of the information given is relevant and there is some detail involved. ***[3 to 4 marks]***

Level 3: The answer fully covers the how refuge areas reduce the spread of Bt corn resistance and the implications of reducing the spread of Bt resistance for human populations. The answer has a clear and logical structure. The information given is relevant and detailed. ***[5 to 6 marks]***

Indicative scientific content may include:

<u>How refuge areas reduce the spread of Bt corn resistance</u>

Without refuge areas, the only European corn borers that survive long enough to reproduce would be resistant ones, so their offspring would inherit the alleles for resistance and the whole population of European corn borers would continue to be resistant.

In refuge areas, European corn borers may be either resistant or non-resistant, because there is no pesticide acting as a selection pressure. This means that Bt-resistant European corn borers may mate with non-resistant individuals from refuge areas to produce non-resistant offspring. This would reduce the number of resistant corn borers in the population.

Implications for human populations

By reducing the spread of Bt corn resistance, the destruction of Bt corn crops by European corn borers can be kept to a minimum. This would help to feed the growing human population, and prevent farmers from losing large amounts of their income to pest damage.

Reducing the spread of Bt corn resistance would also mean that farmers do not need to turn to alternative pesticides, which may be less effective and less specific, killing insects that are beneficial for the crop (such as pollinators).

Finding an adequate replacement pesticide might require the research and production of new pesticides, which costs time and money.

Module 5 : Section 1 — Communication and Homeostasis

Pages 74-77: Communication and Homeostasis — 1

1 C *[1 mark]*

2 A *[1 mark]*

3 a) There are more positive ions outside the cell than inside the cell *[1 mark]*.

b) E.g. at rest, sodium-potassium pumps move sodium ions/ Na^+ out of the neurone cell / across the cell membrane to side A *[1 mark]*. This means that there will be more sodium ions outside of the cell compared to inside the neurone cell, as is shown in Figure 1 *[1 mark]*.

c) When a neurone is at rest sodium ion channels are not open / the cell membrane is not permeable to sodium ions *[1 mark]*.

d) The potassium ions are moved into the cell by sodium-potassium pumps *[1 mark]*, so the concentration of potassium ions is higher inside the cell than outside the cell *[1 mark]*. This causes potassium ions to diffuse out of the cell, down their concentration gradient, through potassium ion channels in the cell membrane *[1 mark]*.

e) The sodium ion channels will mainly be found at the nodes of Ranvier *[1 mark]*. This is because the rest of the axon is covered with a myelin sheath which acts as an electrical insulator *[1 mark]*. As depolarisation only takes place at the nodes of Ranvier, this is where the sodium ion channels are most densely located *[1 mark]*.

4 a) An endotherm is an animal that controls its body temperature internally by homeostasis *[1 mark]*.

b) Any two from: e.g. more sweat is secreted from sweat glands *[1 mark]*. As the water evaporates from the skin it takes heat from the body *[1 mark]*. / Erector pili muscles relax, so the hairs on the skin lie flat *[1 mark]*. This means less air is trapped, so the skin is less insulated *[1 mark]*. / Arterioles near the surface of the skin dilate *[1 mark]*. This means more blood flows through capillaries in the surface layers of the dermis, so more heat is lost from the skin by radiation *[1 mark]*.

c)* How to grade your answer:

Level 0: There is no relevant information. ***[No marks]***

Level 1: The answer gives some explanation of the responses which allow African wild dogs to maintain their body temperature at night or why most lizard species are not active at night. The answer has no clear structure. The information given is basic and lacking in detail. It may not all be relevant. ***[1 to 2 marks]***

Level 2: The answer gives some explanation of the responses which allow African wild dogs to maintain their body temperature at night and why most lizard species are not active at night. The answer has some structure. Most of the information given is relevant and there is some detail involved. ***[3 to 4 marks]***

Level 3: The answer gives a full explanation of the responses which allow African wild dogs to maintain their body temperature at night and why most lizard species are not active at night. The answer has a clear and logical structure. The information given is relevant and detailed. ***[5 to 6 marks]***

Indicative scientific content may include:

Responses which allow the African wild dog to maintain its body temperature at night:

In the African wild dog, thermoreceptors in the skin detect when the external temperature is too low, and send signals to the hypothalamus.

The hypothalamus then sends signals to effectors.

This triggers various responses, such as their hairs to stand upright, shivering, vasoconstriction of their blood vessels, reduced sweating, and release of adrenaline and thyroxine.

These physiological responses mean more heat is produced and conserved by the body.

The African wild dog can also change its behaviour to conserve heat at night, e.g. by sleeping.

Explanation for lizards not being active at night:

Lizards are ectotherms, so they can't control their body temperature internally.

Their internal temperature depends on the external temperature.

This means they will be less active at a lower temperature in order to conserve heat.

d) E.g. by sitting in a shaded area / by burrowing underground *[1 mark]*.

e) A larger body size means that heat takes longer to leave the body *[1 mark]*. Therefore, once Komodo dragons have initially warmed up, they can more easily maintain their body temperature throughout the day *[1 mark]*.

5 a) The lamellae will deform and press on the sensory nerve ending *[1 mark]*. This will cause the sensory neurone's cell membrane to stretch, opening the stretch-mediated sodium ion channels *[1 mark]*. The resulting influx of sodium/Na^+ ions will produce a generator potential *[1 mark]*.

b) The generator potential established as a result of the change may not reach the threshold needed to trigger an action potential *[1 mark]*.

c) The generator potential established as a result of the change may have been caused by a big stimulus, which would lead to several action potentials being produced *[1 mark]*.

d) a transducer *[1 mark]*

e) E.g. each type of receptor only responds to a specific stimulus *[1 mark]*, so different types of receptor are needed to detect the different types of mechanical stimuli *[1 mark]*.

Pages 78-81: Communication and Homeostasis — 2

1 a) The nerve impulses are conducted from one node of Ranvier to the next node of Ranvier / between patches of bare membrane / by saltatory conduction ***[1 mark]***.

b) E.g.

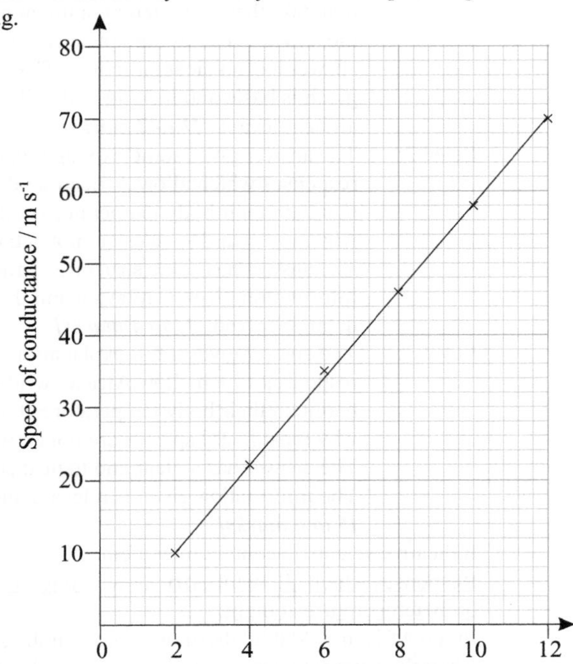

[2 marks — 1 mark for scatter graph with axon diameter on the x-axis (with correct units) and speed of conductance on the y-axis (with correct units), 1 mark for correct plotting of data points and correct line of best fit]

A line of best fit should pass through or near to as many data points as possible, ignoring any anomalous results.

c) 40 m s^{-1} ***[1 mark for an answer between 38 and 42]***

d) The speed of conductance would have been slower at each axon diameter, compared to the myelinated neurones ***[1 mark]***.

2 a) GABA hyperpolarises the postsynaptic membrane of Neurone D. / GABA makes the potential difference across the postsynaptic membrane of Neurone D more negative. ***[1 mark]***

b) Acetylcholine is released at an excitatory synapse, because when Neurones A and B are stimulated together, an action potential is initiated in Neurone D ***[1 mark]***.
GABA is released at an inhibitory synapse, because when Neurone C is stimulated along with either Neurone A or B, it prevents an action potential being initiated in Neurone D ***[1 mark]***.

c) When Neurones A, B and C are stimulated, the spatial summation of Neurones A and B is enough to counteract the inhibitory effect of Neurone C ***[1 mark]***. However, when only Neurones A and C are stimulated, there is not enough excitation to overcome the inhibition and generate an action potential ***[1 mark]***.

d) Metrifonate would prevent the breakdown of acetylcholine by inhibiting acetylcholinesterase/AChE ***[1 mark]***. This would mean that acetylcholine would remain on the receptors on the postsynaptic membrane of Neurone Y, so Neurone Y would continue to be depolarised/generate an action potential ***[1 mark]***.

3 a) $9.8 - 7.6 = 2.2$ mmol dm^{-3}
$(2.2 \div 9.8) \times 100 =$ **22.4%** (to 3 s.f.) ***[1 mark]***

b) The high GI food with the supplement caused the blood glucose concentration to rise more slowly after the food was eaten ***[1 mark]*** and to reach a lower maximum value of 7.6 mmol dm^{-3} compared to the high GI food without the supplement ***[1 mark]***.

c) Type 2 diabetes arises due to β cells not producing enough insulin / receptors not responding properly to the presence of insulin ***[1 mark]***. This means that the blood glucose concentration gets too high ***[1 mark]***, so the food supplement could be useful as it would help people with Type 2 diabetes manage their blood glucose concentration ***[1 mark]***.

d) Any two from: losing weight (if necessary) / eating a healthy, balanced diet / taking regular exercise / taking glucose-lowering medication / using insulin injections ***[2 marks]***.

4 a) Any four from: e.g. a stimulus excites the cardiac cell membrane, causing sodium ion channels to open ***[1 mark]***. This increases the permeability of the membrane to sodium ***[1 mark]***, so sodium ions diffuse into the cardiac cell, down their electrochemical gradient, making the cardiac cell membrane less negative ***[1 mark]***. If the potential difference reaches the threshold, voltage-gated sodium channels open, and more sodium ions diffuse into the cardiac cell ***[1 mark]*** by positive feedback, which depolarises the membrane ***[1 mark]***.

b) E.g. this means that the neurone/cardiac cell membrane is less permeable to potassium ions / fewer potassium ions can diffuse out of the neurone/cardiac cell ***[1 mark]***. So the potential difference across the cell membrane takes longer to change ***[1 mark]*** and therefore slows down the depolarisation stage of an action potential ***[1 mark]***.

c) E.g. disopyramide can increase the duration of the action potentials, resulting in fewer action potentials (in a certain amount of time) ***[1 mark]***. This may slow down the rate of heart muscle contractions, and therefore slow the beating of the heart/heart rate ***[1 mark]***.

Pages 82-85: Communication and Homeostasis — 3

1 a) cortex ***[1 mark]***

b) Adjacent cell signalling ***[1 mark]***. The stimulus is detected by the nervous system, and the nerve impulse is passed directly between neurones until it reaches the neurones in the hypothalamus, which then release CRH ***[1 mark]***.

c) Distant cell signalling ***[1 mark]***. ACTH travels through the blood from the anterior pituitary in the brain to the adrenal gland above the kidney ***[1 mark]***.

d) Cortisol levels will remain high ***[1 mark]*** because the negative feedback mechanism will no longer inhibit it ***[1 mark]***, which could result in the immune system being suppressed for longer / blood volume and pressure remaining high / glucose continuing to be produced by the breakdown of proteins and fats ***[1 mark]***.

2 a) Insulin binds to specific receptors on the liver and muscle cells/target cells ***[1 mark]***. It increases the permeability of the muscle/liver/target cells to glucose ***[1 mark]***.

b) E.g. insulin activates enzymes responsible for the conversion of glucose to glycogen/glycogenesis ***[1 mark]***.

c) Any five from: e.g. glucose enters the β cells by facilitated diffusion ***[1 mark]***. An increased amount of glucose in the β cells causes the rate of respiration to increase, meaning that more ATP is produced ***[1 mark]***. This triggers the potassium ion channels in the plasma membranes of the β cells to close, so potassium ions can't get through the membrane ***[1 mark]***. This means that the inside of the β cells become less negative, so the plasma membranes start to depolarise ***[1 mark]***. This triggers calcium ion channels in the membranes to open, so calcium ions diffuse into the β cells ***[1 mark]***. This causes vesicles to fuse with the plasma membranes of the β cells, releasing insulin ***[1 mark]***.

d) Glucagon acts to increase the concentration of glucose circulating in the blood ***[1 mark]***.

e) E.g. glucagon activates enzymes involved in the breakdown of glycogen into glucose/glycogenolysis ***[1 mark]***. Glucagon activates enzymes involved in the production of glucose from glycerol and amino acids/gluconeogenesis ***[1 mark]***.

f) E.g. adrenaline activates glycogenolysis/the breakdown of glycogen to glucose ***[1 mark]***, which increases the amount of glucose available for muscle cells to respire ***[1 mark]***.

3 a) To keep the internal environment roughly constant within certain limits ***[1 mark]***, so that cells/enzymes can function normally and are not damaged ***[1 mark]***.

b) When a physiological level deviates from its normal state, a mechanism returns the level back to within the normal range ***[1 mark]***.

c) A temperature above 40 °C may cause enzymes to be denatured ***[1 mark]***. This changes the shape of the enzyme's active site so that it no longer works as a catalyst, and as such the metabolic reactions are less efficient ***[1 mark]***.

d) Positive feedback ***[1 mark]*** because the body will no longer be cooled by sweating and so the body temperature will continue to rise ***[1 mark]***.

4 a) To ensure that the blood glucose concentration was not affected by any food consumed ***[1 mark]***.

b) People with Type 1 diabetes have a much higher blood glucose concentration than those without diabetes ***[1 mark]***. This is because their β cells/islets of Langerhans in the pancreas produce no/little insulin ***[1 mark]***, so they can't regulate their blood glucose concentration ***[1 mark]***.

c) i) Student's t-test ***[1 mark]***, because the mean values of two groups are being compared ***[1 mark]***.

ii) There is a significant difference between the blood glucose concentrations of patients with Type 1 diabetes and those without diabetes ***[1 mark]***, and there is a less than 5% probability that the results are due to chance ***[1 mark]***.

d) Type 1 diabetes is caused by an auto-immune disease ***[1 mark]***, in which the body attacks and destroys the β cells in the islets of langerhans ***[1 mark]***.

e) i) GM bacteria ***[1 mark]***

ii) It is less likely to trigger an allergic response / be rejected by the immune system ***[1 mark]***.

f) Stem cells could be grown into β cells ***[1 mark]***. The β cells would then be implanted into the pancreas of a person with Type 1 diabetes ***[1 mark]***. This means the person would be able to make insulin as normal ***[1 mark]***.

g) If blood glucose concentration is too low there won't be enough energy released from respiration for cells to carry out normal activities ***[1 mark]***.

Module 5 : Section 2 — Excretion

Pages 86-88: Excretion — 1

1 C ***[1 mark]***

2 A ***[1 mark]***

Ultrafiltration takes place in the glomeruli and Bowman's capsules, which are located in the kidney cortex. This is the outer part of the kidney, just below the renal capsule.

3 D ***[1 mark]***

1 g = 1000 mg, so you can multiply by 1000 to convert the amount of paracetamol ingested by each individual in g into mg. Then divide this number by the weight of each person in kg. Options A, B and C all give less than 150 mg per kg body weight.

4 a) i) It is the rate at which blood is filtered from the glomerulus into the Bowman's capsule ***[1 mark]***. A low glomerular filtration rate indicates that the kidneys aren't working properly because blood is being filtered more slowly than normal ***[1 mark]***.

ii) GFR ($ml/min/1.73m^2$) = $(0.41 \times \text{height in cm}) \div \text{creatinine in mg/dl}$

So creatinine in mg/dl = $(0.41 \times \text{height in cm}) \div \text{GFR } (ml/min/1.73m^2)$

$= (0.41 \times 165) \div 10.7$

$= 6.3224...$ mg/dl × 10 = **63.2 mg/l** (3 s.f.)

[2 marks for correct answer, otherwise 1 mark for (0.41 × 165) ÷ 10.7]

b) Proteins are normally too large to be filtered out of the blood ***[1 mark]*** so the presence of albumin in the urine may indicate a problem with the kidneys ***[1 mark]***.

c) i) The partially permeable membrane allows waste products and excess water to diffuse from the blood into the dialysis fluid ***[1 mark]***, but prevents blood cells and large molecules (e.g. proteins) from leaving the blood ***[1 mark]***.

ii) E.g. it maintains a concentration gradient from the blood into the dialysis fluid, so that waste products and excess water diffuse in the right direction ***[1 mark]***.

d) Any two from: e.g. urea may build up in the blood, causing vomiting and weight loss ***[1 mark]*** because urea can't be removed by the kidneys ***[1 mark]***. / Fluid may accumulate in the tissues, causing swelling ***[1 mark]*** because excess water cannot be removed by the kidneys ***[1 mark]***. / Bones may become brittle ***[1 mark]*** due to an imbalance in electrolytes/calcium and phosphate ions ***[1 mark]***. / A person may develop anaemia ***[1 mark]*** due to a lack of haemoglobin in the blood ***[1 mark]***.

5 a) Any two from: e.g. she should ensure that the kidneys all come from adult sheep and pigs ***[1 mark]*** as the relative size of the medulla may change as the animals develop/grow ***[1 mark]***. / She should also ensure that the kidneys are not diseased in any of the samples ***[1 mark]*** as diseased kidneys may be misshapen/hard to measure/have differently sized medullas ***[1 mark]***. / She should ensure that the kidneys have not begun to decompose ***[1 mark]*** as it may be more difficult to measure the size of the medullas if they have ***[1 mark]***.

b) How to grade your answer:

Level 0: There is no relevant information. ***[No marks]***

Level 1: The answer covers dissection, measurement or calculation. The answer has no clear structure. The information given is basic and lacking in detail. It may not all be relevant. ***[1 to 2 marks]***

Level 2: The answer covers dissection and either measurement or calculation. The answer has some structure. Most of the information given is relevant and there is some detail involved. ***[3 to 4 marks]***

Level 3: The answer covers dissection, measurement and calculation. The answer has a clear and logical structure. The information given is relevant and detailed. ***[5 to 6 marks]***

Indicative scientific content may include:

Dissection

Put on a pair of lab gloves and an apron/lab coat.
Place the kidneys on a dissecting tray.
Cut the kidneys in half lengthways using a scalpel/dissecting scissors.
Hold the kidney halves in place using dissecting pins.

Measurement

Identify the medulla for each kidney — this is the lighter area beneath the cortex.
Use a ruler to measure the width of each kidney and the width of the medulla in each kidney.

Calculation

For each kidney, divide the width of the medulla by the width of the whole kidney to obtain the relative width of the medulla to the kidney.

Add together the relative widths of the medulla for the three kidneys of each species. Divide this total by three to give the mean/average relative medulla width for each species. The average relative widths can then be compared between sheep and pigs.

Pages 89-91: Excretion — 2

1 a) A: glomerulus ***[1 mark]***
B: Bowman's capsule ***[1 mark]***

b) i) E.g. width of image = 9 mm
$9 \text{ mm} \times 1000 = 9000 \ \mu\text{m}$
actual size = size of image ÷ magnification
$= 9000 \ \mu\text{m} \div 300$
$= \mathbf{30 \ \mu m}$
[Accept values between 25 µm and 35 µm. 2 marks for a correct answer, otherwise 1 mark for the correct rearrangement of the magnification formula]

ii) Osmoreceptors in the hypothalamus detect a drop in the water content of the blood ***[1 mark]***. The hypothalamus sends nerve impulses to the posterior pituitary gland ***[1 mark]*** to release antidiuretic hormone/ADH into the blood ***[1 mark]***. ADH travels to the kidney and acts on the walls of the distal convoluted tubules and collecting ducts, making them more permeable to water ***[1 mark]***.

2 a) i) hepatic artery ***[1 mark]***, hepatic portal vein ***[1 mark]***

ii) Kupffer cells ***[1 mark]***

iii) Hepatocytes, since these cells are responsible for breaking down harmful substances ***[1 mark]***.

b) E.g. a test strip may be used to test for the presence of unprocessed bilirubin in the urine ***[1 mark]***. The test strip may contain bound diazo reactant on its surface ***[1 mark]***. When urine containing bilirubin is added to the test strip a colour change will occur, indicating that the patient may have some liver damage ***[1 mark]***.

3 E.g. it could mean that ammonia isn't processed for excretion quickly enough ***[1 mark]***. This could lead to a build-up of ammonia, which is toxic ***[1 mark]***.

4 a) i)

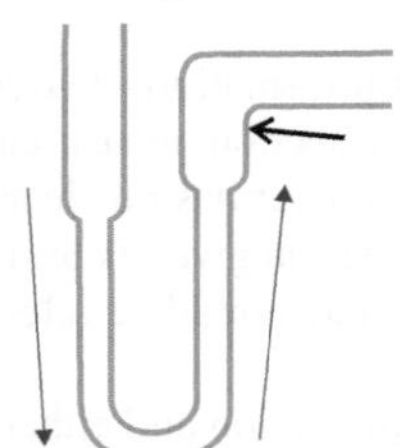

[1 mark]

ii) Actively transporting ions into the medulla increases the concentration of ions in the medulla and lowers its water potential ***[1 mark]***. This causes water to move out of (the descending limb of) the loop of Henle into the medulla by osmosis ***[1 mark]***. This reduces the water content of the filtrate in the loop of Henle so it becomes more concentrated ***[1 mark]***.

b) Animals that live in dry conditions need to conserve more water than those in wetter conditions ***[1 mark]***. Long loops of Henle mean that more water is absorbed from the filtrate ***[1 mark]*** and so more water is retained by the body/less water is lost in the urine ***[1 mark]***.

Module 5 : Section 3 — Animal Responses

Pages 92-95: Animal Responses — 1

1 D ***[1 mark]***

2 C ***[1 mark]***

Although the knee-jerk reflex does not involve a relay neurone, it does involve a motor neurone in the spinal cord (which is part of the CNS).

3 C ***[1 mark]***

The peripheral nervous system connects the brain and spinal cord to the rest of the body — the autonomic nervous system is a functional system within the peripheral nervous system. It controls unconscious activities.

4 a) i) cerebrum / cerebral cortex ***[1 mark]***

ii) Any two from: e.g. vision / hearing / learning / thinking ***[2 marks]***

b) i) Structure B/the hypothalamus stimulates the pituitary gland to release the hormone ACTH ***[1 mark]***. ACTH causes the adrenal glands to release steroidal hormones involved in the 'fight or flight' response ***[1 mark]***. / Structure B/the hypothalamus activates the sympathetic nervous system ***[1 mark]***, which stimulates the adrenal glands to release adrenaline ***[1 mark]***.

ii) Any two from: e.g. the muscles around the bronchioles relax. / Glycogen is converted to glucose. / Muscles in the arterioles supplying the skin and gut constrict. / Muscles in the arterioles supplying the heart, lungs and skeletal muscles dilate. / Erector pili muscles in the skin contract. ***[2 marks]***

iii) Structure C/the medulla oblongata receives and processes information from receptors indicating that heart rate needs to increase ***[1 mark]***. It then sends impulses along sympathetic motor neurones/the accelerator nerve to the SAN/sinoatrial node ***[1 mark]***. The sympathetic neurones/ the accelerator nerve release(s)noradrenaline, which binds to receptors on the SAN/sinoatrial node, causing it to increase heart rate ***[1 mark]***.

5 a)

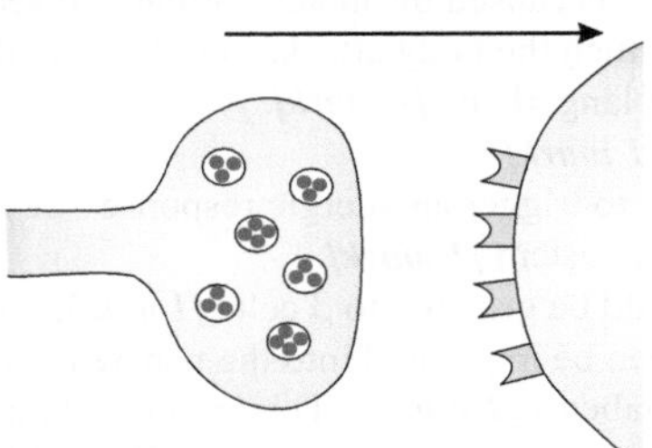

[1 mark for drawing an arrow pointing to the right.]

b) The receptors for the neurotransmitter are only found on the postsynaptic membrane ***[1 mark]***, so the neurotransmitter can only trigger an action potential at the postsynaptic membrane ***[1 mark]***.

c) The action potential depolarises the sarcolemma ***[1 mark]***, and this depolarisation spreads down the T-tubules to the sarcoplasmic reticulum ***[1 mark]***. The depolarisation of the sarcoplasmic reticulum causes the release of calcium ions throughout the muscle fibre ***[1 mark]***.

d) Calcium ions result in tropomyosin being pulled out of the actin-myosin binding site ***[1 mark]***, which allows the attachment between myosin and actin to occur ***[1 mark]***. Calcium ions activate the enzyme ATPase ***[1 mark]***, which breaks down ATP to provide the energy needed for muscle contraction ***[1 mark]***.

e) E.g. at neuromuscular junctions, curare would compete with acetylcholine for acetylcholine receptors on the postsynaptic membrane ***[1 mark]***. At a high dose, curare would block all of the acetylcholine receptors and prevent acetylcholine binding ***[1 mark]***. This means that acetylcholine released from the motor neurone wouldn't lead to the generation of a response in the muscle cell ***[1 mark]***. So the presence of curare would inhibit muscle contraction / prevent muscle contraction being triggered ***[1 mark]***.

6 a) I-band ***[1 mark]***

b) H-zone ***[1 mark]***, because this part contains only myosin filaments and no actin filaments ***[1 mark]***.

c) i) H-zone and I-band ***[1 mark]***.

ii) E.g. the myosin heads bind to the binding sites on the actin filaments, forming cross bridges ***[1 mark]***. The myosin heads then bend and pull the actin filaments along the length of the myosin ***[1 mark]***. Many cross bridges form and break very rapidly, pulling the actin filaments along and shortening the sarcomere ***[1 mark]***.

iii) ATP is hydrolysed by ATPase ***[1 mark]*** to release the energy needed to move the myosin head and to break the actin-myosin cross bridges ***[1 mark]***.

Pages 96-98: Animal Responses — 2

1 a) i) $\bar{x}_1 = 70$ $\bar{x}_2 = 87$

$s_1 = 3.12$ $s_2 = 3.93$

$$t = \frac{70 - 87}{\sqrt{(3.12^2 / 8) + (3.93^2 / 8)}}$$

$t = \mathbf{-9.58}$ (2 d.p.)

[2 marks for the correct answer, otherwise 1 mark for the correct working.]

ii) The scientist should reject the null hypothesis because the critical value, 2.15, is lower than the test statistic, 9.58 ***[1 mark]***. ***[Award 1 mark for the wrong answer carried forward, with a correct explanation.]***

You can ignore the minus sign when comparing your test statistic to the critical value.

b) Any four from: e.g. the difference in the means for each group is statistically significant, suggesting this stress test did increase heart rate ***[1 mark]***. However, the investigation only included one stressful scenario, so other forms of stress may produce different results ***[1 mark]***. The sample size was very small, so the results might show bias ***[1 mark]***. The results may be different for women rather than men / for a different age group ***[1 mark]***. Overall, the scientist's conclusion is not valid for these results ***[1 mark]***. ***[Maximum of 4 marks available.]***

2* How to grade your answer:

Level 0: There is no relevant information. ***[No marks]***

Level 1: The answer gives some explanation of how the structure or properties of one muscle are related to its function. The answer has no clear structure. The information given is basic and lacking in detail. It may not all be relevant. ***[1 to 2 marks]***

Level 2: The answer gives some explanation of how the structures or properties of two of the muscles are related to their function. The answer has some structure. Most of the information given is relevant and there is some detail involved. ***[3 to 4 marks]***

Level 3: The answer gives an explanation of how the structures or properties of all three muscles are related to their function. The answer has a clear and logical structure. The information given is relevant and detailed. ***[5 to 6 marks]***

Indicative scientific content may include:

<u>Deltoid muscle</u>

The deltoid muscle is skeletal muscle.

This means it's made up of many muscle fibres, which are each made up of many myofibrils.

Myofibrils are specialised for contraction because they contain protein myofilaments of myosin and actin, which move past each other to make the muscle contract.

The muscle fibres also contain lots of mitochondria to provide the ATP that is needed for muscle contraction.

The deltoid muscle is used for short, quick bursts of contraction only, e.g. to lift the arm up, so is likely to fatigue easily.

<u>Muscularis externa</u>

The muscularis externa is an involuntary muscle.

This means that it doesn't require a decision to function, so it can constantly keep food moving through the body.

The muscle fibres contract slowly, so nutrients can be absorbed from the food as it's moved through the intestines.

The muscle fibres don't fatigue, so food is kept moving through the intestines.

<u>Cardiac muscle</u>

Cardiac muscle cells are myogenic, so they contract on their own.

The muscle fibres in cardiac muscle are connected by intercalated discs. These have low electrical resistance, so electrical impulses can pass freely between cells.

Each muscle fibre is also branched, so electrical impulses pass quickly through the whole muscle.

This allows the muscle fibres in cardiac cells to contract quickly and rhythmically. This means that blood is kept constantly flowing round the body at a controlled rate.

Cardiac muscle fibres don't fatigue. This means there's no interruption to blood flow.

3 a) i) Individual 3: = ((96 − 81) ÷ 81) × 100 = **18.5%** (1 d.p.) ***[1 mark]***

Individual 4 = (85.8 − 69) ÷ 69) × 100 = **24.3%** (1 d.p.) ***[1 mark]***

The formula for calculating percentage difference is:
% difference = ((final value − original value) ÷ original value) × 100.

ii) Mean percentage increase = (22.7 + 7.9 + 18.5 + 24.3) ÷ 4 = **18.4%** (1 d.p.) ***[1 mark for correct answer, and if incorrect answer(s) are carried forward from 3 a) i), give full marks for correct working]***

b) E.g. as creatine is part of creatine phosphate, creatine supplements might increase the amount of creatine phosphate available in the muscles ***[1 mark]***. This could mean that the muscles will be able to generate more ATP in a given time, as creatine phosphate is broken down to make ATP ***[1 mark]***. More ATP present could mean that there's more energy available for muscle contraction,which might improve a weightlifter's performance ***[1 mark]***.

c) E.g. the weightlifters may have been tired already since they had lifted weights previously in the same day, which may have meant they were not fully recovered before the second lifting session and performed worse as a result. / The creatine may only be effective over a long period of time/when taken at particular times before or after exercising, therefore the investigation might not have assessed the impact of taking creatine effectively ***[4 marks available — 1 mark for each reason and 1 mark for each corresponding supporting explanation]***.

There are other possible answers for this question. Award yourself marks for other reasonable reasons (and explanations) too.

Module 5 : Section 4 — Plant Responses and Hormones

Pages 99-102: Plant Responses and Hormones

1 C ***[1 mark]***

2 A ***[1 mark]***

Thigmotropism is plant growth in response to contact with an object and here the tentacles grow in response to contact with the insect.

3 D ***[1 mark]***

Statement 2 would have been correct if it read 'In shoots, auxins move to the more shaded part of the plant and stimulate cell elongation, thus causing the shoot to bend towards the light'. Statement 3 would have been correct if it read 'In roots, auxins move to the more shaded part of the plant and inhibit cell elongation, thus causing the root to bend away from the light.'

4 a) positive phototropism ***[1 mark]***

b) The results suggest that indoleacetic acid/IAA is produced in the shoot tip ***[1 mark]***, because seedling B didn't curve towards the light but seedling D did ***[1 mark]***.

c) Any two from: e.g. the distance the shoot was from the light source. / The intensity of the light source. / The temperature that the seedling was grown at. / The amount of water available to the seedling. ***[2 marks]***

d) **A**: light did not reach the shoot tip since it was covered in tin foil, so light couldn't influence the distribution of indoleacetic acid/IAA and stimulate cell elongation in the shoot ***[1 mark]***.

B: the shoot tip had been removed, so indoleacetic acid/IAA didn't diffuse down the shoot and stimulate cell elongation ***[1 mark]***.

e) The light caused the indoleacetic acid/IAA to accumulate on the shaded side of the shoot (and stimulate growth there) in both seedlings ***[1 mark]***.

5 a) herbivory ***[1 mark]***

b) i) Any two from: e.g. plants may release alkaloids ***[1 mark]***, which are poisonous to many insects ***[1 mark]***. / Plants may release tannins ***[1 mark]***, which can bind to proteins in the animal's gut, making the plant hard to digest ***[1 mark]***. / Plants may release pheromones ***[1 mark]***, which are chemical signals that may produce a defence response in other, nearby plants ***[1 mark]***.

ii) E.g. lack of water/drought ***[1 mark]***

c) i) Ethene stimulates enzymes that break down cell walls / break down chlorophyll / convert starch into sugars ***[1 mark]***. This helps to make the fruit soft, ripe and ready to eat ***[1 mark]***.

ii) E.g. auxins are used in selective weedkillers (herbicides) ***[1 mark]***. Auxins make weeds produce long stems instead of lots of leaves ***[1 mark]***. This makes the weeds grow too fast, so they can't get enough water or nutrients, so they die ***[1 mark]***. / Auxins are used as rooting hormones (e.g. in rooting powder) ***[1 mark]***. Auxins make a cutting (part of the plant, e.g. a stem cutting) grow roots ***[1 mark]***. The cutting can then be planted and grown into a new plant ***[1 mark]***.

6 a) As the concentration of GA_3 increased, the number of seeds that successfully germinated also increased, from 11.7% at 0 mg dm^{-3} to 83.3% at 1000 mg dm^{-3} of GA_3 ***[1 mark]***. This is because GA_3 is a gibberellin, so it stimulates seed germination by triggering the breakdown of starch into glucose in the seed ***[1 mark]***, which the plant embryo can then use to begin respiring and release the energy it needs to grow ***[1 mark]***.

b) To reduce the effect of random error on the experiment ***[1 mark]***, which makes the results more precise ***[1 mark]***.

c) E.g. they could have taken 10 cm^3 of the 1000 mg dm^{-3} solution and added 90 cm^3 of distilled water — this would have given them a 100 mg dm^{-3} solution ***[1 mark]***. They could have then taken 50 cm^3 of the 100 mg dm^{-3} solution and added 50 cm^3 of distilled water — this would have given them a 50 mg dm^{-3} solution ***[1 mark]***.

Module 5 : Section 5 — Photosynthesis

Pages 103-106: Photosynthesis — 1

1 A ***[1 mark]***

2 B ***[1 mark]***

3 a) Chlorophyll a absorbs most light at 410-425 nm and 675 nm ***[1 mark]***. There is no/very little absorption between 450-600 nm ***[1 mark]***. / Chlorophyll a absorbs violet/blue light and orange/red light ***[1 mark]***. There is no/very little absorption of green/yellow light ***[1 mark]***.

b) The light energy excites the electrons in the chlorophyll, leading to their release from the photosystem ***[1 mark]***.

c) To make ATP from ADP and inorganic phosphate/for the photophosphorylation of ADP ***[1 mark]***. To make reduced NADP from NADP ***[1 mark]***. To split water into protons/ H^+ ions, electrons and oxygen/for the photolysis of water ***[1 mark]***.

d) Carbon dioxide concentration / temperature ***[1 mark]***.

4 a) E.g. rate of uptake of carbon dioxide ***[1 mark]***.

b) By controlling all the variables, so only the effect of light intensity on the rate of photosynthesis was being tested ***[1 mark]***.

c) Any four from: e.g. at both low and high CO_2 concentrations, the rate of O_2 release increases with decreasing distance from the lamp, up until 0.5 m ***[1 mark]***, so light is the limiting factor up until 0.5 m ***[1 mark]***. Then at 0.5 m for each CO_2 concentration the rate of O_2 release levels off ***[1 mark]***, as CO_2 becomes the limiting factor ***[1 mark]***. The values for high CO_2 concentration level off at a higher O_2 release rate as high CO_2 concentration becomes limiting less quickly ***[1 mark]***. ***[Maximum of 4 marks available.]***

d) E.g. set up more than one beaker containing an aquatic plant at each CO_2 concentration and record a mean of the rate of photosynthesis/rate of O_2 release ***[1 mark]***.

e) Plot distance on the x-axis and the rate that O_2 is released on the y-axis ***[1 mark]***. Plot data as a line graph ***[1 mark]***, because the data is continuous ***[1 mark]***.

f) light intensity = $1 / d^2$

light intensity = $1 / 0.5^2$ = **4** arbitrary units ***[1 mark]***

In the table, from 0.5 m to 0.25 m, the rate of O_2 release does not increase for the aquatic plant exposed to a low CO_2 concentration, so 0.5 m is the distance at which photosynthesis has become limited.

5 a) The electrons from photosystem II move along the electron transport chain in the thylakoid membrane ***[1 mark]***, which results in the release of energy ***[1 mark]***. Some of this energy is used to generate a proton gradient across the thylakoid membrane ***[1 mark]***. Protons move down their concentration gradient into the stroma, via ATP synthase, which releases energy that allows ADP and P_i to combine and form ATP ***[1 mark]***.

b) ATP provides the energy ***[1 mark]***, and reduced NADP provides the H^+ ions/protons, to turn glycerate 3-phosphate/GP into triose phosphate/TP ***[1 mark]***. ATP also provides the energy to regenerate RuBP ***[1 mark]***.

Pages 107-108: Photosynthesis — 2

1 a) Any four from: e.g. extract the pigments from some of the plant's leaves by grinding up the leaves and adding, e.g. anhydrous sodium sulfate, a few drops of propanone and then some petroleum ether ***[1 mark]***. Take some of the liquid pigment extract and build up a concentrated spot/point of origin on a thin layer chromatography plate ***[1 mark]***. Put the chromatography plate in a glass beaker containing a small volume of solvent ***[1 mark]***. Put a lid on the beaker and leave it to develop ***[1 mark]***. When the solvent has almost reached the top of the plate, remove the plate and mark on the solvent front ***[1 mark]***. Calculate the R_f values of the separated pigments in order to identify them ***[1 mark]***. ***[Maximum of 4 marks available]***

b) E.g. wear gloves / wear goggles because many of the chemicals involved are toxic ***[1 mark]***. Use a fume cupboard when using volatile chemicals like petroleum ether because the vapours are hazardous ***[1 mark]***.

c) R_f value = distance travelled by solute ÷ distance travelled by solvent
R_f value = 9.3 cm ÷ 9.7 cm = 0.958... = 0.96
Pigment X = carotene ***[1 mark]***

You can see from table 1 that the closest R_f value to 0.96 is 0.95, which is the R_f value for carotene, so pigment X is most likely carotene.

d) The mobile phase moves through/over the stationary phase ***[1 mark]***. The pigments spend different amounts of time in the mobile phase and the stationary phase ***[1 mark]***. The pigments that spend longer in the mobile phase travel faster/further, so different pigments are separated out ***[1 mark]***.

e) They could demonstrate that their results are repeatable by repeating the experiment themselves and getting similar results ***[1 mark]***. They could demonstrate that their results are reproducible by someone else repeating the experiment and getting similar results ***[1 mark]***.

2 a) RuBisCo/ribulose bisphosphate carboxylase ***[1 mark]***

b) RuBP allows the light-independent reaction to continue because CO_2 reacts with RuBP to form GP ***[1 mark]***. Glucose is used as an energy source for respiration / used to make other important molecules, e.g. cellulose ***[1 mark]***.

c) Reducing the length of time that stomata are open for will reduce the amount of CO_2 that enters the plant ***[1 mark]***. This means the amount of GP/glycerate 3-phosphate being made would decrease ***[1 mark]***, as there is less CO_2 available for RuBP to combine with ***[1 mark]***.

When working out the answers to questions on the light-independent reaction it's a good idea to sketch out the reaction (like below) to see exactly what will be affected when different factors are changed.

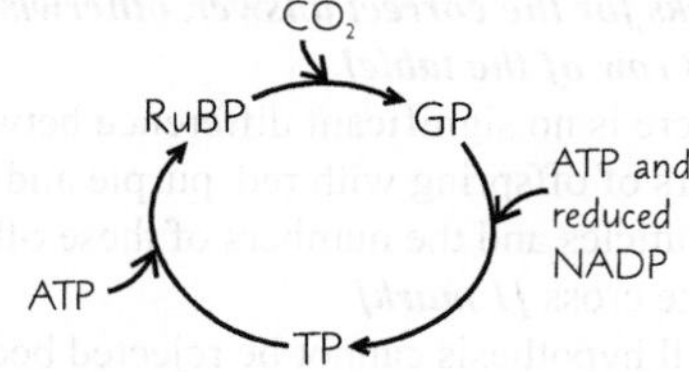

Module 5 : Section 6 — Respiration

Pages 109-110: Respiration — 1

1 D ***[1 mark]***
2 C ***[1 mark]***
3 A ***[1 mark]***

You need to be able to recall this equation for your exam:
RQ = Volume of CO_2 released ÷ Volume of O_2 consumed
In this case, 8 molecules of carbon dioxide are produced and 5 molecules of oxygen are consumed. 8 ÷ 5 = 1.6

4 a) X = cytoplasm, Y = mitochondrial matrix ***[1 mark]***

b) i) Glucose is phosphorylated by adding two phosphates from two molecules of ATP ***[1 mark]***. This creates one molecule of hexose bisphosphate ***[1 mark]*** and two molecules of ADP ***[1 mark]***.

ii) Pyruvate is decarboxylated, forming one molecule of CO_2 ***[1 mark]***. One molecule of NAD is reduced to NADH ***[1 mark]***, by collecting hydrogen from pyruvate ***[1 mark]***. This changes pyruvate into acetate ***[1 mark]***. Acetate then combines with coenzyme A to produce acetyl coenzyme A ***[1 mark]***.

c) i) During anaerobic respiration pyruvate is converted into lactate ***[1 mark]*** using reduced NAD/NADH ***[1 mark]***. This regenerates oxidised NAD ***[1 mark]***, which can be used to oxidise substance B/triose phosphate into pyruvate and therefore maintain glycolysis ***[1 mark]***.

ii) Anaerobic respiration only includes one energy-releasing stage, which is glycolysis ***[1 mark]***. The energy-releasing reactions of the Krebs cycle and oxidative phosphorylation need oxygen, so they can't occur in anaerobic conditions ***[1 mark]***.

Pages 111-112: Respiration — 2

1 a) As more CO_2 is released by the respiring yeast, the pH of the solution may fall, which will affect the results ***[1 mark]***. This decreases the validity of the experiment because not all of the variables have been controlled ***[1 mark]***.

b) The curves plateau/level off ***[1 mark]***. This is because glucose is used up / the yeast cells start to die due to toxic build up of ethanol ***[1 mark]***.

c) E.g.

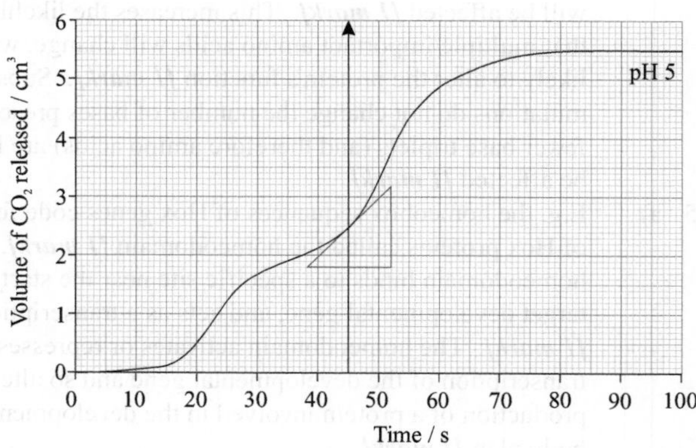

Rate at pH 5: 1.4 ÷ 14 = 0.10 $cm^3\ s^{-1}$
[2 marks for correct answer, 1 mark for correct working — accept answers between 0.09 and 0.11 cm^3s^{-1}]

2 a) NAD ***[1 mark]***
FAD ***[1 mark]***

b) i) She could have added methylene blue to glucose in the absence of yeast / in the presence of boiled/inactive/dead yeast ***[1 mark]***. All other conditions would be kept the same ***[1 mark]***.

ii) E.g. temperature ***[1 mark]*** – used a water bath ***[1 mark]***. pH ***[1 mark]*** – added a buffer ***[1 mark]***.

c) Shaking the tube would mix the solution with oxygen ***[1 mark]***. This would oxidise methylene blue / methylene blue would give up its electrons ***[1 mark]***.

d) The electrons released pass down the electron transport chain, releasing energy ***[1 mark]***. This energy is used to pump protons from the mitochondrial matrix to the intermembrane space, forming an electrochemical gradient ***[1 mark]***. Protons then move down the electrochemical gradient, back into the mitochondrial matrix, through ATP synthase, resulting in the generation of ATP ***[1 mark]***.

Module 6 : Section 1 — Cellular Control

Pages 113-115: Cellular Control

1 A ***[1 mark]***
2 D ***[1 mark]***
3 D ***[1 mark]***

RNA polymerase must bind to the promoter for transcription to begin. The operator does not code for a protein — it is a sequence of DNA that transcription factors (in this case the lac repressor) bind to.

4 a) i) The introns in the primary mRNA sequence would be removed (by splicing) resulting in a mature mRNA molecule ***[1 mark]***.

ii) E.g. the transcription factor that is needed to switch on the lactase gene is expressed in the cells of the small intestine but not in other body cells ***[1 mark]***.

b) i) E.g. it could increase the rate at which the gene is transcribed ***[1 mark]***. This would mean that more lactase mRNA gets produced, so more lactase will be made, compared to a wild-type adult without the lactase persistence mutation ***[1 mark]***.

ii) E.g. it allows adults to consume and derive nutrients from milk/dairy products ***[1 mark]***.

c) i) Any two from: e.g. the mutation could produce a base triplet that still codes for the same amino acid ***[1 mark]***. / The mutation could produce a base triplet that codes for a chemically similar amino acid, so that it functions like the original ***[1 mark]***. / The mutation could produce a base triplet that codes for an amino acid that's not involved with the protein's function ***[1 mark]***.

ii) E.g. insertion and deletion mutations change the number of bases present in the DNA sequence ***[1 mark]***. This changes the way the base sequence is read, so multiple base triplets will be affected ***[1 mark]***. This increases the likelihood that multiple/important amino acids will change, which is likely to alter the protein's function ***[1 mark]***. Substitution mutations do not change the number of bases present, so fewer base triplets (and therefore amino acids) are likely to be affected ***[1 mark]***.

5 a) E.g. the homeobox sequences of Hox genes code for a part of Hox proteins called the homeodomain ***[1 mark]***. The homeodomain binds to a specific site near the start of its target developmental gene, and acts as a transcription factor ***[1 mark]***. The homeodomain activates or represses the transcription of the developmental gene and so alters the production of a protein involved in the development of the body plan ***[1 mark]***.

b) E.g. it controls the number/size of digits in the limb ***[1 mark]***.

c) An internal/external stimulus triggers apoptosis in the cells that make up the webbing ***[1 mark]***. This causes enzymes inside the cells to break down the cell components ***[1 mark]***. This causes the cells to break up into fragments, which are engulfed and digested by phagocytosis ***[1 mark]***.

Module 6 : Section 2 — Patterns of Inheritance

Pages 116-119: Patterns of Inheritance — 1

1 D ***[1 mark]***
2 D ***[1 mark]***

A dihybrid cross between two heterozygotes always produces a 9 : 3 : 3 : 1 ratio in the offspring (unless there's linkage or epistasis involved).

3 B ***[1 mark]***

If you struggled with this question, you could have sketched a quick genetic diagram to help you work out the answer, e.g.

	X^M	Y
X^M	X^MX^M Unaffected	X^MY Unaffected
X^m	X^MX^m Unaffected	X^mY Has Menkes disease

4 a) i) Because both alleles are expressed in the phenotype, so the insects appear both red and purple ***[1 mark]***. Neither allele is recessive / dominant over the other ***[1 mark]***.

ii) A homozygous genotype is one where the organism has two copies of the same allele, e.g. P^RP^R / P^PP^P / P^yP^y ***[1 mark]***. A heterozygous genotype is one where the organism has two different alleles for the same gene, e.g. P^RP^y / P^PP^y / P^PP^R ***[1 mark]***.

b) E.g.

Gametes' alleles

Gametes' alleles	P^R	P^y
P^R	P^RP^R Red	P^RP^y Red
P^P	P^PP^R Red with purple spots	P^PP^y Purple

possible genotypes and phenotypes of offspring

Expected phenotypic ratio: **2:1:1 (red : red with purple spots : purple)**

[3 marks — 1 mark for the correct gametes, 1 mark for the correct genotypes of offspring, plus 1 mark for the correct phenotypic ratio]

c) i)

Phenotype	Expected Result (E)	Observed Result (O)	(O – E)	$(O-E)^2$	$\frac{(O-E)^2}{E}$
Red cuticle	44	48	4	16	0.364
Purple cuticle	22	19	-3	9	0.409
Red cuticle with purple spots	22	21	-1	1	0.045
Total	88	88	–	–	0.818

$\chi^2 = \mathbf{0.818}$

[3 marks for the correct answer, otherwise 1 mark for each correct row of the table]

ii) E.g. there is no significant difference between the observed numbers of offspring with red, purple and red with purple spots cuticles and the numbers of these offspring expected from the cross ***[1 mark]***.

iii) The null hypothesis cannot be rejected because the chi-squared value is lower than the critical value ***[1 mark]***.

iv) There is a greater than 5% probability that the difference between the observed and expected results is due to chance ***[1 mark]***.

5 a) coloured full and colourless shrunken ***[1 mark]***
b) E.g. there are more coloured full and colourless shrunken offspring than expected ***[1 mark]***. This suggests that the heterozygous parent plant produced mostly CS and cs gametes ***[1 mark]***. For the alleles to be inherited together like this, the colour and shape genes must be autosomally linked / on the same chromosome/autosome ***[1 mark]***.
c) E.g. chlorosis (which is where plants don't produce enough chlorophyll and turn yellow) ***[1 mark]*** is caused by environmental factors such as a lack of magnesium in the soil ***[1 mark]***. / Etiolation (which is where plants grow abnormally long and spindly) ***[1 mark]*** is caused by the plant not getting enough light ***[1 mark]***.

Pages 120-122: Patterns of Inheritance — 2

1 a) E.g.

Gametes' alleles	G	g
g	Gg grey	gg non-grey
g	Gg grey	gg non-grey

(rows: Gametes' alleles; cells: possible genotypes and phenotypes of offspring)

Expected phenotypic ratio: **1:1 (grey : non-grey)**
[3 marks — 1 mark for the correct gametes, 1 mark for the correct genotypes of offspring, plus 1 mark for the correct phenotypic ratio]

b) i) Epistasis ***[1 mark]***.
ii)

Genotype	Pigment produced
EeWw	none
Eeww	black
eeww	red

[1 mark for three correct phenotypes]

iii) E.g. parental genotypes: WwEe × wwee
So the genotypes of the offspring and pigments produced are:

	WE	wE	We	we
we	WwEe (white/ none)	wwEe (black)	Wwee (white/ none)	wwee (red)

Probability of offspring producing black pigment: ¼ / 25% / 0.25
[3 marks — 1 mark for the correct parental genotypes/ correct gametes, 1 mark for the correct genotypes of the offspring, and 1 mark for the correct probability]

iv) It means that the genes are (autosomally) linked ***[1 mark]***. This means that their alleles are more likely to be inherited together by the offspring ***[1 mark]***, which will alter the phenotypic ratio in the offspring ***[1 mark]***.

2 a) i) RM and rm ***[1 mark]***
ii) All offspring will have multiple red flowers per stem ***[1 mark]***.
All of the offspring would have the genotype RrMm.

b) i)

Phenotype	Expected Result (E)	Observed Result (O)	O – E	$(O - E)^2$	$\frac{(O-E)^2}{E}$
Multiple red flowers	36	46	10	100	2.778
Single red flower	12	11	-1	1	0.083
Multiple yellow flowers	12	7	-5	25	2.083
Single yellow flower	4	0	-4	16	4.000
					8.944

χ^2 = **8.944**
[3 marks for the correct answer, otherwise 1 mark for column $(O - E)^2$ being correct and 1 mark for column $(O - E)^2/E$ being correct]

ii) Yes there is a significant difference, because the chi-squared value is larger than the critical value of 7.82 at $p = 0.05$ ***[1 mark]***. This means we can be 95% confident that the results are not due to chance / there is only a 5% probability that the difference is due chance ***[1 mark]***.
iii) Any two from: e.g. the genes could exhibit autosomal linkage ***[1 mark]***, making some certain combinations of alleles in the gametes more likely than others ***[1 mark]***. / The genes could exhibit epistasis ***[1 mark]***, resulting in some genotypes being hidden/overrepresented in the phenotypic ratio ***[1 mark]***. / The genes could be sex-linked ***[1 mark]***, resulting in the phenotype being more likely in males than females or vice versa ***[1 mark]***.

c) Because offspring produced by asexual reproduction/ mitosis are genetically identical/clones ***[1 mark]***, whereas sexual reproduction involves meiosis ***[1 mark]*** and the random fusion of gametes at fertilisation, both of which create genetic variation in a population ***[1 mark]***.

Module 6: Section 3 — Evolution

Pages 123-125: Evolution — 1

1 B ***[1 mark]***
Allopatric speciation is when new species develop as a result of geographical isolation. This is what's being described here — two squirrel populations have been geographically isolated by the canyon and evolved into two separate species.

2 C ***[1 mark]***
Stabilising selection is when individuals with alleles for characteristics towards the middle of the range are more likely to survive and reproduce. In this instance, it means that extremes of fur colour become less common.

3 D ***[1 mark]***

4 a) E.g. the Hardy-Weinberg principle assumes that immigration/emigration isn't happening, but the flow of genes suggests that it is ***[1 mark]***.
b) Because the two populations are geographically isolated, alleles are not passed between them ***[1 mark]***. Due to different selection pressures/genetic drift, the allele frequencies will change independently in each population ***[1 mark]***. This could increase the differences/variation between the gene pools of the two populations ***[1 mark]***, eventually leading to reproductive isolation ***[1 mark]***.
c) The flow of genes may reduce/stop ***[1 mark]*** because members of population two are no longer able to attract members of population one ***[1 mark]*** and the two populations stop interbreeding ***[1 mark]***.

5 a) i)

Latitude / ° N	Allele frequency 'W'	Allele frequency 'w'
64	0.62	**0.38**
66	**0.67**	0.33
68	**0.83**	0.17
70	0.92	0.08

[1 mark]

p + q = 1, so the allele frequencies should add up to 1.0 here.

ii) p = 0.92 and q = 0.08.
Frequency of white fur phenotype = $p^2 + 2pq$ = $(0.92^2) + (2 \times 0.92 \times 0.08)$ = **0.99** (to 2 s.f.)
[2 marks for the correct answer, otherwise 1 mark for $p^2 + 2pq = (0.92^2) + (2 \times 0.92 \times 0.08)$]

The question tells you that the 'W' allele is dominant, so to work out the frequency of the white fur phenotype you need to calculate the frequency of the heterozygous individuals (2pq) as well as the frequency of the homozygous dominant individuals (p^2).

b) E.g. the snowy weather acts as a selection pressure on the rodents ***[1 mark]***. The 'W' allele results in the white fur phenotype, which will provide camouflage in snow ***[1 mark]***. Rodents with the white fur phenotype at higher latitudes are more likely to survive and pass on their alleles (including the 'W' allele) than rodents with the brown fur phenotype ***[1 mark]***. After many generations, the frequency of the 'W' allele will have increased in the populations at higher latitudes ***[1 mark]***.

c) The allele frequencies do not add up to 1, suggesting that there are more than two alleles for fur colour in this population ***[1 mark]***.

Pages 126-127: Evolution — 2

1 a) Artificial selection will have reduced the gene pool, because only the highest yielding plants were chosen for breeding ***[1 mark]***. This means that if a new disease appears, there's less chance of the alleles that offer resistance to that disease being present in the population ***[1 mark]***.

b) E.g. the genetic material of the ancestor species, which has not undergone any artificial selection, is being preserved ***[1 mark]***. This could allow useful alleles that have been lost during artificial selection (e.g. alleles that offer disease resistance) to be reintroduced to commercially grown tomato populations in future ***[1 mark]***.

c) E.g. artificial selection in animals can cause health problems / increase the incidence of genetic disease ***[1 mark]***.

2 a) q^2 = the yellow phenotype frequency = 0.25, so $q = \sqrt{0.25}$
$p = 1 - q = 1 - \sqrt{0.25}$
The frequency of the heterozygous genotype = 2pq
$= 2 \times (1 - \sqrt{0.25}) \times (\sqrt{0.25})$ = **0.5**
[3 marks for the correct answer, otherwise 1 mark for $q^2 = 0.25$ and 1 mark for $2pq = 2 \times (1 - \sqrt{0.25}) \times (\sqrt{0.25})$]

Because the yellow phenotype can only arise when the individual contains two copies of the recessive allele, the frequency of the homozygous recessive phenotype (yellow) is equal to the frequency of the homozygous recessive genotype (q^2), which is why you can use 'q^2 = 0.25' in this equation.

b) The phenotype frequencies seem to be changing randomly ***[1 mark]***, but if selection was acting on the trait then there would be a trend/direction to the change ***[1 mark]***. This is because one phenotype would increase an individual's chance of survival, so it would become more common ***[1 mark]***.

c) E.g. because of genetic drift ***[1 mark]***.

3 a) During the drought, *Geospiza fortis* individuals were out-competed for the reduced number of big seeds by other finch species with larger beaks ***[1 mark]***. *Geospiza fortis* individuals with smaller beaks were better adapted to eat the remaining small seeds ***[1 mark]***, so were more likely to survive than those with larger beaks and average beak size fell the following year ***[1 mark]***.

b) E.g. because a population of Galapagos finches is likely to be smaller than a population of finches on the mainland ***[1 mark]***.

Module 6: Section 4 — Manipulating Genomes

Pages 128-131: Manipulating Genomes — 1

1 D ***[1 mark]***

2 A ***[1 mark]***

DNA fragments are negatively charged, so they travel towards the positive electrode. Smaller fragments travel faster than larger fragments.

3 C ***[1 mark]***

Computational biology involves using computers to study biology, e.g. by creating simulations or mathematical models. The use of computer software to analyse biological data is bioinformatics.

4 a) The blood sample will only contain very small amounts of DNA ***[1 mark]***, so amplification is needed to provide enough DNA for the bands produced to be visible ***[1 mark]***.

b) Complementary base pairing allows primers that mark the start and end of the DNA fragment being copied to bind to the DNA ***[1 mark]***. Complementary base pairing allows DNA polymerase to synthesise a new DNA strand using the original fragment as a template ***[1 mark]***.

c) i) E.g. an agarose gel tray is prepared and placed in a gel box/tank with electrodes at either end ***[1 mark]***. DNA samples are added to wells in the gel ***[1 mark]***. The gel box/tank is connected to a power supply and an electric current is passed through the gel ***[1 mark]***.

ii) The genome contains areas of repetitive, non-coding base sequences ***[1 mark]***. Different individuals have different numbers of repeats at different loci ***[1 mark]***. In a DNA profile, DNA fragments corresponding to different numbers of repeats are separated according to size ***[1 mark]***. The pattern of bands produced corresponds to the number of repeats an individual has at each locus ***[1 mark]***.

iii) The blood from the crime scene is a mixture of the victim's and suspect C's ***[1 mark]***.

iv) E.g. the proteins have to be denatured so that they all have the same charge ***[1 mark]***. This means they will all move towards the same electrode when an electric current is run through the gel ***[1 mark]***.

5 a) Somatic cell gene therapy, because it involves altering the DNA of body cells rather than sex cells/gametes ***[1 mark]***.

b) i) E.g. a DNA fragment containing the functional IL2RG gene could be isolated from a healthy cell using a restriction enzyme ***[1 mark]***. The virus DNA could then be cut open using the same restriction enzyme ***[1 mark]***, so that it has sticky ends that are complementary to the sticky ends of the DNA fragment ***[1 mark]***. A DNA ligase enzyme could then be used to join the DNA fragment and viral DNA together, so that the virus has recombinant DNA ***[1 mark]***.

ii) The virus infects the white blood cells and inserts its DNA into their DNA ***[1 mark]***. This provides the white blood cells with the functional copy of the IL2RG gene ***[1 mark]***.

c) Recessive, because inserting a functional copy of the gene restores its function (which would not be the case if the mutation was dominant) ***[1 mark]***.

d) Any two from: e.g. the effects of the treatment may be short lived ***[1 mark]***. / The patient may have to undergo multiple treatments ***[1 mark]***. / The body may start an immune response against the virus vector ***[1 mark]***. / The gene may be overexpressed with adverse consequences ***[1 mark]***. / The gene may be inserted in the wrong place in the DNA causing more problems, e.g. cancer ***[1 mark]***. / The treatment would not affect the germ line so the patient's children could still inherit the disease ***[1 mark]***.

6 a) Positive: e.g. could lead to the development of a vaccine/ drug that more people can use for cryptosporidiosis, reducing the suffering caused by the disease ***[1 mark]***. Negative: e.g. there may be a small risk that the scientists researching the pathogens could become infected with the live pathogen and cause a mass outbreak of disease ***[1 mark]***. / There may be a risk that knowledge of how to genetically engineer pathogens could be used to create agents for biological warfare ***[1 mark]***.

b) Modifying *Cryptosporidium* using traditional methods of genetic engineering would involve inserting DNA transferred directly from another organism ***[1 mark]***, whereas modifying *Cryptosporidium* through synthetic biology would involve inserting DNA created from scratch ***[1 mark]***.

c) E.g. it could be used to produce genetically modified animals that are able to produce a drug/vaccine against *Cryptosporidium* ***[1 mark]***.

One example of animal 'pharming' is the creation of sheep or goats that are able to produce a pharmaceutical drug in their milk.

Pages 132-133: Manipulating Genomes — 2

1 a) The genetic code and mechanisms of transcription and translation are universal / the same in all species ***[1 mark]***.

b) E.g. because all the *E. coli* cells produce the enzyme, whereas only some of the plant cells produce the enzyme. / Because the *E. coli* produce the enzyme all the time, whereas the plant cells only produce the enzyme at certain times ***[1 mark]***.

c) Restriction enzymes recognise specific DNA sequences either side of the gene of interest ***[1 mark]***. They then catalyse a hydrolysis reaction that breaks the DNA at these sequences (cutting the gene of interest out of the plant DNA) ***[1 mark]***.

d) The ampicillin gene serves as a marker gene for cells that have successfully taken up the plasmid ***[1 mark]***. Only *E. coli* that have successfully taken up the plasmid and possess the ampicillin resistance gene will be able to grow on the growth medium ***[1 mark]***.

e) They may have used electroporation to create an electric field ***[1 mark]***, which would have increased the permeability of the *E. coli* cell membranes ***[1 mark]***, so that they took in the recombinant plasmids ***[1 mark]***.

2 a) i) E.g. 240 000 × 6 = 1 440 000 base pairs to be read in total
1 440 000 ÷ 12 000 = 120 minutes = **2 hours**
[2 marks for the correct answer, otherwise 1 mark for a correct conversion from minutes to hours]

ii) E.g. unlike older techniques, high-throughput sequencing methods are automated and very fast ***[1 mark]*** so it allows whole genomes to be sequenced quickly and more cheaply ***[1 mark]***.

b) Advantages: any two from: e.g. the new crop could help increase global food production/reduce the risk of famine ***[1 mark]***. / The new crop could allow maize to be grown on land that is currently unusable because it is too cold ***[1 mark]***. / The new crop could allow maize to be produced locally in cold areas, reducing the need for transport of the crop and the associated energy cost/pollution ***[1 mark]***.
[Maximum 2 marks available]
Disadvantages: any two from: e.g. farmers may begin to practice monoculture with the new crop, reducing biodiversity ***[1 mark]***. / If all the new plants are genetically identical, the crop will be more susceptible to disease ***[1 mark]***. / If a large corporation owns the patent to the technology, it may be very expensive for farmers ***[1 mark]***.
[Maximum 2 marks available]

Module 6 : Section 5 — Cloning and Biotechnology

Pages 134-136: Cloning and Biotechnology — 1

1 B ***[1 mark]***

2 C ***[1 mark]***

3 A ***[1 mark]***

Species A grows best under the optimum conditions of 25 °C and pH 4, so the number of microorganisms will be at their highest in total, and will grow fastest, under these conditions. The growth conditions for curve X (28 °C, pH 6) are further from the optimum conditions than options B, C and D, so a greater number of microorganisms would be grown under options B, C and D, compared to curve X. This means that the curves of these options would be higher than curve X. Option A is the only option with conditions that are further from the optimum than curve X, so it must be curve Y.

4 a) Any four from: e.g. use a scalpel/sharp secateurs to take a cutting from the stem of the plant ***[1 mark]***. Remove the leaves from the lower end of the cutting, leaving just one at the tip ***[1 mark]***. Dip the lower end of the cutting in rooting powder, which contains hormones that induce root formation ***[1 mark]***. Plant the cutting in a suitable growth medium ***[1 mark]***. Grow the cutting in a warm, moist environment until roots have formed, and the plant can be grown elsewhere ***[1 mark]***.

b) As vegetative propagation is a cloning technique, the offspring are all genetically identical to the parent plant, and so the desired petal colour is guaranteed to be passed on to all offspring ***[1 mark]***. In contrast, seeds are produced by sexual reproduction, and so only a proportion of the offspring will inherit the desired petal colour, and the other offspring will not be saleable ***[1 mark]***.

c) i) Unlike cells from other parts of the plant, these cells are stem cells and so can differentiate into any type of cell ***[1 mark]***.

ii) The sterilisation step is important to kill any microorganisms present ***[1 mark]***, as these microorganisms would compete with the plants cells for nutrients, thus reducing their growth rate ***[1 mark]***.

iii) Any four from:
Advantages, e.g. less space is required for tissue culture than would be needed to produce the same number of plants by vegetative propagation. / Tissue culture can produce more plants than vegetative propagation because the number of cells that can be taken from the parent plant is greater than the number of cuttings that could be taken.
Disadvantages, e.g. tissue culture is more expensive than vegetative propagation due to higher energy use and the specialist equipment required. / Tissue culture is more complicated than vegetative propagation and requires more training to be achieved successfully. / Tissue culture is less suitable for small scale production than vegetative propagation due to the higher costs. / Contamination of the tissue cultures with microorganisms could cause complete loss of the plants being cultured. ***[4 marks]***

5 a)i) Colonies would be formed on the plate ***[1 mark]***.
ii) Aseptic techniques prevent contamination of the cultures with microorganisms from other sources ***[1 mark]***, which could give a false-positive result in the test ***[1 mark]***.
iii) Bacteria that aren't resistant to methicillin or any of the other antibiotics used in the test ***[1 mark]***.
b) By making serial dilutions of the MRSA in broth and then plating them onto the agar ***[1 mark]***.

Pages 137-140: Cloning and Biotechnology — 2

1 a) Any two from: e.g. the ideal growth conditions for microorganisms are easy to create, meaning that large numbers of microorganisms can be grown easily. / Microorganisms have a short life-cycle, so they can be grown rapidly and the enzymes made quickly. / Microorganisms can be grown on a range of inexpensive materials, so they are economical to use. / Microorganisms can be grown at any time of year, so their use isn't restricted. ***[2 marks]***
b) i) Any two from: e.g. the vessel has a pH probe so that the pH can be monitored and kept at the optimum level for the microorganism's enzymes to work efficiently. / The vessel has a water jacket so that the temperature can be kept at the optimum level for the microorganism's enzymes to work efficiently. / The vessel has paddles which stir the medium so that nutrients are adequately circulated to all microorganisms. / Sterile air is pumped into the vessel ensuring that the microorganisms always have access to oxygen for respiration. ***[2 marks]***
ii) Naturally secreted enzymes will be cheaper ***[1 mark]***, because expensive processes that are usually required to extract the enzyme are avoided ***[1 mark]***.
c) i) Stage W is the lag phase, where the population size increases slowly, because the microorganisms have to make enzymes and other molecules, before they can reproduce ***[1 mark]***. Stage X is the exponential phase, where the population size increases quickly, because the culture conditions are at their most favourable for reproduction ***[1 mark]***. Stage Y is the stationary phase, where the curve levels off and the population size stays the same, because there is no longer enough food and poisonous waste products start to build up ***[1 mark]***. Stage Z is the decline phase, where the population size decreases due to the build-up of toxic waste products and the scarcity of nutrients ***[1 mark]***.
ii) E.g. in continuous fermentation, there would be no decline phase ***[1 mark]***, because nutrients are continually put in and waste products are taken out at a constant rate ***[1 mark]***.
d) i) E.g. the lactase enzymes could be encapsulated in alginate beads ***[1 mark]***, trapped in a silica gel matrix ***[1 mark]*** or covalently bonded to cellulose or collagen fibres ***[1 mark]***.
ii) Any two from: e.g. extra equipment is required, which can be expensive to buy. / Immobilised enzymes are more expensive to buy than free enzymes, so they're not always economical for use in smaller-scale production. / The immobilisation of the enzymes can sometimes lead to a reduction in the enzyme activity because they can't freely mix with their substrate. ***[2 marks]***
iii) E.g. penicillin acylase in the production of semi-synthetic penicillins. / Glucoamylase for the conversion of dextrins to glucose. / Glucose isomerase for the conversion of glucose to fructose. / Aminoacylase for the production of pure samples of L-amino acids. ***[1 mark]***

2 a) How to grade your answer:
Level 0: There is no relevant information. ***[No marks]***
Level 1: There are a couple of points made about the cloning process, but these are not linked to the context of the Pyrenean ibex. One disadvantage of the process has been given briefly. The answer has no clear structure. The information given may be basic and lacking in detail. It may not all be relevant. ***[1 to 2 marks]***
Level 2: There is a brief description about the cloning process, which is linked to the context of the Pyrenean ibex. Two disadvantages of the process are given briefly. The answer has some structure. Most of the information given is relevant and there is some detail involved. ***[3 to 4 marks]***
Level 3: There is a full and detailed description of the cloning process, which is clearly linked to the context of the Pyrenean ibex. More than two disadvantages of the process are clearly described. The answer has a clear and logical structure. The information given is relevant and detailed. ***[5 to 6 marks]***

Indicative scientific content may include:
<u>Detail about the cloning process:</u>
The scientists used somatic cell nuclear transfer to clone the Pyrenean ibex.
First, nuclei were extracted from the fibroblast cells of the Pyrenean ibex.
Then the nuclei were removed from oocytes from the domesticated goat.
The fibroblast nuclei and enucleated oocytes were fused together.
The cells were stimulated to divide forming embryos.
An embryo was transplanted into a surrogate mother and then a Pyrenean ibex developed and was born.
<u>Detail about the disadvantages of the cloning process:</u>
Animal cloning is very difficult/time consuming/expensive.
There is no genetic variability in the cloned population, so all of the cloned animals will have any undesirable characteristics possessed by the parent/will be susceptible to the same diseases.
The cloned animals may not live for very long/have health defects.
Using cloning to resurrect an extinct species may be viewed as unethical.

b) i) As the Pyrenean ibex is extinct, it would not be possible to obtain egg cells and sperm to create the embryo, and so artificial embryo twinning could not be used ***[1 mark]***.
ii) The clones are all genetically identical, so any variables that come from genetic differences are removed ***[1 mark]***.
iii) E.g. in agriculture, to increase the number of animals with desirable characteristics. / To save endangered animals from extinction. ***[1 mark]***

3 a) rate = change in y / change in x
Number of bacteria at 5 hours = 10^3
Number of bacteria at 12 hours = $10^{7.8}$
$(10^{7.8} - 10^3) \div 7 = 9013533.492...$
= 9 013 533 cells $hour^{-1}$
= 9 000 000 cells $hour^{-1}$ (2 s.f)
[2 marks for correct answer, otherwise 1 mark for $(10^{7.8} - 10^3) \div 7$]

b) Any two from: e.g. lactic acid bacteria are used in cheesemaking/yoghurt production, to convert the lactose in milk into lactic acid, which makes the product solidify/thicken. / Genetically modified bacteria are used to make human insulin, by having the gene for human insulin inserted into their DNA. / Pollutant-removing bacteria are used in bioremediation, where they break down pollutants into less harmful products in order to clean up an area. ***[2 marks]***

Module 6 : Section 6 — Ecosystems

Pages 141-143: Ecosystems — 1

1 D ***[1 mark]***

2 B ***[1 mark]***

The colonisation of an area of grassland after a bush fire is an example of secondary succession, because some soil is still present. The other two examples are primary succession because they are occurring in areas where soil has not yet formed.

3 C ***[1 mark]***

You need to convert both amounts into the same units here before you can do a percentage efficiency calculation. You divide by 1000 to convert J to kJ, so 2.4 × 10^6 J = 2400 kJ. So the percentage efficiency is: (2400 ÷ 18 000) × 100 = 13.3%.

4 a) i) Sandwort and sea couch ***[1 mark]***.

ii) Their organic material is decomposed after they die, forming a basic soil ***[1 mark]***. They make the abiotic conditions less hostile, so new organisms can survive there ***[1 mark]***.

b) Any one from: e.g. woodland is the most complex community that the ecosystem can support ***[1 mark]***. / Woodland is the steady state reached when the ecosystem has passed through all stages of succession ***[1 mark]***.

c) Any four from: e.g. marram grass would only have been able to survive after a thin layer of soil was created by plants such as sandwort and sand couch ***[1 mark]***. Marram grass may have adaptations that make it particularly suited to growing at the third stage, e.g. being able to survive without much shelter ***[1 mark]***. Once the marram grass had stabilised the sand dunes, a larger number of plants were able to survive there ***[1 mark]***. More plants colonising the area created more competition between plant species ***[1 mark]***. As the abiotic and biotic conditions changed, the marram grass was no longer the best adapted plant species, and was out-competed by the shrubs ***[1 mark]***. ***[Maximum 4 marks available]***

d) E.g. the ecosystem would not reach the final stage of succession / succession would be deflected ***[1 mark]*** because the cattle would eat any young woody plants beginning to grow, so that it would not be possible for woodland to be established ***[1 mark]***.

5 a) E.g. pests/insects eating the crop ***[1 mark]***.

b) Nitrogen compounds are broken down/converted into ammonia by decomposers in the soil ***[1 mark]***. Ammonia is converted to ammonium ions ***[1 mark]***. Then nitrifying bacteria/*Nitrosomonas* convert ammonium ions to nitrites ***[1 mark]*** and other nitrifying bacteria/*Nitrobacter* convert nitrites to nitrates, which growing plants can use as a source of nitrogen ***[1 mark]***.

c) Under anaerobic conditions, there is a greater number of denitrifying bacteria, which convert nitrates into nitrogen gas ***[1 mark]***, so waterlogging would reduce the amount of nitrates in the soil ***[1 mark]***. This reduces the amount of nitrates available to the plants for growth, so will reduce crop yield ***[1 mark]***.

Pages 144-146: Ecosystems — 2

1 a) Any one from: e.g. temperature / soil type / soil pH / availability of space/water ***[1 mark]***.

b) E.g. the quadrats could have been placed (next to each other) along a belt transect ***[1 mark]***.

c) i) A scatter graph ***[1 mark]*** because the student is investigating whether there is a correlation between two discrete variables (ground vegetation cover and light intensity) ***[1 mark]***.

ii) E.g. if the measurements were not taken simultaneously, they will not account for the fact that light levels will vary depending on the time of day/the weather ***[1 mark]***.

2 a) As the mass of fertiliser increases, the yield of crop increases ***[1 mark]***, until a peak in crop yield is reached at 160 kg ha^{-1}, after which the crop yield begins to decrease ***[1 mark]***.

b) 7.3 – 4.5 = 2.8
(2.8 ÷ 4.5) × 100 = **62%** (to 2 s.f.) ***[1 mark]***

c) E.g. the water content of the freshly harvested crop may vary, which would create variation in mass that is unrelated to the investigation ***[1 mark]***.

d) E.g. test the fertiliser in different soils/different locations. / Test the fertiliser on different crop plants. / Test the fertiliser at different times of the year/seasons. ***[1 mark]***

e) E.g. by using herbicides to kill weeds ***[1 mark]***, so crops face less competition and therefore obtain more energy to put into growing biomass ***[1 mark]***. / By using fungicides to kill fungal infections ***[1 mark]***, so crops don't have to expend energy fighting an infection and can use the energy for growing biomass instead ***[1 mark]***. / By using insecticides to kill insect pests ***[1 mark]***, so less biomass is lost to insects eating the crop ***[1 mark]***. / By introducing natural predators to remove pest species ***[1 mark]***, so less biomass is lost to organisms eating the crop ***[1 mark]***.

3 How to grade your answer:

Level 0: There is no relevant information. ***[No marks]***

Level 1: There is a brief description of one or two ways that carbon moves through the ecosystem. The answer has no clear structure. The information given is basic and lacking in detail. It may not all be relevant. ***[1 to 3 marks]***

Level 2: There is a description of several ways that carbon moves through the ecosystem, with reference to biological, chemical or physical processes. The answer has some structure. Most of the information given is relevant and there is some detail involved. ***[4 to 6 marks]***

Level 3: There is a full description of most of the ways that carbon moves within the ecosystem, with reference to biological, chemical and physical processes. The answer has a clear and logical structure. The information given is relevant and detailed. ***[7 to 9 marks]***

Indicative scientific content may include:

<u>Biological processes</u>

Carbon is removed from the air/water when plants/algae/phytoplankton photosynthesise.

This carbon is then stored in the tissues of the plants/algae/phytoplankton.

It is passed on to fish and other aquatic animals when the plants/algae/phytoplankton are eaten.

The aquatic organisms all carry out respiration, which releases carbon into the air/water in the form of carbon dioxide.
When the organisms die, some of the carbon compounds in their remains are broken down by decomposers, such as bacteria. The decomposers also respire and release carbon dioxide.
Chemical and physical processes
Some of the remains of the dead organisms are not decomposed and are instead turned into fossil fuels over millions of years. Carbon is released into the air as carbon dioxide when the fossil fuels are burnt/combusted.
Some of the remains of dead organisms, e.g. shells, become compressed over time to form rocks such as limestone on the ocean floor. The carbon compounds in these organisms become part of the rocks.
Some of these rocks may be drawn down into the Earth's crust, where they undergo chemical changes and release carbon dioxide. This carbon dioxide can be released into the air/water by volcanic eruptions.
If the rocks become exposed, then they can be chemically or physically weathered. This can cause the release of ions from the rock into solution. These ions enter the groundwater and are carried back to the ocean in rivers.
Carbon dioxide from the atmosphere also dissolves directly into the ocean. It can be carried around the ocean by deep underwater currents for many years before returning to the ocean surface and being released back into the atmosphere.

Module 6 : Section 7 — Populations and Sustainability

Pages 147-150: Populations and Sustainability

1 D ***[1 mark]***

In predator-prey relationships, the size of the predator population increases in response to an increase in the number of their prey, so the peak for the predator species comes after the peak for the prey species. You know it's negative feedback because whenever the populations increase or decrease, they get pushed back towards a stable state.

2 D ***[1 mark]***

Statement 1 is false because it refers to preservation, not conservation. Statement 3 is false because conservation ecosystems provide economically important resources that can be traded, so there is an economic as well as ethical benefit to conservation.

3 a) Sustainability means meeting the needs of people today without reducing the ability of people in the future to meet their own needs ***[1 mark]***.

b) The grazing animals will feed on plants, including young shrubs and trees, preventing the larger plants from growing ***[1 mark]***. This prevents the fens from developing into carr woodland / maintains the fen ecosystem ***[1 mark]***.

c) i) E.g. if the fens are lost, then future generations won't be able to enjoy the scenery and wildlife / use the area for boating ***[1 mark]***.

ii) E.g. there may be a conflict between the need to conserve the habitat for the species that live there, and the need to allow tourists to visit and generate income for the area ***[1 mark]***.

4 a) i) E.g. walkers can cause footpath erosion ***[1 mark]***, which can lead to soil being washed into waterways, disturbing the aquatic wildlife ***[1 mark]***. / Walkers/cyclists may fail to keep to paths and trample/ride over ground vegetation ***[1 mark]*** which may damage/destroy sensitive species ***[1 mark]***.

ii) E.g. regular repair and maintenance work can be carried out on the paths. / Walkers/cyclists can be educated about the importance of keeping to the paths. ***[1 mark]***

b) i) E.g. clearing one large area would expose a lot of ground, resulting in soil erosion (which would make it more difficult for newly planted trees to grow) ***[1 mark]***. Clearing small patches exposes less soil, resulting in less soil erosion, so trees can grow back more quickly ***[1 mark]***.

ii) E.g. coppicing / planting native tree species to improve biodiversity / attaching newly planted trees to posts to provide support / growing newly planted trees in plastic tubes to protect them from grazing animals / avoiding planting trees too close together ***[1 mark]***.

Any suggestion that helps trees to reach maturity faster or grow back more quickly will help to make timber production more sustainable.

5 a) As the population size increased, there were fewer resources (e.g. food, water, space) available per individual, so intraspecific competition increased ***[1 mark]***. Eventually, the amount of resources became limiting and the population declined ***[1 mark]***. When the population size was low, there was less intraspecific competition for resources. This meant more of the crabs could survive and reproduce, causing the population to grow again ***[1 mark]***.

b) 65 (accept between 60 and 70) ***[1 mark]***

The population size is fluctuating around the carrying capacity. When it's below the carrying capacity, it's able to increase, and when it gets too far above the carrying capacity, it decreases.

6 a) i) Any two from: e.g. unwanted species get caught in the fishing nets ***[1 mark]***. / Pollution from fishing boats damages their habitat ***[1 mark]***. / Catching fish for human consumption removes a food source for their natural predators ***[1 mark]***.

ii) E.g. introducing fishing quotas ***[1 mark]***. Setting limits on fishing net mesh size ***[1 mark]***.

b) Any one from: e.g. they could bring diseases to the native plants and animals ***[1 mark]***. / Introduced animal species could eat native species, reducing their populations ***[1 mark]***. / Introduced species could out-compete native species ***[1 mark]***.

7 Advantages: e.g. it provides the local people with an alternative source of income to livestock farming, so they are no longer in conflict with the wild animals that could kill livestock ***[1 mark]***. It gives the local people an incentive not to hunt the large predators, as these are attracting tourists to the region, which increases their income ***[1 mark]***.
Disadvantages, any two from: e.g. large numbers of tourists might disturb the wildlife ***[1 mark]***. / Parts of the ecosystem might be lost due to the need to develop infrastructure for ecotourism, e.g. roads, hotels, visitor centres ***[1 mark]***. / Farming/keeping livestock might be an important part of Maasai culture that they are no longer able to do ***[1 mark]***.
[Maximum 4 marks available]

Mixed Questions

Pages 151-152: Mixed Questions — 1

1 C ***[1 mark]***

Fish have a closed, single circulatory system. Both sides of the heart pump blood to the gills and to the rest of the body. Veins take blood back to the heart.

2 B ***[1 mark]***

A pyrimidine base contains a single carbon-nitrogen ring, so it must be B. Molecule D contains two carbon-nitrogen rings joined together — it's a purine base. Molecule A is α-glucose, and molecule C is an amino acid.

3 A ***[1 mark]***

You can tell that this image was taken using a scanning electron microscope because you can see more detail than you could with a light or laser scanning confocal microscope, and the image is 3D (transmission electron microscopes only produce 2D images).

4 A ***[1 mark]***

Epistasis is when one gene masks the expression of the alleles of other genes. In this example, having a copy of a dominant allele for the suppression of synthesis gene means that the malvidin pigment will not be produced even if the dominant allele for malvidin synthesis is present.

5 D ***[1 mark]***

Pages 153-157: Mixed Questions — 2

1 a) Carbohydrate / disaccharide ***[1 mark]***

b) i) E.g. the reaction/breakdown of lactose is a hydrolysis reaction ***[1 mark]***, which requires the addition of a water molecule ***[1 mark]***.

ii) Any two from: e.g. the temperature of the solutions. / The concentration of the lactose and lactase solutions. / The type of glucose test strip used. / The person observing the colour change of each glucose test strip. ***[2 marks available — 1 mark for each reasonable suggestion]***

For this question there are other correct answers that aren't listed here. For an answer to be valid, the variable needs to have an impact on the results, and be something that's possible to control in an experiment.

c) i) E.g. that lactase is only active below pH 8 / lactase is inactive at pH 8 or above ***[1 mark]***. Lactase breaks lactose down into glucose and galactose, therefore, if glucose is present/the strip is green, it indicates lactase is active / if glucose is absent/the strip is yellow, it indicates that lactase is inactive ***[1 mark]***.

ii) Above and below its optimum pH, every enzyme is affected by the H^+ and OH^- ions found in acids and alkalis ***[1 mark]***. These ions interfere with the ionic and hydrogen bonds that hold the enzyme's tertiary structure together ***[1 mark]***. This changes the shape of the enzyme's active site ***[1 mark]***.

iii) E.g. increase the number of reactions carried out between pH 7 and 8 ***[1 mark]*** because it is between these pH values that lactase activity stops ***[1 mark]***.

Accurate results need to be close to the true answer, so increasing the number of reactions carried out between pH 7 and 8 would let the student narrow down where lactase activity stops. E.g. the investigation could show that the activity stops between pH 7.2 and 7.3 rather than between pH 7 and 8.

d) E.g. phagocytes may identify the milk proteins as foreign antigens ***[1 mark]***. They would then move their cytoplasm around the proteins, engulfing them ***[1 mark]***. The milk proteins would then be broken down in the phagocytes by digestive enzymes ***[1 mark]***. The phagocytes would then present the fragments on their surfaces to activate other immune cells ***[1 mark]***.

2 a) i) spindle fibre ***[1 mark]***

ii) Cell B because the diagram shows the homologous pairs being separated, not the sister chromatids ***[1 mark]***.

b) 20 ***[1 mark]***

c) i) Meiosis because the chromosome number changes from diploid/2n in the sporophyte to haploid/n in the spores ***[1 mark]***.

ii) When a sperm fertilises an egg, a diploid/2n fertilised gametophyte is formed ***[1 mark]***. This must mean that both the egg and sperm are haploid/n ***[1 mark]***. The spores are also haploid/n and to maintain a haploid number of chromosomes between the spores and gametophytes, stages 1 and 2 must represent mitosis ***[1 mark]***.

d) i) E.g. there may be lots of variation in habitat in each area ***[1 mark]*** and she may want to make sure that the different habitats are sampled in proportion ***[1 mark]***.

ii) E.g. repeat the sampling at least three times and calculate a mean for each area ***[1 mark]***.

3 a) Cl^- ions move from the epithelial cells lining the ileum, through the open Cl^- channel proteins and into the ileum lumen ***[1 mark]***. The build up of Cl^- ions lowers the water potential of the lumen ***[1 mark]***. This causes water to move by osmosis out of the epithelial cells into the lumen ***[1 mark]***. This lowers the water potential of the epithelial cells, causing water to move out of the blood into the cells ***[1 mark]***.

b) i) E.g. *V. cholerae* will have a cell wall, the ileum epithelial cell will not. / *V. cholerae* will not have a nucleus/ membrane-bound organelles, the ileum epithelial cell will. / *V. cholerae* will have smaller ribosomes than the ileum epithelial cell ***[1 mark]***.

You're being asked to compare the structure of a prokaryotic cell (V. cholerae) to that of a eukaryotic animal cell (the ileum epithelial cell) here.

ii) Any four from: e.g. diffusion of nutrients across the outer surface alone would be too slow to meet a human's needs ***[1 mark]***. This is because it would take too long for substances to travel from the outer surface to the cells deep within the body ***[1 mark]***. Not enough substances would be exchanged across the outer surface, which is small relative to the volume of a human ***[1 mark]***. Humans have a relatively high metabolic rate, so diffusion across the outer surface would be too slow to keep up with metabolic demand ***[1 mark]***. Therefore humans need a specialised exchange surface to improve the efficiency of nutrient absorption ***[1 mark]***. ***[Maximum of 4 marks available]***

c) Any two from: e.g. drink only boiled/treated water. / Cook food thoroughly. / Wash hands often with soap and water. / Improve sewage/water treatment. / Keep sewage outlets away from sources of drinking water. ***[2 marks]***.

d) E.g. in an environment containing an antibiotic/the body of a cholera patient being treated with an antibiotic ***[1 mark]***, *V. cholerae* bacteria with alleles for resistance to that antibiotic will be more likely to survive and reproduce than *V. cholerae* bacteria without those alleles ***[1 mark]***. Over time the alleles for antibiotic resistance become more frequent in the population ***[1 mark]***. This is directional selection because antibiotic resistance is an extreme trait ***[1 mark]***.

Pages 158-159: Mixed Questions — 3

1 a) A: glycerate 3-phosphate/GP ***[1 mark]***
B: NADP ***[1 mark]***
C: ribulose bisphosphate/RuBP ***[1 mark]***

b) E.g. the rate at which glucose is produced as a result of the light-independent reaction would be reduced ***[1 mark]***. This would mean that there is less glucose available for respiration, and so less energy available for plant growth ***[1 mark]***. / The rate at which amino acids are produced as a result of the light-independent reaction would be reduced ***[1 mark]***. This would mean that there are fewer amino acids available for making proteins, and so fewer proteins available for plant growth ***[1 mark]***.

c) i) One or more bases in the sequence of DNA are swapped for another ***[1 mark]***.

ii) The mutation could alter the amino acid sequence of the RuBisCo protein ***[1 mark]***, which could change the shape of RuBisCo's active site ***[1 mark]***. This could increase the rate of RuBisCo activity and therefore the rate at which molecule A/GP is produced (allowing the whole of the light-independent reaction to progress faster) ***[1 mark]***.

If the active site changes so that its substrate fits even better than previously, this could increase enzyme activity.

d) It helps to convert CO_2 from the atmosphere into the organic compounds that make up plant tissues ***[1 mark]***. This allows carbon to be passed from plants to the animals that eat them as part of the carbon cycle ***[1 mark]***.

2 a) Liver cell membranes become more permeable to glucose ***[1 mark]***. Glucose is converted into glycogen ***[1 mark]***.

b) Any four from: e.g. the human insulin gene could be cut out of human DNA using restriction enzymes ***[1 mark]***. The insulin gene could then be inserted into a vector/plasmid/bacteriophage ***[1 mark]***. The insulin gene would be joined to the vector/plasmid/bacteriophage DNA using ligation/a ligase enzyme ***[1 mark]***. The vector would then be used to transfer the human insulin gene to the *E. coli*/the *E. coli* could be encouraged to take up the plasmids/the *E. coli* could be infected with the bacteriophage DNA ***[1 mark]***. The *E. coli* would then transcribe and translate the human insulin protein ***[1 mark]***. ***[Maximum 4 marks available]***

c) Stem cells could be made to produce ß/beta cells and implanted into the pancreas of a person with Type 1 diabetes ***[1 mark]***, so that they are able to produce their own insulin ***[1 mark]***.

Pages 160-162: Mixed Questions — 4

1 a) i) motor ***[1 mark]***

ii) Any two from: e.g. it takes time for the depolarisation caused by the action potential to spread from the sarcolemma of the muscle fibre to the sarcoplasmic reticulum. / It takes time for the sarcoplasmic reticulum to release its stored calcium/Ca^{2+} ions into the sarcoplasm. / It takes time for calcium/Ca^{2+} ions to bind to the protein that moves tropomyosin out of the way. / It takes time for the actin-myosin cross bridges to form. ***[2 marks — 1 mark for each correct answer]***

b) Calcium/Ca^{2+} ions leave their binding sites and are transported back into the sarcoplasmic reticulum ***[1 mark]***. This causes the tropomyosin molecules to move back so that they block the actin-myosin binding sites again ***[1 mark]***. This allows the muscles to relax because no myosin heads are attached to the actin filaments/there are no actin-myosin cross bridges and the actin filaments slide back to their relaxed position ***[1 mark]***.

c) i) The muscle fibre is short of oxygen ***[1 mark]***.

ii) E.g. the link reaction produces acetyl coenzyme A and reduced NAD ***[1 mark]***. Acetyl coenzyme A goes into the Krebs cycle, which produces reduced NAD and reduced FAD ***[1 mark]***. The oxidation of the reduced NAD and FAD during oxidative phosphorylation, releases electrons ***[1 mark]***. The energy carried by these electrons is used to produce ATP (the cell's energy store) which can be used for muscle contraction ***[1 mark]***.

2 a) Petite mutants are able to grow on a substrate containing glucose because they can still generate energy from glucose via glycolysis ***[1 mark]***, which occurs in the cytoplasm and does not require the mitochondria ***[1 mark]***. However, they form smaller colonies than normal cells because glycolysis alone produces much less ATP from each molecule of glucose than the full respiratory chain ***[1 mark]***, so the cells will not be able to release as much energy for growth as normal cells ***[1 mark]***.

b) As petite mutants have inactive mitochondria/can only form small colonies, they are less fit than non-mutant cells and are therefore less likely to survive and reproduce ***[1 mark]***. As a result, a lower proportion of the next generation will inherit the petite mutation, and the petite mutants will largely be eliminated from the population by natural selection ***[1 mark]***.

c) The NRF-1 transcription factor binds to specific DNA sequences near the start of its target genes ***[1 mark]***. It then increases the rate of transcription of these genes ***[1 mark]***.

3 a) How to grade your answer:

Level 0: There is no relevant information. ***[No marks]***

Level 1: The answer describes some elements of how the founder effect may have led to speciation. The answer has no clear structure. The information given is basic and lacking in detail. It may not all be relevant. ***[1 to 2 marks]***

Level 2: The answer covers most of the elements of how the founder effect may have led to speciation. The answer has some structure. Most of the information given is relevant and there is some detail involved. ***[3 to 4 marks]***

Level 3: The answer covers founder effect and how this may have led to speciation in detail. The answer has a clear and logical structure. The information given is relevant and detailed. ***[5 to 6 marks]***

Indicative scientific content may include:

The island population of beetles was started by a small group, which meant that the number of alleles in the initial gene pool was small.

As the beetles are flightless, and the population was separated from the original population by water, there was no gene flow between the two populations.

The small gene pool and lack of gene flow meant that the population would have been heavily influenced by genetic drift, so that certain alleles (e.g. the allele for black colouring) were passed on more often by chance.

The new population would have grown with reduced genetic variation. This is the founder effect.

Eventually, the founder effect may have led to speciation, as the two populations changed so much that they were no longer able to breed together to produce fertile offspring.

b) E.g. the genome sequences of the two species can be compared using computer software ***[1 mark]***. The more similar the DNA sequences, the more closely related the species are ***[1 mark]***.

BRAQ71